John Lawrence

THE
TOTAL QUALITY
CORPORATION

· THE ·
TOTAL QUALITY

FRANCIS McINERNEY
AND SEAN WHITE

CORPORATION

HOW 10 MAJOR COMPANIES TURNED
QUALITY AND ENVIRONMENTAL
CHALLENGES TO COMPETITIVE
ADVANTAGE IN THE 1990S

TRUMAN TALLEY BOOKS/DUTTON
NEW YORK

TRUMAN TALLEY BOOKS/DUTTON

Published by the Penguin Group
Penguin Books USA Inc., 375 Hudson Street, New York, New York 10014, U.S.A.
Penguin Books Ltd, 27 Wrights Lane, London W8 5TZ, England
Penguin Books Australia Ltd, Ringwood, Victoria, Australia
Penguin Books Canada Ltd, 10 Alcorn Avenue, Toronto, Ontario, Canada M4V 3B2
Penguin Books (N.Z.) Ltd, 182–190 Wairau Road, Auckland 10, New Zealand

Penguin Books Ltd, Registered Offices:
Harmondsworth, Middlesex, England

First published by Truman Talley Books/Dutton,
an imprint of Dutton Signet,
a division of Penguin Books USA Inc.
Distributed in Canada by McClelland & Stewart Inc.

First Printing, October, 1995
1   3   5   7   9   10   8   6   4   2

Copyright © North River Ventures, Inc., 1995
All rights reserved

ISBN 0-525-93928-8
CIP data is available

Printed in the United States of America
Set in Times New Roman and Gill Sans
Designed by Steven N. Stathakis

To our children

CONTENTS

CONTENTS

PART TWO

THE
TOTAL QUALITY
CORPORATION

INTRODUCTION

RIDING THE GREEN WAVE

"A penney saved is two pence clear. . . ."
—BENJAMIN FRANKLIN, *Necessary Hints*
to Those That Would Be Rich

The idea behind this book took us by surprise. In February 1990, we visited a manufacturing facility in North Carolina where Canadian supplier Northern Telecom builds its flagship computerized telephone exchanges. Our objective was to see how Northern, a leader in a fiercely competitive industry, kept costs down. The plant manager was Allan Toomer, a down-to-earth ex-submariner who had navigated his company through some very dangerous waters by improving the efficiency of his operations with quiet determination.

Years ago, Toomer first taught us that there is a direct connection between market share and cleanliness. We have since inspected many plants in America, Japan, and Europe, and have found the best are invariably the simplest: clear layout and no clutter. Efficiency and simplicity seem to go together. If the plant looks like a mess, the company *is* a mess and performance reflects it. At plants operated by some of the world's high-tech giants, we've seen shop floors as confusing as a New Jersey highway interchange, little old ladies hand-dipping computer parts into vats of solder the way chocolate is put on a Dairy Queen cone, rafter-high piles of inventory that made Canal Street sweatshops look well kept, and homemade production equipment held together with rubber bands. Al Toomer's factory was spotless, and he had the sales (and profits) to show for it.

As we toured his plant, Toomer remarked that Northern had decided to eliminate CFCs from printed-circuit-board production. CFCs, best known by the trade name Freon, were widely used in electronics manufacturing to clean parts after soldering. CFCs are versatile, inexpensive, nonflammable, and nontoxic. They were universally considered harmless; then scientists discovered that they destroy the ozone layer, which protects people from cancer-causing ultraviolet rays. These chemicals will now be banned worldwide after the year 2000. Northern, anticipating change, had decided to eliminate CFCs from its own factories well ahead of government requirements.

Toomer explained to us that his engineers had experimented with a variety of other solvents to replace CFCs in the cleaning process. Then an idea occurred to them: Why not eliminate the cleaning process altogether? By tightening up production tolerances, they obviated the need for cleaning. Without cleaning, they found that they didn't need CFCs or any other solvent. Then came the most startling news: Toomer told us that with this change, Northern had reduced costs and improved quality quite dramatically into the bargain. In 1993, the company estimated that by eliminating CFCs it would save more than $50 million in direct costs during the remaining years of the decade.

During the 1980s, Northern Telecom faced deregulation, rapid technological change, and many well-financed Japanese and European competitors. Northern overcame these challenges using a simple and direct strategy: relentless cost reduction. In ten short years, Northern had risen from the Canadian backwaters to top billing. The company became and remained the low-cost producer in its market, beating out its much bigger competitors. With smart managers like Al Toomer, Northern had used a potentially expensive government mandate (CFC elimination) to strengthen its market leadership.

This lesson made one thing clear to us: pollution is a certain sign of poor management. Pollution means waste, and waste means inefficiency. In short, pollution indicates that costs are needlessly high. Eliminate an environmental problem and you solve a competitive one.

After we returned from our trip to North Carolina, we started looking around. Despite all the commotion about the "costs" of environmental regulation, we saw that Northern Telecom was not alone. While many tried to turn back the clean-environment tide, a few, like Northern Telecom, were turning environmental pressure to advantage, riding the Green Wave to lower costs and higher efficiencies.

For the past fifteen years, we have closely monitored the performance of American, Japanese, and European electronics giants (their failures as well as their successes), and advised them on all aspects of competitive survival. In particular, we have analyzed the cost-reduction strategies of these major worldwide firms. We have come to understand what makes a winner (or a loser) in the world's most competitive markets. After our Northern Telecom plant tour, we realized that environmental indicators, which are widely available, could be used as a proxy for production or operational efficiencies, which are normally closely guarded secrets.

At the time we visited North Carolina, we had just left Northern Business Information, the world's leading publisher of research on the telecommunications industry, which we had founded in 1976 and sold to McGraw-Hill in 1988. Since then, we have turned our hand to identifying high-tech companies with long-term investment potential. To assess an organization's value, we must gauge its efficiency. The "green is lean" test has remained unfailingly reliable.

POLLUTION SPELLS MISMANAGEMENT

After years of research we have reached a simple conclusion: zero waste equals zero defects. Those companies that pollute the least have the highest-quality products and services. From the same observations, we have also concluded that waste, or pollution, is a key indicator of unnecessary cost, and, most important, inattentive routine management.

Today, competitive companies around the world are successfully meeting the challenges of the 1990s with continual efficiency improvements. These mavericks are riding the Green Wave, raising their financial performance by reducing the environmental impact of their operations, often dramatically. For them, pollution is a cost, as well as a red flag for poor quality.

While competitors restructure to stave off bankruptcy, slashing workers by the tens of thousands, those on the crest of the Green Wave are turning adversity to advantage. They are capitalizing on the precipitous drop in the cost of information to substitute knowledge—better thinking—for machinery, labor, and natural resources. Their efforts place a premium on training and productivity while uncoupling growth from the consumption of energy and raw materials, the source of pollution. They will, many of them, survive the contest for high-growth opportunities because they are the low-cost producers in their markets.

These leaders have, as a business strategy, adopted some of the toughest environmental standards in the world, constantly challenging their employees to rethink operations from end to end. They are driven by men and women with a vision, iconoclasts who can see beyond conventional management methods to a better, and more profitable, way of doing business.

This book tells the stories of ten internationally successful companies that have recently improved their market share and lowered their costs by drawing the connection between waste, margins, and quality. These companies have consciously revolutionized their operations, meeting their environmental obligations in order to increase profits. We also explore the impact of the Green Wave on Europe, Japan, the United States, and the fast-growing economies of the Third World.

Inefficiency is at the very heart of the economic problems we face in the 1990s: trade deficits, bankruptcies, white-collar layoffs, and "restructuring." One national champion after another, from General Motors to IBM, from Volkswagen to Philips, has responded to financial disaster by slashing jobs with unprecedented ruthlessness. This book is good news for shell-shocked readers looking for a better way for business to reduce costs and regain competitiveness.

Overwhelmingly, we all call ourselves environmentalists, concerned about the health of ourselves and our children. But while we want to breathe clean air, we must also put food on the table. Sure we can clean up pollution, but will the price be too high? How many jobs will we lose? Will our biggest manufacturers shift production to Third World countries with few if any environmental standards?

We are all looking for a brand of environmentalism that is not antibusiness. Many citizens are skeptical of the "can't do" attitude of corporate leaders who resist environmental improvements every step of the way, an attitude frequently reinforced by misdirected government policy and misguided ideas of what competitiveness is all about. At the same time, nobody wants to put his or her job on the block to save the ozone layer.

There is a better way. We don't have to balance environmental responsibility and competitive realities, because they are one and the same.

Through their governments and their spending habits, consumers everywhere are forcing companies to shoulder the environmental consequences of their activities. Consumers around the world have become "green." Environmental fervor ebbs and flows with the economic and political tide. When people are worried about losing their jobs, their concerns about the environment recede. Calls for change reach fever pitch after disasters like the *Exxon Valdez* oil spill, the Bhopal, India, chemical plant explosion, or the Chernobyl nuclear power plant catastrophe. With or without these headline-grabbers, the direction of public opinion is headed in one direction only: greener. As citizens, people expect their governments to do something about the environment. They also expect the companies they buy from to meet their clean-environment obligations in ways that go well beyond advertising and public relations. Biodegradable trash bags and compostable diapers are no longer enough. We call this environmental trend the "Green Wave."

DEMATERIALIZATION AND THE POSTINDUSTRIAL ECONOMY

During the past thirty years, industrial growth has been "dematerialized," or uncoupled, from the consumption of the earth's natural resources. What we buy today, from cars to soda cans, is made with less metal, oil, and water; what we turn on, from lightbulbs to refrigerators, uses less electricity; our cars run on less gas. Examples abound. In 1972, container manufacturers got twenty-two cans out of a pound of aluminum; by 1992, they were stretching more than twenty-nine cans out of each pound. Furthermore, more than two-thirds of those cans were being recycled, up from negligible levels two decades ago.[1] During this same period, the fuel economy of American cars doubled.

Better technology and more efficient production are partially responsible for dematerialization. But in addition, as consumers grow richer, they spend more and more of their income on services, like entertainment, travel, and dining out. Clearly fewer natural resources go into fifteen dollars' worth of cable TV shows than into fifteen dollars' worth of charcoal for the barbecue. Perhaps most important of all, the "information economy" has swelled, as computers have found their way into virtually every aspect of human activity. The raw-material content of a $250 computer microprocessor or a $500 computer program can be measured in cents. Their value derives not from any materials they contain but from the knowledge of the producers who make them, and the service they provide to the people who use them.

Concern about the environment—and about wasteful consumption, for that matter—is not new. But real pressure to use our natural resources more carefully began only twenty-five years ago. The first OPEC oil embargo in 1973 delivered a striking lesson to the world's consumers. While this event was entirely man-made, it was seized by environmentalists and neo-Malthusians as an object lesson on the limits to growth. Waiting in gas lines, everyone could consider the fragile link between industrial development and the environment.

Around the world, governments, business, and consumers reacted often with fear, then with action. The result was a great reduction in the use of natural resources, particularly energy. Voluntarily, and in response to price increases and government regulation, people turned out the lights, turned down the thermostat, and started thinking about structural changes. Homeowners invested in attic insulation and storm windows, not to mention more fuel efficient cars. Industry upgraded inefficient electric motors, incandescent lights, and old trucks. The amount of energy required to generate another dollar's worth of production began to fall, in some countries quite sharply. In the 1970s, as oil prices spiked up, this reduction in "energy intensity" of the world's economy was sharp. In the 1980s, when oil prices declined, efficiency improvements slowed, but continued nonetheless.

During the past generation, pollution-control laws have also had a dramatic effect on air and water quality. In the industrialized world, for example, air emissions of sulfur oxides, particulates, and lead have fallen dramatically, despite increased industrial activity.[2] In the United States, the power industry generates 2½ times as much electricity for each ton of pollution produced, compared to 1970.[3] After the Love Canal disaster in the United States spotlighted the potential ill effects of small quantities of industrial by-products, toxic-waste disposal was recognized as a serious problem, resulting in tighter controls. Then concerns about garbage-disposal problems resulted in new recycling requirements around the world.

Pollution laws have forced industry to reduce its use of raw materials, hastening the process of dematerialization. Less lead is used in gasoline, less mercury in batteries, less coal is needed to produce a kilowatt-hour of electricity. In the 1970s, many predicted that the world would run out of key commodities if we didn't change. Well, people did change, and most raw material supplies are now in surplus. Industry continues to wean itself from the consumption of natural resources. "Sustainable growth," the current mantra of the environmental community, is becoming a reality.

"Global warming" became the apocalypse of choice in the early 1990s. Carbon dioxide is not in itself harmful, but its growing concentration in the atmosphere is apparently causing the earth's average temperature to rise. While other pollutants have been controlled in large measure, CO_2 emissions have climbed persistently over the past twenty years, raising questions about the cumulative effect of human activity on the planet as a whole. The global warming frenzy reached a crescendo at the United Nations–organized Conference on Environment and Development (better known as the "Earth Summit"), which took place in Rio de Janeiro in 1992.

In preparation for the Earth Summit, the European Union proposed a new tax on hydrocarbon fuels (primarily coal, oil, and natural gas) based on their carbon content, or their ability to cause global warming. While the response of President Bush's administration was lukewarm to say the least, Japan also indicated its willingness to levy a carbon tax in order to reduce carbon dioxide emissions. The thin end of a long wedge has been inserted between consumers and their fuels of choice, even if it takes some years before a "carbon tax" is widely adopted. Carbon taxes will eventually sever growth from oil and coal once and for all.

THE OPPORTUNITIES

Environmental opportunities are vast, covering markets as diverse as cars that get better gas mileage and processes that remove toxins from contaminated soil. At the core is environmental technology: techniques, products, and services that reduce pollution before it is generated, save energy, or clean up environmental messes that have already occurred.

On pollution controls, the large industrial countries spend well over 1 percent of their GNP every year,[4] pushing this market above $150 billion in the United States alone. Total worldwide expenditures for environmentally related products and services will soon top $500 billion, exceeding the car market and reaching half the size of the information technology market. By some measures, the environmental industry is growing faster than biotechnology, telecommunications, or computer software.[5] Every new government regulation makes this market bigger, and one resource the world will never run short of is government regulations.

Environmental technology will have a bright future only if suppliers show their customers how to eliminate wasteful practices to the benefit of their own customers. Leadership in ET will go not to those with the best hardware, but to those who can solve real problems. It's not enough to deliver flue gas scrubbers; pulp mills are concerned about paper quality and costs. It's not enough to sell water-based paints; car companies want to make their products more attractive and more durable. It's not enough to deliver more fuel-efficient airplanes; airlines want to improve load factors and on-time performance. It's not enough to reduce pollution; ET suppliers must save money and improve quality for their customers.

Many companies are trying to increase the "green content" of products to appeal to consumers, eliminating toxic ingredients and excess packaging, as well as making them recyclable, returnable, more energy efficient, or simply relabeling them as "environmentally friendly."

With three-quarters or more of consumers calling themselves

environmentalists,[6] the green appeal is a natural for marketers. Selling to the environmental concerns of consumers can help move products, if it is done judiciously. But there has been something of a backlash in recent years. Green marketing got out of control in the late 1980s with eyepoppers like ozone-friendly deodorants and "Supergreen" gasoline.[7]

For decades, direct labor costs have been a declining share of total costs for most manufacturers, to the point where in some industries, like semiconductors, they are a minor cost factor. Material costs are often high, particularly if semifinished goods are purchased for further processing. In many companies, carrying costs for work-in-progress and finished goods are greater than for labor. Speeding the flow of goods from suppliers, through the factory, and on to customers is what really reduces costs today. In other words, the producer with the lowest costs (and most profits) is the one with the highest rate of inventory turnover.

Like inventory control, zero emissions requires new thinking about how materials are handled throughout the manufacturing process. Northern Telecom, as we saw, tried water cleaning to reduce its use of CFCs, but then settled on no cleaning at all, installing parts to more precise standards instead. This change depended on more accurate handling of computer parts, but several steps in the manufacturing process were eliminated, as were all solvents (CFC or water based). Furthermore, production was sped up and fewer parts were damaged due to rough handling.

In another case discussed later in this book, car manufacturer Nissan required its suppliers to send parts in reusable plastic crates. Not only were fewer workers required to unpack parts, but parts also went more quickly to the production line. What's more, the plastic crates were designed to deliver smaller quantities to the line more frequently. Line workers had fewer steps to take to reach what they needed, because crates were smaller. Parts-inventory carrying costs declined. Quality improved because the parts were handled by fewer people.

Redoubling their efforts to reduce emissions will enable Green Wave riders to set new standards in manufacturing. Many competitors remain focused on quality alone (measured in defective parts per million, for example). They all too often ignore the waste involved in achieving high levels of quality.

Companies that wish to be successful Green Wave riders will want to ask themselves, Which war are we fighting, this one or the last? We visited one electronics factory in Germany that prides itself on quality, quality achieved through rigorous inspection. Defective pieces were simply junked or reworked by hand at considerable expense. Even the Deming Prize, the apex of achievement in manufacturing in Japan, recognizes quality without regard to the waste it may take to get there. Today, quality must be achieved without waste. For the smartest competitors, first-rate quality will be the *result* of eliminating waste.

GREEN PRODUCTIVITY

This book is not about a "kinder, gentler" business world that puts people before profits. On the contrary, we think industry should *put profits first.* To invest in its workers and technology, to pay high wages and maintain good benefits, to provide the products and services that customers around the world will pay for, companies must make money.

We also know that to maximize profits, managers must minimize waste. To do so quickly, cheaply, and continuously, they must have their employees "on side." All those waiting for the layoff ax to fall will be thinking about their own problems, not the company's. And MBAs sending out memos from headquarters will not improve efficiency any better than Soviet apparatchiks could reduce waste at farm collectives in the Ukraine with directives from Moscow.

Many of the world's biggest companies, some of them major exporters, have let the costs get out of line with those of foreign and domestic upstarts. This problem is going to get worse before it gets better. Jack Welch, the widely respected CEO of General Electric, told *Fortune,* "There's going to be global price competition like you've never seen. It's going to be brutal."[8] Financial pressure, not renewed vision, is what finally forces companies to respond to market realities. Each must reduce costs to survive. In this fight for survival, they can't leave any stone unturned when wringing costs out of operations. And they can't restructure their way to success without attacking the root of their problems.

Restructuring has become a code word for big-time layoffs. Even *layoffs* is something of a misnomer. At one time, those laid off, usually blue-collar workers, got hired back when demand picked up. Today when you get laid off, that's it. You get fired and they don't ever ask you back.

Sometimes layoffs are necessary. Deregulation of markets can make large bureaucracies redundant, and new technology can put thousands of jobs in jeopardy at the flip of a switch. Radical improvements in productivity can reduce the need for factory labor significantly and suddenly. But however necessary, restructuring looks like "slash and burn" management to most people: slashing their jobs and burning their futures.

All too often, companies under extreme cost pressures see mass layoffs as a way out. Yet this approach does not improve financial results in most cases, according to a 1992 Right Associates survey of 1,200 American companies. Some 900 of these companies had laid off workers during the previous five years, but three-quarters of them said layoffs did not boost their financial results. Two-thirds said productivity did not improve.[9]

Indeed, on the road to lean management, layoffs, as we have said, are the easy part. You get a quick cut in costs and your earnings per share suddenly look better. What happens after the cutting is another matter. That's when the real work begins, and that's the subject of this book.

A friend of ours works in human resources at a large New York bank, which like many others restructured in a big way after the stock market crash in 1987. In one year, this bank reduced employment by nearly 20 percent through a combination of layoffs, attrition, and branch divestitures. Incredibly, little was gained, even in direct labor costs. The bank's wage bill declined a mere 2 percent in the year that followed. The bank also took a huge write-down to cover restructuring costs, mostly severance pay of up to two years. And during this period, budgets for consultants and temps increased fourfold. Within a few years, "head count" crept back up to where it had been. Our friend said that his bank, in a bizarre game of musical chairs, was hiring the deadwood laid off from other New York banks, generally at salaries 25 percent higher than those of the people they replaced. This company incurred enormous costs, thousands of lives were shattered, and little of lasting value was accomplished.

So if all you want is a Band-Aid, a well-publicized restructuring may fit the bill. Our friend's bank boosted enthusiasm for its stock on Wall Street, at least for a while. But to reduce costs fundamentally, you must identify inefficiencies and eliminate the underlying cause of waste. There has to be real change in thinking, in processes and organization.

What's the point of laying people off if, for example, you don't reduce the number of layers of management? What's the point of reducing the number of layers of management if authority is not decentralized?

Restructuring should be an opportunity to go back to basics, to reexamine what your company does best, and, most importantly, to determine what customers value. What do we do best? is not always an easy question to answer. Neither is, Why do customers buy from us? It sounds silly, but most companies don't have the faintest idea. Anything you make or do that your customers do not value is wasted effort and unnecessary cost. This includes packaging your customers throw away, expensive solvents that evaporate into the air in your paint shop, and fuel you burn in your trucks. If your customers won't pay for it, why do it? You must zero in on exactly what customers value about you, your products and services. Then you can deliver what they want, *and no more.* Here lies the real opportunity to reduce costs, raise quality, and improve customer satisfaction—and to improve your environmental performance in the bargain.

In all the companies we have studied for this book, management fiat never reduced costs. Rather, dedicated and creative workers figured out better, more efficient ways of doing business. They applied knowledge to fundamental processes. In almost every case, one person, sometimes high up and sometimes not, got the "green" bug, wanting to do something good for the environment. In the process, these managers often improved their own standing in their organizations, or their own financial rewards. So much the better.

In tough markets, these champions usually had little or no money. They faced tight budgets, and could not raise prices to pay for their programs. They certainly could not sacrifice the quality of their products or services to the environmental cause. With nowhere else to turn, they started evangelizing. As others were caught up in their ideas, they asked questions and found solutions. Do we need to layer plastics to produce bumpers? Will our guests care if their towels are changed only once a day? What will happen if we stop spraying pesticides? Such self-examination produced small, ongoing, continuous improvements, what the Japanese call *kaizen*.

ZERO WASTE EQUALS ZERO DEFECTS

To improve their competitive position, not incrementally but radically, forward-looking companies from around the world are embracing the ultimate environmental goal: zero emissions. This means no smoke up the stack, no toxic chemicals down the drain, no trash to the dump. What drives them to this goal is continual, relentless cost reduction and quality improvement. Employees, especially PR types, will tell you that going "green" is the right thing to do. But zero emissions is not just feeling good about yourself. Nor is it a one-time quick fix. It is about cost and quality.

We have profiled ten environmental mavericks for this book. They see environmental improvement not as public-relations gloss and legal spin control, but as better organization, better management, and better products. To squeeze out waste, they redirect their efforts in light of genuine customer expectations. They focus on what customers really value about their products, and shed the rest.

The companies in this book operate in different industries and countries, and vary greatly in size. But they have much in common. First, they are growing and successful, despite adverse economic conditions. Second, they have not responded to problems simply by removing thousands of employees. Rather, they decided to boost the productivity of their workers by improving efficiency. For all, better environmental performance reduces costs. Third, and perhaps most important, CEOs and top managers driving change at these organizations are iconoclasts: they break the rules in their companies and industries.

There are a number of common elements in their approaches to environmentally based efficiency:

- They have all drawn the connection between waste and quality.
- They all use the waste-quality relationship to drive management decisions.
- They all use waste reduction to remove inefficiencies in customer service.
- They all use the environment as a catalyst to force organizational issues to the surface, where they can be solved.
- They all use environmental measures to increase shareholder value.

Here's how you can achieve the same results:

Go where the money is. The companies in this book identified the pockets of waste that represented significant potential savings.

Pinch pennies. Small, seemingly inconsequential improvements add up, particularly when many customers are served. In fast-growing markets lots of problems can be swept under the rug; in slow-growth, competitive ones, success lies in the details.

Ask, Why are we doing this? These companies have rethought what they do from the customer's point of view and found that many activities can be eliminated because nobody values them; less activity means less waste means less environmental damage and more profit.

Set tough goals. Ambitious targets like zero emissions and organic certification soon reveal good ideas and creative thinking. Continuous, incremental improvements make goals a reality; those who set their sights low are seldom disappointed. All the companies in this book have voluntarily set standards higher than regulators require. To approach zero emissions, they rethink what they do far beyond the factory gates, from product conception to final disposal.

Run ahead of the regulators. At these ten companies, management worries about customers, not fighting the government. They don't have to worry about today's legal levels of pollution becoming tomorrow's big lawsuit. This advantage alone gives them a lead on competitors.

Go mainstream and empower employees. The companies in this book do not rely on a VP environment any more than they do on a VP quality. Environmental performance, like quality, is everybody's job, visibly led by top management, and front-line employees are encouraged to effect change.

Focus on thinking, not technology. For our ten companies, the judicious application of new technologies and new investment play a role, but innovative ideas result in the most profitable changes.

Forget about recycling. Recycling is a way to deal with a problem *after* it occurs, and seldom pays, except when it forces changes that eliminate the need for recycling in the first place.

Don't count on suppliers. In most cases, the companies in this book had to drag their suppliers kicking and screaming into the future.

WHY NOW? WHY THEM?

In each case, the companies in this book substitute knowledge—worker brainpower—for natural resources. But why should anyone substitute information for energy consumption when fuel is the cheapest it's been since the 1950s? For the same reason companies adopt the toughest quality standards in the world: to build market share, to cement relations with customers, to increase profits.

Many companies are constantly improving quality, for example, by meeting the stringent international ISO 9000 standards, which specify quality control methods.[10] They do so not just to remain players in Europe, where these standards are widely used, but also to be competitive throughout the world. Environmental standards are similar catalysts to improved performance. Anyone who thinks it's cheaper to waste materials and energy than to fix the real problem has not been attentive to what's going on. A company that pollutes has a problem with top management, its processes, or its products.

A decade ago, many business leaders thought quality cost more. They know now that improving quality reduces costs. In our own experience in information technology, the low-cost producer *always* has the highest quality. The same goes for pollution. If you are worried about costs, pollution indicates inefficiency. It provides an opportunity to save money. Moving to other countries where standards are lower will not help if you do not face the root problem. You cannot waste raw materials, which may be cheap, without wasting other resources, which are expensive. Wasteful practices indicate a poor organization living on borrowed time. We've seen a lot of factories, and you can eat off the floor in the ones with the lowest costs.

Many people feel they lead two lives. At home, as private citizens, they are environmentalists. We asked one woman we met in Hong Kong about what will happen when China takes over the territory from the British in 1997. She responded, "I'm more worried about the nuclear power plant at Daya Bay that the Chinese are building than about 1997." At the same time, at work, some people still feel that pollution and paychecks go together.

Some observers argue that it is possible to be green and save money too. But they miss the essential finding that can be learned from the companies in this book: You *must* be green and you *must* eliminate waste to be competitive today. There is no choice between cost reduction and environmentalism. Our ten companies show why.

Some markets will simply be closed to those unable to meet very high green standards. Many countries, including the United States, Germany, and Japan, are already using environmental laws to protect domestic producers in a broad range of industries. The only way to avoid this problem is to be the greenest kid on the block. If you want the sale, the performance of your product better be the best, and your production costs, including energy and raw materials, better be rock bottom.

The companies profiled in this book don't have to worry about environmental barriers. These leaders have already made the decision to go beyond compliance with the law. They are not waiting around for governments to develop coherent policies. For them, legal tests are irrelevant since their goal is to approach the limit: zero emissions. They operate to the toughest standards in effect anywhere. While all large, our ten companies have not widely publicized their environmental achievements. For them, the Green Wave is not about Earth Day press releases. They are not subordinating profits to saving the planet. Rather, they are forging stronger organizations with better thinking.

Eight of these ten companies are based outside the United States, although in three cases we discuss their American operations. Our choice of organizations is not accidental; another finding in this book is that many Canadian, European, and Japanese companies are way ahead of their U.S. rivals in recognizing the power of environmentally driven cost reduction.

The first part of this book consists of one chapter for each company. For these profiles, we rely on firsthand experience. We have visited their factories, offices, and stores, talked to their managers, and questioned their customers. Our book is about real people at work, making real decisions—and real money.

In the second part of our book, we consider how government action can encourage (or discourage) waste reduction and efficiency. In four chapters, the book contrasts policies in the United

States, Europe, Japan, and in the rapidly expanding economies of Singapore and Hong Kong for their effect on competitiveness.

This book's penultimate chapter is about the "real" information revolution. We believe that the plummeting cost of information is driving the Green Wave. Those countries (and companies) with the best-educated workers will be the ones that most successfully profit from this historical shift. Knowledge is today's most valuable resource. Only those with knowledge can substitute cheap information for more expensive natural resources.

This book is written for anyone concerned about the future, certainly, but mostly for CEOs and top managers who are responsible for making their companies prosper. Decision-makers facing global pressures on their markets need to act now. Pushed and pulled by government regulation, by customer demands for greener products, and by foreign competition, they will find here information they can translate into action. With the lessons learned from the following ten environmental leaders, they can enhance their own market leadership driven by efficiency.

PART ONE

NISSAN DRIVES DOWN PLANT EMISSIONS

GOING FOR ZERO EMISSIONS

In a hotly contested market like cars, survival means relentless cost reduction. Manufacturers can turn the screws on employees and suppliers to produce incremental savings. But to gain lasting advantage, to reduce costs permanently, they must rethink production, if not their entire business, every day. Unfortunately, managers cannot use traditional methods to evaluate new ideas. Shifts in thinking, by definition, defy measurement. Waste reduction can at first look like a poor investment, but with the right philosophy it will always pay—often in unexpected ways.

When Nissan announced its losses for 1993, the business world was stunned. Sales had dropped by 3 percent, pushing the company into the red—to the tune of ¥56 billion ($483 million)—for the first time in forty years. At home, the bottom fell out of the car market as worried consumers tightened their purse strings. In the United States, sales skidded as Nissan's share fell in a tough market. Things got so bad that the company was borrowing money to keep its factories running.[1]

Yoshifumi Tsuji, appointed president in mid-1992 just as the extent of Nissan's woes were becoming painfully clear, decided that there was only one solution: cut costs. Nissan could not grow its way out of this hole. Consumer confidence was in the doldrums throughout the industrialized world. At the same time, competitors were opening new plants at a record pace, making overcapacity endemic in all major markets. With sales prospects flat at best, profits could only come through cost reduction. Acknowledging financial problems is not easy for any company, but for one of Japan's most successful export giants, the experience was especially painful. But instead of heading for cover, Tsuji decided to face the music.

Perhaps even more shocking than Nissan's losses was Tsuji's reaction. Late in 1992, the company announced that, through attrition, employment would be reduced by 4,000, or 6 percent of the total, over the next three years. Then early in 1993, to the shock of lifelong workers, Nissan announced it was closing its flagship Zama plant outside Tokyo.[2] For a Japanese company of Nissan's stature, a pillar of Japan's employment-for-life edifice, such moves would have been unthinkable just a few years earlier.

Through these and other measures, Tsuji, a no-nonsense, hands-on engineer with a manufacturing background, wanted to improve productivity by 10 percent annually. During the fat years of the 1980s, Nissan had let production costs rise while market share in Japan and the United States slid. Rapid sales growth covered a multitude of sins. Nissan was spending more to build its cars than arch-rival Toyota in Japan and Ford in the United States.[3] From its neck-and-neck position in 1979 with Toyota as the largest Japanese supplier in the United States, Nissan had slid to the number-three spot behind Honda. The slump of the early 1990s hit all the car companies hard, but Nissan was taking it right on the nose.

Nissan's U.S. operations did not escape the cost-reduction imperative, and the company came under enormous pressure to raise profits to help cover losses at home. In April 1993, 115 employees were laid off and the president of the U.S. sales company quit.[4] Further staff cuts were expected over the next two years.[5] Then the company bagged its race-car program, sacking seventy workers.[6] For a decade, Nissan had been investing billions in production, development, and sales in the United States. Suddenly the open checkbook slammed shut.

Times had certainly changed since the late 1980s, when management initiated an ambitious environmental program at Smyrna, Tennessee, the location of Nissan's only production facility in the United States. Back then, profits were at record levels, as sales grew with relentless predictability every year. In 1989, Nissan announced that it would double U.S. production capacity at Smyrna, at a cost of nearly $500 million. In 1991, Nissan could speak expansively of "the harmonious coexistence of people, automobiles, and nature." It was not long before cutbacks and cost reduction, not peace and harmony, were the words on everyone's lips.

The job of slashing costs at Smyrna fell squarely on the shoulders of Emil Hassan, senior vice president of operations. An urbane man yet an engineer to the core, Hassan has been a rising star at Nissan since joining the company in 1981. With two dozen years of car-manufacturing experience behind him, Hassan is someone who understands what is happening on the shop floor. In short, he was cut from the same cloth as Tsuji, his boss in Tokyo. Hassan has met the challenge laid down by Tsuji, cutting costs with single-minded determination—and boosting quality in the bargain. Smyrna has met its cost-reduction goals, and its quality is now as good as anything produced by Nissan in Japan. Central to Hassan's success has been his program for waste reduction and environmental improvement.

THE CHALLENGE

Nissan Motor Manufacturing Corp. makes cars and trucks at its Smyrna plant, located on 782 acres of old cornfields and well-tended orchards three miles from I-24, twenty miles south of Nashville. As we come over a rise in the two-lane county road, the plant is suddenly in view. The scale of the place, in the middle of nowhere, is breathtaking: a low, vast building more than a mile across, occupying more than 5 million square feet, or thirty-three acres. From the outside, there is no sign of activity except a lone plume of steam drifting upwards.

Nissan broke ground at Smyrna in 1981, and has gradually expanded the building, now about half again as large as the original. In front, facing a landscaped parking lot, is the administration area, through which visitors enter. Here are housed the general managers of the plant, as well as hundreds of engineers in spartan but pleasant surroundings. For the most part, office areas are open, the atmosphere casual but businesslike. In engineering, employees wear dark blue polo shirts with the Nissan logo stitched on the breast pocket.

The administration area opens into the three main parts of the plant, all of roughly equal size, stretching as far as the eye can see in each direction. To the north is trim and chassis production; to the east, the paint shop; and to the south, body, frame, and stamping, where vehicles are finally assembled. Smyrna is the biggest car-manufacturing facility under one roof in the United States, and Nissan maintains a fleet of golf carts just for getting around inside the building.

Visiting a manufacturing site like this is always a thrill, and Smyrna is no exception. The real work of industry is done in places like this, turning steel and other raw materials into everyday products—in this case, those icons of American culture, automobiles. Under twenty-foot ceilings, the scale of things is awesome, from the huge stamping presses to endless overhead conveyors. Activity is ceaseless: forklifts cross back and forth, partially assembled cars travel along their tracks, robots advance with feverish motions, welding and painting. Everywhere, workers move quickly and with determination.

Representing an investment of $1.2 billion, Smyrna produces 450,000 vehicles per year, and employs nearly 6,000 workers on two shifts. Some 60 percent of the vehicles Nissan sells in the United States are made here, and nearly three-quarters of the people the company employs in North America work at the site. In addition to the final assembly of small and medium-sized cars and compact pickup trucks, the plant also produces engines, gas tanks, bumpers, and other body parts. In the decade after the plant opened in 1983, 2 million vehicles rolled off the production line.

Sound like this plant should produce a lot of waste? Smyrna used to account for as much garbage as a small city. What's more, operations here once sent tons of paints and solvents into the air or down pipe drains every year. Today it's a different story. Nissan has approached the goal it set for itself in 1988: no smoke up the chimney, no fifty-five-gallon drums of toxic chemicals to storage, no garbage to the landfill. Zero emissions.

During the past decade, recycling has become a reality for most American households. At home, Americans have grown used to sorting their trash into a half-dozen piles and listening to lectures from their children on the evils of ozone depletion, rainforest destruction, and pitching out newspapers with the coffee grinds. But in the United States, as in other developed nations, businesses, not households, account for most garbage. In recent years, industry has accounted for over 80 percent of all solid waste produced.[7] In other words, we don't see three-quarters of the garbage we produce—and pay for. This mess results from the products and services we buy, before we buy them.

When Nissan decided to do something about its environmental impact, the challenge it faced was extraordinary. Perhaps even more daunting than the engineering and management challenge of eliminating mountains of garbage and tons of air and water pollutants was that greatest of forces: organizational inertia.

Although it was generating trash on a monumental scale, the direct costs to Nissan were low. Tennessee had welcomed the company with open arms, and, generally, neither Nissan's employees, its neighbors, nor the state thought a little pollution was too much too pay for thousands of high-wage jobs. For many, the attitude was, What's the problem?

At the same time, the potential for disrupting production for the sake of a little recycling was a strong argument against change. Making cars is an immensely complex process. Thousands of parts must be brought together at just the right time by thousands of people. Production lines are like tightly wound clocks, put together over months and years. You don't mess with them unless there's a compelling reason, like reducing costs, improving quality, or raising safety standards. And, as we have seen, Nissan, in a tough market, was in no position to throw money at feel-good causes, whatever the public-relations benefit.

Led by Emil Hassan, the advocates for environmental change prevailed at Smyrna. Hassan is expansive about his environmental plans. A nearby resident and active in local affairs, he thinks this part of Tennessee is beautiful, and he does not want to spoil it. And Nissan does not want its neighbors to smell the plant or to see any effects of its presence beyond the factory gates. When Nissan was first lured to Tennessee in 1980, the local county government agreed to take its garbage come what may. Nissan could have said, "This stuff is your problem." It did not. With authority, Hassan adds, "We want to make green cars." Green means fuel efficient, of course, but Nissan also wants to minimize the impact of manufacturing.

In the process, Nissan has learned that reducing waste pays big dividends, and that these returns often come from unexpected quarters. The company made many changes on faith without knowing exactly what the benefits would be. Yet Emil Hassan knew that environmental improvement at Nissan was not a whim for a company with money to burn. Like all its investments, Nissan's pollution-control programs had to pay their own way. Hassan wants to make "green cars," but, as one of the engineers working for him told us, "he could see the potential savings from the beginning."

DOWN AND DIRTY

To avoid disrupting its existing production lines, Nissan decided to focus its cleanup efforts on a new model, the Altima, a midsized four-door sedan. While staking out new ground with the Altima avoided the problems of disrupting the company's ongoing business, it added a new element of risk. The Altima was to be a bold move by Nissan into a segment of the market in which Nissan's performance had been disappointing.

The first Altima rolled off the production line in June 1992 after three years of preparation. Annual capacity is 200,000 units, a little less than half of Smyrna's total output. Since most environmental damage at a car plant is caused by painting and parts packaging, this is where the most radical changes were made. The lessons learned with the Altima were gradually applied to other production lines.

When the Altima was conceived, Smyrna produced twenty long Dumpsters of garbage every single day. Four years later, this figure was down to just two daily landfill-bound loads; another year later, down to about one. To give an idea of how much this represents, if each employee threw out four soda cans per day, one Dumpster would be filled. Another way to look at solid waste is the amount per car. When the program began, Smyrna generated 180 pounds of trash per vehicle; four years later the plant-wide average was down to 30 pounds. Another twelve months on, the average was down to 14 pounds per unit. Plans call for this small volume of trash to be reduced a further 90 percent. These are plant-wide figures; even less is produced for the Altima, which is farther along than the other production lines.

Nissan effected this dramatic reduction by switching to reusable containers for parts and components that it buys from other suppliers. Now, over 97 percent of the 9,750 different parts Nissan buys come in reusable containers; the balance are delivered in containers that can be recycled.[8] Before, parts containers were simply trashed.

Buying clout helps when you want to make suppliers change. Globally, Nissan makes nearly 3 million vehicles annually, so it can throw its weight around. Suppliers are responsive to Nissan suggestions, to say the least. Furthermore, many of its suppliers have been doing business with Nissan for years, if not decades, so relations are tight. To some extent, supplier changes were made by fiat; Nissan simply said, "This is the way we are doing business." The stick that Nissan wields is obvious; the carrot is long-term contracts that give suppliers stable, predictable revenues and cash flows.

Despite Nissan's purchasing power, any big change involving suppliers, if it is to be successful, requires selling them on the benefits, and working closely with them. To get results, Nissan sometimes paid higher prices, sometimes lower. Typically, for example, it might cost the supplier $7.50 for a throwaway package and $10.00 for a reusable one. Suppliers have to figure out how to make this pay. Unfortunately for them, they must sometimes use different reusable containers for other car makers (a packaging association is trying to standardize across the car industry). To some extent, Nissan simply shifted its garbage problem to suppliers. Those that delivered their parts using unrecyclable materials like foam (for example, as blocks between stacks of windshields) were required to take their own garbage back. This proved a strong incentive for them to change.

Masterminding the return of thousands of reusable crates is no small task. Nissan hired some managers from another car company to run the container-handling system. This competitor had tried to switch to reusable crates, was unable to manage the logistics of getting them back to suppliers, and ultimately abandoned the idea. Nissan, with more patience, has benefited from this rival's failure.

One of the biggest remaining logistical concerns is containers for the parts that come from Japan. The company's Japanese plants rely more heavily on landfills than Smyrna does. In Tennessee, Nissan started with a clean slate, without any environmental skeletons in the closet. Much of the effort companies like General Motors and General Electric (or Nissan in Japan, for that matter) expend on environmental affairs is for cleaning up sites that are 50 or even 100 years old. Starting fresh helps.

For parts packaging, recycling does not play a big role. Nissan doesn't want mountains of trash, whether it can be recycled or not. The idea is to eliminate waste altogether, with reusable containers. Nevertheless, for a very small number of parts, the company will accept delivery in containers like corrugated cardboard, that can be baled up and sold for scrap. For example, the factory receives enough fuses to last for two weeks in one cardboard box; it just doesn't make sense to have special containers for such small parts that are ordered infrequently. And in its offices, the company continues to recycle paper and aluminum cans.[9]

For process wastes, like trimmings from plastic moldings and metal stamping, Nissan relies heavily on recycling. There is a ready market for steel, which can be reused to make more steel. Originally the company simply gathered up trimmings into loose piles and threw them into a truck to be hauled off to the scrap yard. Then Smyrna purchased a machine for crushing scrap metal into small cubes, which fetch more than loose trimmings.

Plastic is another story. Plastic recycling is in its infancy, so there is little market for scrap. The economics of plastic recycling are unproved, to say the least, and landfilling and incineration remain the most cost-effective means of disposal.

Sometimes unpainted plastic trimmings or defective parts can easily be ground up and reused for the same purpose. Generally, however, reuse is difficult because plastic is easily contaminated. For example, trimmings from plastic bumpers cannot simply be ground up and turned into more bumpers because the paint gets mixed in with the plastic and makes it inflexible. Nissan sends painted plastic scraps to a company that turns them into plastic lumber, parking stops, and other items Nissan buys back at inflated prices. Nissan is stimulating demand for its scrap by specifying the recycled content of the plastic products it buys. Here, again, is where buying clout helps: Nissan asked Rubbermaid, for example, to use scrap from Smyrna in the garbage cans and other products Nissan buys.

To avoid "cascading" (whereby plastic is recycled into less valuable products until it is finally worthless landfill), Nissan is trying to reuse plastic for its original purpose. If you are spending a lot of money to produce high-quality plastic, you don't want to pay someone to take it away to make park benches. Until the Altima was introduced, Nissan only made bumper parts at Smyrna; now it also makes plastic gas tanks. At its labs in Japan,

Nissan figured out how Smyrna could shred and reuse multilayer plastic gas tanks. And the labs also developed a process for removing paint from bumpers so they can be recycled as bumpers.[10]

These kinds of high-tech fixes are expensive. To simplify its task, Nissan is also reducing the number of plastics used in its cars (the proliferation of plastic types itself makes recycling difficult), and to redesign some parts to use plastics that can be recycled more easily. But the real opportunity for savings, and the next challenge Nissan has set for itself, is to "design out" process waste. Changes in manufacturing as well as in car design will be necessary. We were told at Smyrna, "Over the next five years, we may have to start influencing the design more to keep reducing waste." By reducing the number of parts, by designing parts that are easier to make, by operating machines to closer tolerances, and by reducing defects (i.e., fewer parts that need to be scrapped), Nissan can stop a lot of problems before they start. And avoid a lot of headaches: no waste, no need for complicated recycling technologies. And no need to worry about the vagaries of the scrap market.

Once the garbage monster was tamed at Smyrna, Nissan turned to the next biggest mess, the paint shop. With traditional painting techniques, cars and trucks are painted by workers (or robots) with spray guns, but only about half the paint reaches the car. Most of the rest evaporates into the air, and some residual amount finds its way into the drains on the floor as sludge. Paint contains petroleum-based chemicals, called volatile organic compounds (VOCs), that are a major component of smog. Twenty years ago, VOCs overwhelmingly came from motor vehicle emissions and flue gases from power plants. These sources have been cleaned up, but the smog persists. So in the late 1980s, the government started casting around for other sources, like paint shops, that were once considered marginal contributors to the country's poor air quality.

Half a million vehicles take a lot of paint and, in the bad old days, created a lot of VOC emissions. So, beginning with the Altima, Nissan switched to water-based paints, which contain only a tiny fraction of the petroleum that the old paints did. The change was not easy: Nissan had to develop new paints and a new application system. The biggest concern was finish quality. Other car makers had switched to water-based primers, but kept oil-based finishes for the final coat, to hedge their bets. Nissan decided to switch over completely for the Altima, and claims it was the first car company to go to 100 percent water-based paint for any model.

Nissan did not want to spend a lot of money on a new paint shop while it was still wasting half the paint it sprays on its vehicles. So the company's engineers chose a state-of-the-art electrostatic system, which gives the surface to be painted an electrical charge, causing it to attract the metal in the paint like a magnet. Unfortunately, this system would not work with the water-based paints, and Nissan's paint suppliers said it simply could not be done. Other technical difficulties had to be overcome as well. For example, cleaning the new system proved much more difficult than the old. But after considerable wrangling with suppliers and the complete reformulation of all its paints, Nissan eventually got the system to work. VOC emissions are down 75 percent compared to the old process, and are well under legal limits.

Another by-product of the painting process is sludge, the residue that collects from the paint that doesn't get on the car. By switching to electrostatic painting, Nissan greatly reduced the amount of sludge it produces. And by using water-based paints, the paint shop produces sludge that is less toxic than if oil-based mixes were used. A small amount of sludge remains, which would normally be landfilled. Nissan built a $4 million incinerator to dispose of paint sludge (even water-based paints contain some hydrocarbons that can be burned), as well as wood and broken shipping pallets that cannot be reused. Some other solvents may also be burned. This incinerator is an expensive way to dispose of paint sludge, since it is not considered hazardous. But there are a number of benefits. There is less potential legal liability than in sending it to a landfill, where it might come back to haunt the company later. Landfill charges are avoided. And costs are partially recouped by using heat from the incinerator to help heat and cool the plant. Capturing energy that would otherwise be wasted has helped Nissan reduce the amount of energy it takes to make a car by 35 percent over the past two decades.

Incinerating process by-products (particularly toxic ones) to produce electricity or steam is a popular means of disposal outside the United States. "Thermal recycling," as it is euphemistically called, is considered efficient and environmentally benign in Japan and Germany. But in the United States, where competitiveness and environmentalism don't mix well, this approach is not popular. In 1993, Vice President Al Gore (who hails from Tennessee) got into a high-profile fight with the EPA about a new toxic-waste incinerator in Ohio, which resulted in a general tightening of regulations for all incinerators.[11] Nissan did not have any problems with its neighbors when it sought permits for its facility. The incinerator is not burning toxins and is very clean; nevertheless, the company may have found obtaining permits easier in a state that was eager for high-paying jobs.

Paint is not the only source of VOCs in car manufacturing. Many oil-based solvents are used for cleaning. Nissan is experimenting with citrus- and water-based cleaners for its machinery and to prepare sheet metal for painting. In addition, Nissan has switched to "close-loop" systems, which permit solvents to be reused many times before being returned to suppliers. Solvent packaging has also changed. For liquids, refillable containers of up to 600 gallons are used, which eliminates the need for cleaning. In the past, fifty-five-gallon drums created storage, cleaning, and disposal headaches. In total, Smyrna recycles or sells back to its suppliers 92 percent of the hazardous materials used in production.[12]

THE PAYOFF: LOWER COSTS, BETTER CARS

For Japanese car manufacturers such as Nissan, purchases of raw materials and components make up three-quarters of their total expenditures. Labor costs are relatively minor; at the most efficient plants, 5 percent or less of total production costs.[13] Even General

Motors, which is much more vertically integrated than its Japanese rivals, spends four times as much on parts as on labor.[14] For many manufacturers, the cost of carrying inventory (parts, work-in-progress, and finished goods) often exceeds all other expenses, and can spell the difference between profit and loss.[15]

The problem is that scarce cash has been shelled out for all those spare parts and half-finished cars that are gathering dust in the factory. That money could be used for better purposes, like selling cars, developing new ones, or paying dividends. If managers can reduce what's in the pipeline at any given time, they can reduce overheads dramatically. And naturally, if they throw away less of what they buy, they are better off.

In addressing its environmental concerns, Nissan has in fact zeroed in on inventories. If the company is to reduce production costs 10 percent per year, as it believes it must to survive, reducing the cost of raw materials and components has to be its first priority. According to a Nissan executive, "What we are talking about here is twenty-first-century materials handling, which is driven by our green strategy."

If parts and materials are the biggest expense for a car manufacturer, better organization is the best and simplest way to reduce costs. In cars, as in most manufacturing business, automation is an expensive alternative. Car manufacturing is not highly automated. In fact, industry-wide, automation of final assembly is surprisingly limited.[16] While robots do some tasks like painting and welding very well, people do complicated and varied tasks better. Indeed, at first glance, car assembly today probably does not look all that different from Henry Ford's River Rouge plant in 1920.

Small changes that make the process easier also produce large savings. The key is to simplify. We have visited many factories around the world, in North America, Asia, and Europe, and most of them were a mess. Racks of parts and unfinished goods, dirty floors, and cardboard boxes full of coffee cups is the norm. The most efficient plants, invariably operated by extremely successful companies, appear simple, with clear layouts and no clutter. Efficiency and simplicity go together. When they go together well, the result is "green."

If the plant is a mess, the company is probably a mess and performance reflects it.[17] Sloppy operations indicate slack management. On the basis of these observations, we have concluded that there is a high correlation between plant cleanliness and market share. When the factory is well organized, when there are wide aisles and lots of elbow room, employee safety and morale benefit. So do quality, efficiency, and productivity. As someone at Nissan put it, "If the plant is a mess, a worker doesn't care if one more bolt drops on the floor. If it's spotless, he will be careful." Compared with the many plants around the world we have visited, we found Smyrna clean and well organized.

Managing the flow of raw materials into Smyrna is a staggering job. Some 10,000 parts that go into Nissan's cars and trucks are purchased from others, but the material-staging area at Smyrna is a tiny area of the plant. By switching to reusable containers for virtually all the parts it buys, Nissan has simplified the way it assembles cars and trucks. Instead of having a lot of people unwrapping and disposing of boxes, and others feeding them into the right spot on the assembly line, parts come straight into work areas in the right quantity, in containers that are easy for the line workers to use. What's more, there are smaller quantities of parts in the reusable crates than in the throwaway ones that they replaced, so there is less traffic handling materials and less congestion on the line. These changes make housekeeping much easier, and cut parts handling significantly. And since parts do not have to be unwrapped, labor costs are reduced.

Work stations on the assembly line used to be fifteen to twenty feet long, with big boxes of parts needed for each task. Now the containers are smaller, the right size, engineered for each job. Workers spend less time walking and more time working because of the new containers. Labor costs, even if they are a small segment of the total, still add up—every cent counts in this market. With less wasted effort, less labor goes into each car. But most important, controlling the flow of parts in this fashion reduces parts inventory. In the beginning, some suppliers were apprehensive about delivering half or quarter truckloads of parts (the "milk runs," Nissan calls them) instead of the full loads they were used to. But these suppliers have come around.

In two years, there was a 40 percent reduction in parts inventory at Smyrna. This kind of savings, company-wide, would free up as much as $400 million at Nissan, the same amount that Nissan spent to put the Altima into production. And while the entire reduction in parts inventories was not due to reusable containers, better and simpler materials handling was a big factor.

Fewer parts and less clutter have other indirect but real benefits. Less handling means better quality. A worker grabs a windshield out of large delivery tray and swings it into place on a car in one motion—the only time it is touched in the plant. Before, it would have been unwrapped, moved to the production line, then lifted into place: there were three opportunities to break or scratch each one. Custom-designed crates protect parts better. Tire rims, for example, now arrive in big plastic eight-pack pallets, each rim in its own slot. Formerly they came on plywood sheets, stacked up and then shrink-wrapped; not only was there a lot of garbage, but the plywood was expensive, and the rims could rattle around inside, getting dented.

Smaller production runs are possible. Faster delivery of smaller quantities of parts right to the production line makes it easy to switch from one model to another. That means Nissan can match production more closely to demand. For example, the company might want to minimize the number of cars it makes with standard transmissions and no air-conditioning. If nobody wants them, they will end up sitting on dealer lots until they are sold at steep discounts. Car companies also appeal to consumers by increasing the number of options and models they have to choose from. To do so and still make money, production must be flexible.

Less space is now needed for each car produced. When it opened, Smyrna had 3.4 million square feet to make 250,000 vehicles per year; since then, the plant has grown only about 50 percent in size, but vehicle capacity has nearly doubled and engine-assembly and parts-stamping have been added. About one-third less space is now needed per car produced. For each car that rolls out the door, this means a smaller investment in bricks and mortar, lower real estate taxes, less heating and cooling.

Safety has improved. Wider, less cluttered aisles reduce the chance of accidents. Without packages to be unwrapped, there are far fewer injuries from box knives than before. All this adds up to lower medical and workers' compensation costs, fewer sick days, and better employee morale.

And then there are the direct savings. When it originally switched to returnable containers, Nissan expected to lose money, but the change has turned out to be a break-even proposition. First, of course, trash handling and disposal bills are down. By reducing its volume of landfilled trash by 95 percent, Nissan dramatically reduced its trash-disposal costs. In tipping fees alone, the plant cut operating costs by some $5 million per year. As in other parts of the country, tipping fees (i.e., landfill charges) rose quickly during the 1980s, for Smyrna by 200 percent. Furthermore, collecting, compacting, and loading a train's worth of garbage each day took a big organization. In just eighteen months, Nissan was able to eliminate five positions for rubbish handling, a savings in the hundreds of thousands of dollars per year.

On the direct-cost side, Nissan had to set up a special department for handling the return of bar-coded, reusable plastic crates for incoming parts. With this complex system, Nissan loses in crate handling much of what it gains from less unpacking. Recycling cardboard and other materials also requires a sizable collection system.

When these easily identified costs and savings were tallied, Nissan concluded they were a wash as far as the bottom line was concerned. So while it breaks even on direct costs, Nissan benefits from production economies and quality and safety improvements that management does not even try to quantify.

Nissan uses the same criteria to finance an environmental project as any other capital investment, but the company never undertakes any project for financial reasons alone. There is no strict policy that all investments must show a 30 percent rate of return, for example. Other considerations, like safety and quality, also come into play. Each project is judged on its own merits.

When Nissan installed its new electrostatic painting system, for example, the savings on paint alone were large. With the old system, 50 percent of the paint sprayed on a car went into the air or down the drain; with the new one, only 10 to 20 percent is lost. At seventy to eighty dollars per gallon of paint, the savings cover a lot of investment. At the same time, the finish quality of its cars improved ("higher gloss and reflectivity"), and environmental costs and risks went down. For other investments, like Smyrna's incinerator and plastic recycling program, the advantages are long term.

Adding up all these benefits—some small, some large, some easy to quantify, some not—Nissan is confident that its environmental investments have been worthwhile. This approach to process management, which produces consistent results (in this case 10 percent cost reduction per year), is the very essence of *kaizen,* the system of continuous improvement made famous by Japan's large car companies. Perhaps more to the point, the Altima has been a success: sales exceeded expectations in the first year after introduction, raising Nissan's U.S. market share significantly.[18] This was none too soon after a disastrous 1993.

In one respect, results have been disappointing. Nissan's environmental accomplishments did not reduce its compliance burden. Using chemicals on the government's hazardous materials list means paperwork and lots of it, even if those chemicals are not released into the air or water. No matter how much it reduces pollution, Nissan does not expect compliance costs to decrease. "The trend is always up in terms of paperwork, no matter what we do here."

COMMITMENT, NOT SPIN CONTROL

With the ambitious waste-reduction goals Nissan set for itself, management had to do a lot more than skim *Fifty Simple Things*

Business Can Do to Save the Earth for good ideas. Passing out re-usable Nissan coffee mugs would not make a big dent in the amount of garbage coming out of a plant like Smyrna. The company had to rethink how to make cars, reconsidering details others may have overlooked.

You can judge how seriously a company takes the environment by how it is organized. At Smyrna, Nissan assigned an engineer to each of three areas: air, water, and hazardous and solid waste. A fourth managed the group. These engineers controlled their own capital and operating budgets. They were part of the environmental and utilities group, which reported to the director of plant engineering.

The first concern of this small team was to stay current with the permits required by several layers of government. They had to ensure that Nissan stayed within the law, always a quickly moving target. Federal environmental regulations alone are now more extensive than the IRS tax code.

Despite the complexity of compliance, the environmental engineers did not get bogged down in paperwork like those in their position at so many other companies. They were not fighting last year's battle with the government. The difference is management support and leadership. The environmental team was able to look forward because Nissan gave them the authority to translate ideas into action. At Nissan, environmental responsibilities are a line-engineering function. Nissan wants real change, not spin control from public relations, legal affairs, or human resources.

Those in the front line have no doubts about who drives Nissan's environmental goals: it's top management. Clear direction and commitment at the top make life a lot easier for those engineers bringing Nissan's vision to life. And their commitment was believable precisely because the environmental program was viewed right from the beginning as integral to Nissan's productivity goals. As someone told us, "This was a high-visibility project driven from high up in the organization."

Emil Hassan had this vision; he saw the potential savings right from the start. He has been vindicated by the results—and it hasn't hurt his career any. In the five years after the solid-waste reduction program began at Smyrna, Hassan was promoted twice, until he had plant-wide responsibility for manufacturing, engineering, and quality. The people who work for him are quick to give him credit for his accomplishments. Clearly they are all proud of a job well done.

Management backing helped with the naysayers and with the kind of institutional inertia present in any large organization. Nevertheless, change is never easy when 6,000 people are involved. Nissan's environmental engineers still had to work with others with more pressing concerns. At every turn, they had to consult many co-workers.

The Smyrna plant has full control over environmental affairs. There is some contact with Japan, but no formal relationship between environmental staffs. As one manager told us, "It is really very different there in terms of regulation; we let them know what we are doing. They send us questionnaires, but not on a regular basis. Nissan is a worldwide company, but in terms of environment, we are not too connected." This is a Japanese company, to be sure. But these are Americans making the environment pay big dividends.[19]

To make cars more efficiently, Nissan needs the cooperation of its workers, particularly when change involves ongoing process improvements at the shop-floor level. No scheme imposed by fiat would have much of a chance of success if workers on the line—or their union—resisted change. By locating in rural Tennessee, Nissan sidestepped the kind of union work rules that slow down or prevent change elsewhere. This is a "right to work" state, and Nissan is not a union shop. Employees are clearly glad to have their high-paying jobs; the kind of resentment and cynicism that is palpable in many older factories with a history of management-labor tension is not apparent here. Even so, Nissan has earned the confidence of its employees. Despite the layoffs in marketing and sales in the United States, Smyrna has been spared. Recently, the car maker was named one of the "100 Best Companies to Work for in America" for the second time, on the basis of pay and benefits, opportunities, job security, pride in work and company, openness and fairness, and camaraderie and friendliness.[20]

Perhaps the biggest risk at Smyrna is *too* much commitment. Nissan's business is cars, not plastic shipping crates or metal scrap. The company has brought some parts production in-house to facilitate plastic recycling, and expanded its processing of scrap metal. In the scale of things, these are small investments at Smyrna. But in a market as tough as cars, no competitor can afford to take its eye off the ball.

THE VIEW FROM JAPAN

Much of Nissan's corporate environmental policy sounds quaint to an American ear. One brochure from Japan opens with the following Zen-like statement: "At Nissan, our policy on the environment is that nature, people and cars share the same habitat. In other words, we live in symbiosis."[21] However strange this blurb may sound, Nissan has a clear, focused environmental plan that is bearing fruit for itself and its customers.

The activities at Smyrna are only part of Nissan's broader environmental agenda. At the "Earth Summit" in Rio in 1992, Nissan announced its environmental objectives:

- Reduce manufacturing waste
- Improve waste-treatment techniques
- Promote recycling
- Reduce the use of VOCs
- Reduce carbon dioxide emissions through more efficient energy use
- Eliminate the use of CFCs
- Raise fuel economies

The first five of these goals are central to the efficiency gains that have taken place at Smyrna, and all save Nissan money while improving the company's environmental record. Plant emissions is something Nissan can control. At the same time, nuts-and-bolts production economies are critical elements in its strategy for success in a tough car market. Indeed, cost reduction is a matter of life and death right now. But for the long term, eliminating production waste is only part of the challenge. Nissan makes cars, the biggest single source of ecological damage in the First World. Clearly, reduction of auto emissions are beyond the scope of the plant at Smyrna.

To stay ahead of government auto standards, Nissan is developing electric vehicles and engines that run on alternate fuels. Like its competitors, Nissan recognizes that the long-term viability of its business may depend on developing alternatives to conventional internal combustion engines. Switching to new fuels will further reduce conventional pollutants, as well as carbon dioxide, the cause of global warming. In the meantime, Nissan R&D is largely directed at the reduction of tailpipe emissions of its gasoline and diesel engines.[22] Simply improving the fuel economy of its vehicles is probably the best thing Nissan can do for the environment and car sales at the same time.

When cars were mostly steel, recycling them was easy: they were crushed into little cubes, melted down, and turned into more steel. Today, cars are made out of many different materials that are difficult to recycle, particularly plastics. It's also expensive to disassemble cars and to sort all the different types of plastics and metals, even if there is a market for them. Like it or not, auto makers must face this problem. Already the German government requires manufacturers to take their cars back for final disposal. Recycling plastics, as Nissan is trying to do at Smyrna, is key to making this work.[23]

Nissan reacted quickly to the Montreal Protocol, the international agreement on ozone-damaging CFCs. By April 1992, the company had found substitutes for CFCs in manufacturing (as cleaning solvents and plastic foaming agents). Later that year, Nissan began a two-year program to convert its cars to CFC-free air-conditioning (starting with the Altima at Smyrna).

Leadership in this area no doubt has some marketing value.

On the cost side, Nissan will avoid the increasingly heavy taxes that are being placed on CFCs to discourage their use. Nissan claims to be the first car company to equip all its North American dealers to recycle the Freon released from air conditioners being repaired; before, the CFCs just went into the air.[24] There is a rapidly developing market for this increasingly scarce commodity, the price of which has topped $5.00 per pound, up dramatically from the $0.57 per pound it was a few years ago before environmental taxes were imposed.[25]

THE LESSONS

Nissan's environmental strategy for its Smyrna plant has produced clear benefits. Most important for a company in a bitterly competitive market, manufacturing efficiencies have improved. What's more, Nissan has jumped ahead of the compliance curve. While it still has plenty of forms to fill out for regulators, the company has gone beyond what the law requires, in many cases by approaching zero emissions. Nissan managers can worry about making better cars, not fighting the government. And they don't have to worry about pollution that might be legal now coming back to haunt them in the future in the form of a big lawsuit. In short, Nissan's environmental strategy at Smyrna has been a success.

There are several lessons to be learned from Nissan's experience:

Set tough goals. When it decided to go for zero emissions, Nissan's goal seemed absurd to many. But ambitious targets like this flush out the good ideas and creative thinking. Continuous, incremental improvements made the goal a reality.

Take waste reduction seriously. Managers at the highest levels of Nissan were committed to Smyrna's environmental plan right from the start—indeed they initiated it. They charged line engineers with responsibility for pollution. At car companies like Nissan, engineers, not lawyers or public-relations types, have the real power and command respect in the front lines. Nissan has placed its environmental goals at the center of its strategy, and it shows.

Look at the big picture. Nissan would not have realized the benefits of its environmental program using conventional cost-accounting methods. Management had faith in its ideas and people. Faith does not mean "voodoo" accounting, but a willingness to figure unexpected benefits into the equation.

Focus on thinking, not technology. "We are obsessed with technology in this company—we want to be on the leading edge," we were told at Smyrna. Nissan considers itself a leader in technology, but the change taking place at Smyrna is not about technology. Certainly, designing plastic gas tanks so they can be recycled on-site, for example, is no mean task from an engineering point of view. The switch to water-based paints with electrostatic application required state-of-the-art process control. But what drives change here is new ideas, not expensive high-tech fixes.

Forget about recycling. Eliminating waste before it is created is the key to Nissan's success; recycling plays a minimal role. The recycling Nissan does at Smyrna, of plastic, for example, is cumbersome, technology intensive, and expensive—just as it is everywhere else.

Push suppliers. In no small measure, Nissan reduced waste at Smyrna by pushing its problems onto suppliers, but so what? This takes advantage of the creativity of others. Parts suppliers should know more about packaging their products than Nissan. Paint manufacturers know about making paint. Still, getting them to change is never easy. Nissan, like other Japanese car companies, takes a cooperative approach to supplier relations, but many vendors were kicking and screaming all the way along.

Trust employees. By locating in a rural, nonunion location, Nissan has done what it can to avoid the no-can-do attitude of many of its competitors. Nevertheless, management believes that waste reduction and productivity improvement go hand in hand, and is willing to let front-line people make this philosophy a reality. They have the budgets and authority to drive change at Nissan. As one environmental engineer told us, "I have never had a request for a project refused."

Have money. Whatever its financial and market difficulties,

Nissan clearly has access to capital—it wouldn't be in the car business for long if it didn't. Many of its programs took a lot of money to put into place, and couldn't be done on a shoestring budget. And the company's buying clout helped to shift the burden to suppliers. But Nissan's real gains have less to do with massive infusions of cash than with new approaches to old problems, new ideas. These are essentially free.

Start fresh—if you can. Smyrna is no longer new; Nissan broke ground on the plant in 1981. But Nissan does not carry the environmental baggage that many fifty-year-old facilities, and many of its competitors, must deal with. Cleaning up old problems (or "site remediation" as it is called) is not just expensive, it also consumes management time and influences the way a company views the environment. Managers preoccupied with EPA fines—if not jail sentences—are not going to take risks. And they are much more likely to turn problems over to lawyers than to engineers.

EXXON REFINES
ITS STRATEGY

MAKING MONEY ON A
CLEANER ENVIRONMENT

The oil industry has taken a beating over the past decade and a half. After a ten-year run-up, oil prices peaked in 1980. Since then, prices have fallen steadily, except during a couple of upward spikes at times of international crisis. And few other industries have faced such stiff environmental controls as big oil, a visible target for eager regulators. Exxon, the world's largest oil company, has met both of these challenges at once, lowering the cost and the environmental impact of its operations and products at the same time. Despite falling demand, Exxon has increased its revenues. And by cutting waste, the company has also increased profits. Today, there are few investments that Exxon makes that do not simultaneously cut costs and pollution.

Like computer manufacturers, oil companies have grown accustomed to falling prices. But when computers get cheaper, people buy more of them. The computer industry keeps growing faster than prices fall. No such luck for oil. Demand for "black gold" has been essentially flat for two decades, despite falling prices in recent years. In the United States, gasoline prices hit postwar lows (in real terms) in the early 1990s, but demand remained soft because the fuel economy of the average American car has more than doubled since prices first shot up. Consumers and business kept on improving the efficiency of their cars, homes, and factories long after the oil shocks of the 1970s were over.

Survival in this climate depends on nonstop cost cutting. The equation is simple: To make a profit, costs must fall faster than prices. Exxon has excelled at this game, turning in solid financial growth. Since the early 1980s, Exxon's oil and gas production and sales (measured in barrels) have barely budged. Nevertheless, revenues have kept growing, and the company has remained solidly in the black, despite multibillion-dollar outlays for the *Exxon Valdez* tanker disaster. The value of its stock has soared.

While other icons of America's postwar industrial might, like IBM and GM, have stumbled under the weight of their own size, Exxon has remained successful, and surprisingly nimble. One reason is that Exxon has stuck to its knitting, shedding most of its diversified operations (ranging from electronic typewriters to exotic bicycle frames) once the heady days of ever-rising oil prices came to an end. While it has not been spared the restructuring and layoffs forced on other large companies by recession, Exxon has kept control of its own destiny with tight financial management and the perseverance of engineers with a mission. Never-ending cost reduction is part of this culture. And for Exxon, efficiency improvements depend on waste and pollution reduction.

SERIOUS BUSINESS AT BAYTOWN, TEXAS

Exxon's operations at its Baytown, Texas, complex are vast, occupying 3,412 acres, an area about the size of Manhattan below Fourteenth Street. The complex runs some two miles from the state road down to the Houston Ship Channel that connects the city of Houston to Galveston Bay and the Gulf of Mexico. Six enormous Exxon docks receive the tankers that bring two-thirds of its crude to the refinery. The rest arrives by pipeline.

Exxon struck oil in Texas in 1919 and opened the Baytown refinery in 1920, processing 10,000 barrels a day. Today, some 400,000 barrels a day—about 3 percent of U.S. consumption—flow through the endless array of pipes, boilers, smokestacks, and storage tanks at Baytown. The refinery keeps a fifteen-day supply of crude on hand in some sixty tanks scattered around the site. Baytown, Exxon's second largest American refinery, produces fuels (like gasoline and diesel), lubricants (oil and grease), and chemical feed stocks, which go into plastics, solvents, and other products.

On a hot day in June, we visited Exxon's Baytown complex. Refineries are remarkably different from other production facilities. The scale, even compared to a big car plant like Nissan's in Tennessee, cannot be appreciated from the ground. While we toured the site by truck, a view from the air would be necessary to take in the whole place.

Few of the refinery's 1,900 workers were visible, except for several repair crews on the job. A few passed in pickup trucks and several on bicycles (Exxon has a fleet of bikes for getting in and around Baytown). Much of the site is covered with gravel that looks freshly raked. There is no litter or junk piled up anywhere: we didn't see a single fifty-five-gallon drum, that icon of careless environmental control. Many plumes of steam rise from smokestacks, but we saw only a single pipe flaring gas into the sky. And to one visitor who grew up in New Jersey and knows refinery pollution, Baytown was virtually without smell.

Exxon's profits from refining have been strong in recent years, largely because of efficiency improvements. At Baytown, the company's biggest expense is energy. Transforming crude into useful products is extremely energy intensive, involving heating and reheating throughout the process. To save money from its refinery operations, Exxon has to go where the money is.

Over the past two decades, Exxon has improved the energy efficiency of its refinery by several orders of magnitude. Today, the equivalent of about one out of ten barrels of oil is self-consumed in the refining process, only one in twenty in some really efficient operations. Twenty years ago, one in five barrels were needed to transform crude into useful products. As one engineer told us, "When I started, we built up all our costs to figure out the best ways to run refinery. At that time, we allocated sixteen cents per thousand cubic feet for natural gas. Gas was very plentiful then. . . . Now it is much more expensive, and we have to save energy." Today gas costs ten times as much. This is a strong incentive for Exxon to conserve.

Exxon looks to the day when all its operations are as efficient as today's best, when on average, its refineries need the equivalent of just one out of twenty barrels of crude to run the rest. But as one engineer told us, "This is not a destination, but a journey." Exxon's objective is to wring further energy savings out if its refineries forever.

Doubling energy efficiency over the past generation, and doubling it again in the future, will have a profound effect on Exxon's competitive position. For the environment, the effects are equally profound. When Exxon's own energy use drops, less pollution is produced, of course. More important, Exxon is effectively boosting its oil reserves. Twenty years ago, for every 100 barrels of oil entering the refinery, only 80 barrels were turned into Exxon products. Soon, 95 barrels will be turned into jet fuel, gasoline, and heating oil. That's a 19 percent increase in supply without pumping a single additional barrel of crude out of the ground.

Refineries are different from factories in that they run around the clock, essentially automatically. The major components of the refinery—vacuum-pipe stills, reformers, crackers, and cokers—run for years between repairs. That means big improvements take time to put into operation, but everyday sorts of changes can have an effect as well. On our tour, we were shown some of the big and little improvements that have transformed Baytown's energy efficiency.

The most visible sign of activity at this refinery is the steam plumes that rise from stacks throughout the site. Much of the heating and reheating of oil that takes place in the refinery involves water. Steam is also a by-product of some operations. In the past, all steam was simply vented into the air. Steam is not a pollutant, but a great deal of heat went up the stack. Today, nearly all this steam is recaptured, and run through turbines to generate electricity. Cogeneration, as this process is called, displaces hydrocarbon fuels that would otherwise be used to produce electricity, and can save as much as 30 percent of the energy needed to make electricity and steam separately.[1] Now the Baytown site is self-sufficient in electric power; in fact, Exxon produces so much electricity that it has enough to sell to the local utility.

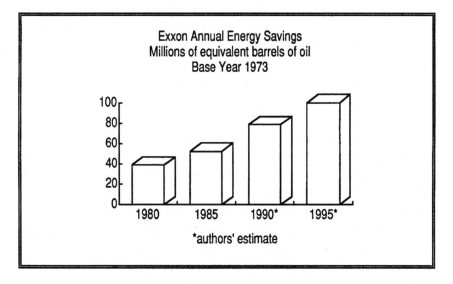

Exxon Annual Energy Savings
Millions of equivalent barrels of oil
Base Year 1973

*authors' estimate

In a similar fashion, the refinery once just vented exhaust gases from its many furnaces into the air. Now these exhaust gases pass through a heat exchanger to preheat the fresh air feeding the furnaces. As a result, less fuel (generally natural gas) is needed to create heat. This cuts costs, reduces fuel consumption, and lowers pollution levels. Company-wide, Exxon reduced energy use by 35 percent between 1973 and 1989, a savings of 70 million barrels of oil a year. The cumulative total is about 650 million barrels, more than Canada's total annual consumption.[2]

During the first stages of the refining process, a barrel of oil is "fractured" into a number of compounds. The lighter ones, like naphtha, can then be readily processed into high-value fuels like gasoline. But too much remains that is of low value, like asphalt and lubricating oils. "Cokers" are used to transform these heavier compounds into lighter fuels. Cokers are key to the economics of refining since there isn't enough of a market for heavier by-products. As one engineer put it, "Cokers turn dirty fuel oil we can't sell into higher-value fuels."

Cokers work by extracting pure carbon, or coke, from heavy gas oils. Typically, 25 percent of a coker's output is coke. If this carbon is very pure, it has a number of specialized uses, including printing inks and anodes for aluminum smelters. However, if there are too many impurities in the carbon, which is normally the case, the coke is just about worthless. Sometimes it can be used by cement kilns for fuel or as fill. Often it is simply landfilled. Thus coking, however essential, has traditionally been very inefficient and wasteful.

Exxon developed a better way. In the late 1980s, the company brought on-line its "Flexicoking" process, developed by Exxon's research labs. With Flexicoking, nearly all the coke by-product is recycled in the coker as fuel. Instead of ending up with 25 or even 30 percent as coke, Flexicoking generates only 1 to 3 percent coke. The energy requirements of the process are greatly reduced, with coke replacing natural gas as a fuel. What's more, the small amount of coke that remains contains high concentrations of materials that Exxon can sell at a profit. The system works so well that Baytown can handle heavy, low-grade crudes, processing them into valuable, lighter products. As one engineer told us, "Flexicoking changed the economics of a refinery like this." Good for Exxon, good for the environment.

Baytown has sixty-five processing units spread out over thousands of acres connected by miles of pipes. Sloppiness—drips, leaks, spills, evaporation—can cause a lot of pollution and cost a lot of money. Every two gallons of gasoline that evaporates into the air takes one dollar right off Exxon's bottom line. With 400,000 barrels going through the refinery every day, the potential losses are enormous.

At one time, for example, excess pressure from oil storage tanks (of which there are sixty at Baytown) was simply vented into the atmosphere. As these tanks were emptied, vapors filled the air above the liquid. Then when the tanks were refilled, this vapor was compressed by the incoming liquid. Simple pressure valves at the top of tank released the pressure before it got too high. This released vapor (gasoline or heating oil, for example) was a pollutant, of course, but also cost the refiner money in lost sales.

Exxon now uses "double top" tanks. Inside, a second top floats on the petroleum, much like a swimming pool cover. The sides of these floating tops are engineered to prevent vapor leaks around the edges. Evaporation losses from these storage tanks have been cut nearly to zero. We asked one manager if the savings covered the extra cost of construction. He answered, "Yes. We don't lose product through evaporation, and we now probably build the tanks for the same amount or less than the old ones." Less waste also means less oil needed to be pumped from the ground, and less noxious gases in the air.

Twenty or thirty years ago, vapors from many other stages in the refining process were flared off, that is, ignited at the end of a pipe like a big Bunsen burner. Flares are still necessary for safety reasons if pressures build up too quickly, but now Exxon recaptures most of the hydrocarbons from vapors and burns them to produce steam (instead of using natural gas). Very little flaring is necessary (and the company adds steam to the flared vapors to ensure complete combustion and minimal pollution). We saw only one lighted flare on our tour of Baytown.

Many of the changes Exxon has made to conserve energy can be called "high-tech." Flexicoking, a proprietary process, represents a big R&D and equipment investment for the company. Cogeneration and the reuse of flue gas and petroleum vapors don't come cheap either: all require significant capital outlays. But some changes depend more on better thinking than on more spending.

Exxon has essentially eliminated the disposal of toxic materials into nearby watercourses. One Exxon Chemical official told us that the plant returns water to the Houston Shipping Channel cleaner than it comes out. However, when new federal regulations required Exxon to eliminate all traces of benzene from its waste stream, the refinery faced equipment outlays in the hundreds of millions of dollars to remove the last, minute quantities of this chemical from water released into the channel. Then, in the words of one manager, "We decided to try changing the company ethic instead."

Before Exxon's new program began, the refinery was "leaking" 800 to 1,000 barrels per day into its drains. Some leakage might seem inevitable in a plant this size. One thousand barrels is only a fraction of 1 percent of the crude flowing through the refinery. And, of course, everything that goes into drains at the Baytown complex, including storm water, is collected and treated in retention basins before entering the channel. Nevertheless, traces of benzene were still getting through.

To plug the leak, Exxon trained all workers to stop the loss of small quantities of oil throughout the refinery. In some cases, the change was as simple as fixing leaky faucets. In others, new procedures were necessary. For example, extra steps now are taken to drain the last bits of oil from tanks and pipes before flushing them out. The program worked. Leakage is down to less than fifty barrels per day, less than 5 percent of the loss before, and an infinitesimal one-hundredth of 1 percent of the oil flowing through the complex.

An ounce of prevention was worth several hundred million dollars of cure, and there is also the value of the extra 1,000 barrels of oil per day Exxon now has to sell—millions of dollars flowing straight to the bottom line every year. Under a McDonald's-like sign at the refinery, Exxon totes its savings in hundreds of thousands of barrels from its "Stop Oil to the Sewer" program.

Like other manufacturers, Exxon has also cut costs by cutting the amount of inventory. At Baytown, while sales have increased, the company has slashed by more than half the amount of product "in the pipeline" at any one time. This frees up capital that would otherwise be tied up in heating oil and jet fuel that had been produced but not sold. Less in the pipeline also means fewer opportunities for leaks through evaporation or into drains.

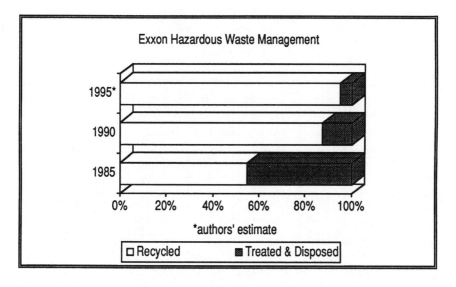

Exxon Hazardous Waste Management

1995*
1990
1985

0% 20% 40% 60% 80% 100%

*authors' estimate

□ Recycled   ■ Treated & Disposed

Similar changes have taken place throughout Exxon's business. During the seventies and eighties, Exxon cut air emissions from its U.S. refineries by more than 75 percent, and made comparable gains overseas. The EPA requires manufacturers to report their discharges of industrial by-products, whether these chemicals are released as air and water pollution or sent somewhere else for disposal. At Exxon, these so-called "SARA releases and transfers" have fallen by well over half since the late 1980s (see chart).

Exxon recycles over 90 percent of the hazardous wastes it still produces. A decade ago, only half was recycled and the balance was treated or landfilled (see chart). At a company the size of Exxon, this shift represents a monumental environmental improvement. Just one drier/incinerator project at the company's Baton Rouge chemical complex reduced waste disposal by 55 percent, which translates into 1,000 truckloads less that get landfilled every year.[3]

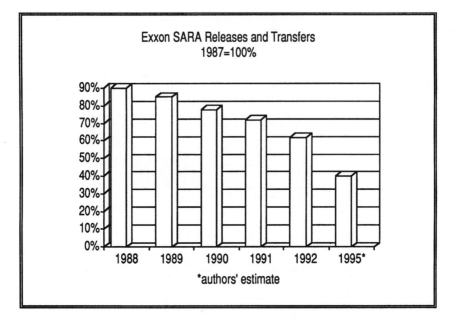

As a result of these efforts, Exxon does not appear on EPA lists of top polluters in the United States, even though the company is the largest oil company by far, and one of the biggest chemical producers. Other chemical and oil companies are still well represented on these EPA scorecards. Even in Texas and Louisiana, where Exxon's biggest facilities are located, the company is not on the EPA list of facilities with the greatest releases of chemicals into the environment.[4]

INVESTMENT OR TAX?

Government regulation drives oil-company outlays for environmental improvement. One industry study estimated that to comply with current and expected regulations in the United States over the next twenty years, oil companies would have to spend at least $166 billion. On an annual basis, this would require current spending levels to double.[5] A British Petroleum executive figured that to comply with environmental laws, U.S. companies must now spend $15 billion to $20 billion per year, not much less than total industry profits. And it's the same story in Europe, where annual compliance outlays of $9 billion are about equal to the profits of Europe's top oil companies.[6] As for Exxon, annual environmental expenditures are running at almost $2 billion per year, between one-third and one-half of its total net income. Over the past twenty years, the company has spent over $20 billion, not counting the cost of the *Exxon Valdez* tanker spill.[7]

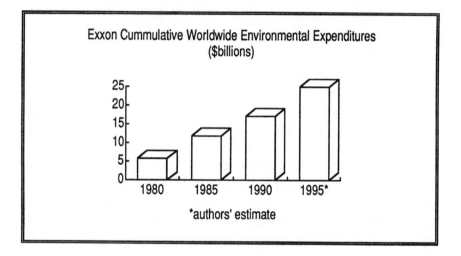

Exxon Cummulative Worldwide Environmental Expenditures ($billions)

Is investment on this scale worth it? Without question, the environment has benefited, if the smell of the air and the look of the Houston Shipping Channel at Baytown are anything to go by. Financially, it's harder to say. Because the oil industry has faced stiff environmental regulation for so long, even insiders can't easily separate what's spent on the environment from other, ongoing investments. For example, most—perhaps all—of the efficiency and quality improvements made by Exxon at Baytown have environmental benefits as well.

Many oil-industry managers are frustrated by heavy-handed regulation more than anything else. Most environmental laws specify not only the results, but the means of achieving them. Engineers would rather have the freedom to determine the most economic way of reducing emissions on their own. Too often regulators don't just tell the oil companies what to do, but how. This approach almost guarantees that the desired environmental benefit is not achieved at the lowest cost.

One unintended result of overmanaged environmental regulation is that small players are squeezed out. As the regulatory ratchet is tightened, small companies cannot afford to comply. Unlike Exxon, they cannot make investments without an immediate payoff. To cut urban smog, for example, the Clean Air Act requires refiners to reformulate gasoline using ethanol or MTBE, a natural gas by-product. At Baytown, Exxon has built a small plant to supply its own MTBE. Other refineries can't afford this investment and may have to shut down.

EXXON IN SINGAPORE

Far from the vast industrial atmosphere of its Baytown complex, we visited Exxon Chemical's research laboratories in the leafy suburbs of Singapore. This small country, halfway around the world from Houston, is a major research, production, and marketing center for Exxon Chemical, one of the ten largest chemical companies in the world.

As oil prices have fallen, Exxon boosted its margins by converting petrochemical building blocks made at Baytown and other refineries into other products. While crude oil is sold by the barrel and jet fuel by the gallon, many petroleum-based products are sold by the ounce. By producing these specialty chemicals—adhesives, plastics, solvents, and other oil derivatives—Exxon gets more revenue out of each barrel of crude. We went to the Singapore labs to find out about one such high-value product, Exxon's "Actrel" line of decreasing agents.

One of the most pressing environmental challenges for industry in recent years has been the elimination of CFCs from production. As a result of international agreements, manufacturers (including several in this book) can no longer use CFCs (better known as Freon) for cleaning metal and plastic parts, as well as electronic components. Exxon has helped solve this problem by going "back to the future."

Three decades ago manufacturers used hydrocarbon-based solvents for parts cleaning. For many applications, like car repair, this meant nothing more than kerosene. Handling petroleum solvents can be dangerous, but there was little alternative. Then engineers began using Freon, primarily a refrigerant until then, because it was safer and better for extra-fine cleaning of small parts, particularly for computers.

Many alternatives to CFCs have been developed. Some, like HCFCs, have proved to be nearly as bad for the ozone layer and have also been banned. Others were too expensive or had their own set of environmental complications. For example, water cleaning, the simplest alternative, requires lots of energy for drying, and contaminated water must be processed before disposal. And "no-clean" systems are not suitable for every application.

Exxon Chemical developed a new product to overcome the drawbacks of old oil-based solvents like kerosene and turpentine. By the end of 1991, Exxon's Singapore labs had developed a range of cleaners for the electronics industry in Asia, targeting VCR, disk-drive, printed-circuit-board, and computer-chip makers, among others. In some applications, Exxon's Actrel fluids have proved superior to the CFCs they replaced. For example, a ball-bearing company reduced the number of steps for cleaning and rustproofing from three to one. Unlike other solvents (including CFCs), Actrel can be matched to the kind of soil that needs to be removed. Exxon can tailor its product exactly for each application.

Actrel and the company's extensive research facilities in Singapore show the high-tech side of Exxon. To be sure, oil is a business where you get your hands dirty. But to maintain margins in a tough field, Exxon must add more knowledge to its products at every stage from well-head to market. Exxon now spends nearly as much on R&D as on exploration.[8]

Research is about turning information into knowledge in its purest form. R&D makes up a greater share of Exxon's spending every year, and could surpass exploration outlays before long. Increasingly, then, Exxon is more in the information business and less in natural resources. When it diversified into computers in the late 1970s, Exxon had the right idea, in a sense. Over the last decade, however, Exxon's knowledge has been far more valuable in its oil-based products than in its computer hardware. As one engineer told us in Singapore, to find an alternative to CFCs, Exxon decided "to fix the old molecules in our portfolio." The complex hydrocarbon molecules that Exxon pumps out of the ground are remarkably versatile—given the right R&D.

Exxon's Singapore operations also show just how closely waste reduction, pollution control, and efficiency improvement are interlinked for the company. Singapore has one of the toughest environmental regimes in the world (see chapter "Singapore and Hong Kong"), and yet Exxon centers its Asian operations there. With its highly educated workforce, Singapore is an obvious choice for R&D activity. But Exxon also has enormous refining and chemical investments in Singapore, which it continues to expand. There's no oil in Singapore, and there are many nearby countries that are not nearly as fussy about environmental requirements. But by operating within Singapore's tough environmental standards, Exxon has improved its financial performance.

DOWNSTREAM IMPACT

Unlike Actrel, most of Exxon's products do not have a good effect on the environment. But there has been great improvement in the cleanliness of petroleum fuels, primarily in response to government mandates. Taking the lead out of gasoline, for example, has dramatically reduced blood levels of that heavy metal all across America. Desulfuring home heating oil, diesel fuel, and gasoline has cut acid rain and other forms of air pollution.

Reformulated fuels are the next frontier. In 1990, Exxon introduced gasolines that lower hydrocarbon emissions by up to 20 percent. In smog-prone areas, Exxon also began selling oxygenated gasolines that reduce carbon monoxide levels. Reformulated gasolines stipulated by the Clean Air Act will cut emissions even further by the end of the decade, although the result may be higher prices and lower gas mileage. Heavy R&D investment makes these new products a reality. Using better environmental performance to sell more products may be more difficult.

Like Exxon, Texaco has been working on this branding/pollution challenge for some time. In 1994, Texaco launched "New Clean System 3," a gasoline product with additives designed to clean carbon from car-engine intake valves and combustion chambers. The additive has to withstand the heat of combustion, clean the engine, and then burn itself up, all without polluting. The result reduces engine deposits by 30 percent and cuts nitrogen oxide emissions by one-fifth compared with Texaco's older System 3 gasoline.[9] This sounds great, of course, but getting people to switch brands for something that is cleaner than competing products is not so easy. Consumers interviewed by the *New York Times* when the new gas was introduced said that they basically didn't care: gasoline is a convenience that they buy on price. One woman said that it wasn't something she gave a lot of thought to; besides, she didn't know much about car engines.[10] Consumers often exhibit contrary traits: at the ballot box they vote for tougher standards, but in the market they buy what's cheapest and easiest to get.

In a business as competitive as oil, branding can help add points to market share—or cut a few points. Few companies are more easily tarred with the opprobrium of pollution than oil companies. Exxon, for example, has been through the miseries of the *Exxon Valdez* oil spill in Alaska's beautiful Prince William Sound. But Exxon still has to protect its valuable brand name in order to sell gasoline to consumers. The *Exxon Valdez* saddled the company with billions in cleanup costs and legal damages, but more importantly, it threatened Exxon's brand.

Some changes are not as visible as reformulated gasolines or oil-tanker spills, but produce real environmental benefits nonetheless. Exxon packages motor oil in one-quart containers made from recycled plastic, cutting waste in the United States by 2 million pounds per year.[11] And Exxon has upgraded storage tanks and pipes at its shipping terminals and gas stations around the world to prevent soil contamination from leaks. For a company such as Exxon, with a 100-year history, cleaning up damage caused in decades past is an ongoing task.

Unlike many other companies we have seen, Exxon is not fighting the last war. With so many old sites around the world, the company diverts plenty of resources to cleanup. But remediation does not dominate its environmental program. You don't get a sense among engineers at Exxon that their goal is to keep the regulatory jackals at bay. Rather, their mission is to improve profitable efficiencies.

Many by-products from Exxon's refineries would be considered pollution if the company could not find a market for them. Exxon can use most hydrocarbon compounds, either recycling them in the refining process or transforming them into chemical products. To avoid disposal problems for the chemicals it generates but can't use itself, Exxon finds other markets. For example, French chemical giant Rhone-Poulenc operates a plant right in the middle of the Baytown complex that takes acid by-products from refining and turns them into sulfuric acid for sale.

A refinery like Baytown produces a lot of sulfur by removing the element from fuels to make them burn cleaner (and also, to a lesser degree, by cleaning its own flue gases). When desulfuring of fuels began, there was some concern about the stuff piling up somewhere. At Baytown, there are no piles of dry sulfur. Exxon keeps it as a hot liquid piped directly to ships for resale. The biggest use for sulfur is fertilizer, but there are also smaller applications for rubber and pharmaceuticals. Exxon sells pure sulfur as a refining by-product, which has driven down the cost of sulfur. This may be bad if you mine sulfur, but good if you buy products made from it, since the price of sulfur has plummeted since desulfurization began. Resale is also good for the environment since there is no need for sulfur mining anymore.

STANDARD OIL: THE MICROSOFT
OF THE NINETEENTH CENTURY

During the past 100 years, oil has transformed the world as radically as information will transform the next. Exxon, successor to John D. Rockefeller's original Standard Oil trust, played a star role in the past century. Its performance over the last decade indicates that it will prosper in the next century as well.

As economies mature, they demand cleaner, lighter petroleum products. In the United States for example, the heavy-fuel-oil market is in decline, while demand for cleaner portable fuels like gasoline, heating oil, diesel, and jet fuel continues to grow. Developing countries need greases, waxes, and heavy fuels. They have primitive machinery that runs on these types of products.

With intensive R&D and heavy capital investment, Exxon can continue to wring more energy out of each barrel of oil and to find more valuable uses for the "hydrocarbon molecules in its portfolio." In the future, biotechnology could dramatically change the amount of energy needed to refine oil, substituting microbes engineered in the laboratory for natural gas. Reformulated gasolines that all but eliminate pollutants may obviate the need for electric cars.

Oil's share of the world's energy supply has fallen dramatically over the last generation, to about one-third today, and will continue to down in the foreseeable future. The trick for Exxon is to ride this trend. Exxon can add more value to its products before they are sold. While gasoline is a commodity, products like Exxon's Actrel solvents can be branded and sold at a premium. In a sense, Exxon increases the information content of these products, making them more valuable and easier to differentiate. In a recent report to shareholders, Exxon's CEO wrote that in Europe and North America the "emphasis is on higher-quality and more environmentally attractive products." The two go hand in hand.

THE LESSONS

There are several lessons to be learned from Exxon's environmental experience:

Don't fight the last war. Exxon kept environmental and efficiency improvement closely connected, despite the demands of the *Exxon Valdez* disaster and the cleanup of old sites.

Go where the money is. In its own operations, Exxon has had the biggest environmental impact where it spends the most money—on energy.

Apply technology to your processes. In a business as capital intensive as oil, big environmental changes usually require big spending. The payoff comes from lower costs and better quality. Environmental improvement is a bonus.

Apply knowledge to your products. Exxon's business is selling natural resources, not information. But Exxon has steadily increased the knowledge content of its products, wringing more valuable fuels out of each barrel of crude. In the process, the company has increased margins and reduced pollution.

Think about the journey, not the destination. For Exxon, efficiency gains and waste reduction are not goals; they are a continuing way of life. Cost reduction—and the pollution reductions that are its by-product—permeates every aspect of this company's operations.

WAL-MART DISTRIBUTES THE WEALTH

TURNING INFORMATION INTO PROFITS

Sometimes the most important changes result not from what you do but from what you don't do—what might be called virtues of omission. By eliminating activities that their customers don't value, or don't even know about, companies can cut their costs, often radically. As these costs fall, the environmental consequences of business activity usually diminish as well. Wal-Mart revolutionized the way merchandise is delivered to customers. By substituting information for truck trips, Wal-Mart made itself the leading retailer in the United States and single-handedly reduced the energy intensity of the American economy.

With a splash of press coverage, Wal-Mart Stores opened its 1,915th discount store in Lawrence, Kansas, in June 1993. This was Wal-Mart's environmental demonstration store, "the centerpiece of Wal-Mart's efforts to build awareness of the air, land and water we share and the actions we can all take to become more responsible stewards of our planet,"[1] according to Mike Benson, the store manager. For its Lawrence site, the company minimized the environmental impact of every aspect of construction and operation. Design work took three years under the guidance of Hillary Clinton, who was a director of Arkansas-based Wal-Mart until her husband was elected president of the United States.

For construction, Wal-Mart selected engineered wood for the roof of the 120,000-square-foot building, eliminating the need for long pieces of old-growth timber, and for steel, which takes more energy to make. With this building material, short lengths of second- or third-growth trees are laminated together to form strong, lightweight wooden I-beams. The engineered-wood process requires 50 percent less wood than a solid wooden beam, and uses three-quarters more of each tree than traditional log planing. Young, eight-inch-diameter trees can be turned into structural beams up to eighty feet long.

To reduce operating energy costs, Wal-Mart took several steps. First, architects placed skylights throughout the store. These were custom designed to allow in the maximum amount of light while providing minimal energy loss. Inside, fluorescent lights with electronic ballasts cut energy use in each fixture 25 to 30 percent compared to standard fixtures used in other Wal-Mart locations. To get the most out of the skylights, photodetectors turn off lights when they are not needed. For heating and cooling, the company selected a state-of-the-art system that can use ozone-friendly refrigerants. In the summer, air conditioners make ice at night when utilities have extra capacity (and electric rates are lower). Then, during the day, the ice is used to cool the air in the store, reducing peak electric demand.

Outside, holding tanks capture and treat rainwater runoff from the roof and parking lot, and gray water from sinks inside. This water irrigates the native buffalo grass and trees planted on the site. In the parking lot, recycled plastics were used for bumper blocks, signs, and cart corrals. Next to the store, Wal-Mart operates a community recycling center for plastic, glass, paper, and aluminum. Shoppers can also dump unwanted packaging in recycling bins near the front doors. The final touch: the big Wal-Mart sign out by the road is powered by solar panels.

After these new ideas are tested in Kansas, Wal-Mart plans to apply them around the country. And building several hundred stores a year, Wal-Mart could reduce its environmental impact significantly within a short time, and cut operating costs into the bargain. For Wal-Mart, a company built on shaving cents off its costs, investment in environmentally friendly buildings must pay its own way. If any company can make this kind of investment work, Wal-Mart can. Others will soon follow. The company has promised to share its findings with competitors.[2]

SHOWING THE GREEN FLAG

While the Lawrence store was a high-profile environmental step for Wal-Mart, the company shows its green colors in every location. Near the front door of each store is a sign that tallies the benefits of Wal-Mart's recycling (261,041 trees saved, according to one store in Pensacola, Florida), and promotes the company's efforts to purchase environmentally friendly products with less packaging. Green products range from "Sam's America's Choice" blue corn chips, made from organic grain, to biodegradable pens, made from cornstarch-based plastics that turn into carbon dioxide and water when left outside for a couple of years. Wal-Mart was a charter member of the Buy Recycled Business Alliance, which promotes the market for products made out of recycled materials.[3]

Consumers expect the companies they buy from to meet their environmental obligations in ways that go beyond public relations. Wal-Mart is trying to meet these expectations. But reducing waste also fits well with Wal-Mart's frugal culture; for this company waste reduction and efficiency have long been inseparable.

Less packaging can be sold as environmentally friendly. But less packaging also means less transportation and less handling in stores. Wal-Mart is not the only retailer to pressure suppliers to eliminate unnecessary packaging. Sears, for example, hangs hand tools like hammers and wrenches in their displays without wrapping, saving seventy-eight tons of plastic a year.[4] That means seventy-eight tons of packaging Sears does not have to buy, transport, unwrap, collect, and pay to haul to the dump. Good design—information—can be substituted profitably for natural resources. By eliminating packaging, the Swiss candy and coffee company Jacobs Suchard cut the amount of fuel needed to transport a carton of its products by half. A range of changes, from simpler packages to reusable shipping pallets, eliminated 10,000 tons of waste in three years. A new coffee package alone cut waste, energy consumption, and water use by more than a third for that product.[5]

THE BUSINESS OF AMERICA IS INVENTORIES

However praiseworthy, Wal-Mart's in-store environmental programs are dwarfed by changes shoppers do not see. The real savings for Wal-Mart and its customers come from better distribution. Wal-Mart may not pay less for Coca-Cola or Pampers than any other large retailer, but Wal-Mart does pay less to move them after they pass the factory gates. Wal-Mart's success is based not only on its ability to "sell" merchandise but also to move thousands of goods efficiently from manufacturer to consumer. Wal-Mart offers everyday low prices and good service, but it can do so only because its cost of bringing goods to market are so low.

In the past, merchandise would go into inventory three times, once at the plant, again at the wholesaler's, and a third time at the retailer's store. Much of what Wal-Mart sells doesn't go into inventory anywhere, but comes right off the production line for delivery to the store, where it will go right onto display, to be sold within days. At other retailers, the stuff sits around for weeks. Most merchandise still flows through the company's own warehouses, but moves on to a Wal-Mart outlet within hours, if not minutes. With the company's innovative "cross-docking" system, truckloads of merchandise come in one side of the warehouse from suppliers, cross the loading dock, and then go right out again on other trucks bound for individual stores. Wal-Mart enjoys big discounts for buying in quantity, and doesn't squander these savings on inventory costs.[6]

For Wal-Mart, this system means less money tied up in inventory, less paid to employees to handle its merchandise, less spent on transportation. For its customers, of course, such efficiency lowers prices. For the environment, less transportation means less energy consumed. Less diesel fuel is burned for each dollar of sales generated. What's more, fewer goods are produced because there is a much smaller pipeline to be filled up with potato chips and folding lawn chairs. Furthermore, because goods flow more quickly, the economy requires smaller factories, warehouses, and stores than would otherwise be necessary. Wal-Mart's sales per square foot of store are almost 50 percent greater than industry averages. Consumers benefit from lower prices, the environment from less development.

Just-in-time delivery is associated with manufacturing, but Wal-Mart applied this process to retailing. By improving communications between buyers and sellers, Wal-Mart has substituted better management for inventory, trucks, and warehouses. According to management expert Peter Drucker, Wal-Mart slashed its costs by one-third, compared to traditional retailers, with its efficient distribution system.[7]

Beginning in the 1970s, when it was a small regional chain, a fraction of its current size, Wal-Mart invested heavily in computers. Because many of its stores were located in remote areas with poor telephone service, the company had to overlay its own satellite-based telecommunications network. Originally the company used this system for basic bookkeeping (like accounts receivable and payable), as well as for training. Wal-Mart founder Sam Walton also liked to give televised pep talks to all his employees around the country. But the real benefit of this network came when the company began experimenting with direct links between its cash registers and the factory computers of its suppliers. Today, when a checkout clerk scans a customer's package of Pampers, Wal-Mart's network passes that information on to Procter & Gamble's computer, where production and store delivery are then scheduled for a new order.

Sounds like common sense, but in the past, retailers tallied sales and reordered only weekly or monthly. Wholesalers, for their part, estimated the retail sales they expected, and then placed orders with the manufacturers. At the plant, managers scheduled production based on their forecasts of sales. Up and down the line, large inventories buffered planners from the inaccuracies of their estimates. Basically, all those involved guessed at what they needed, and then hoped they could shoehorn their stocks into the market.

Wal-Mart turned this process on its head, basing its orders and merchandising decisions on what people actually buy. With its elaborate computer network, the company had the information it needed to determine accurately, and quickly, what customers want, where and when. Wal-Mart now has a four- to five-year lead on its competitors in just-in-time delivery between suppliers and customers.[8] Customers, not Wal-Mart managers with crystal balls, are driving production and delivery schedules. Store managers, in daily contact with customers, have wide latitude to experiment with new merchandise. The role of Wal-Mart headquarters is to make the system work, not to force-feed stores with goods customers don't want.

This efficiency allows Wal-Mart to do what many consider impossible: keep inventories low and shelves well stocked at the same time. Furthermore, while some competitors cut slow-selling items they carry to compensate for inefficiencies in their organization, Wal-Mart can constantly expand its already wide selection of merchandise (as much as 70,000 different items in each store). At the company's Sam's Clubs warehouse outlets, fewer, high-volume items are sold in bulk, and inventory turns are even faster than at other Wal-Mart stores.

On top of rock-bottom prices, Wal-Mart also provides better service. We have visited Wal-Marts across the United States, and have been surprised by how consistently friendly and helpful Wal-Mart "associates" are. We have never encountered the withering "why are you asking me" look. At one location in North Carolina, we were led, practically by the hand, across dozens of aisles to the item we sought. Compared to other retailers, Wal-Mart has sophisticated training, including its company-wide television network and multimedia PCs. Electronic delivery means fewer printed training manuals, fewer trees cut down, and less diesel fuel burned moving them around. Furthermore, the 150 to 200 people at work at each Wal-Mart are not in low-paying "McJobs." On the contrary, 70 percent of Wal-Mart store employees are full-time with full benefits, and no one at Wal-Mart is paid minimum wage.[9] For retailers, merchandise costs, not labor rates, drive profitability. Wal-Mart can pay its people better because it gets goods to customers for less. For anyone planning a career in retail, a stint at Wal-Mart is a free education.

While employees are courteous and helpful, service at Wal-Mart has more to do with well-stocked shelves and fast checkouts. These result from the company's smart use of information technology. The same high-speed satellite network that transmits ordering information directly to suppliers also processes credit card authorizations in seconds, a fraction of the time required on the dial-up lines used at most stores.

This substitute of information for transportation and warehousing is not just happening at Wal-Mart, of course. While Wal-Mart has been the leader, others have followed. For a decade, distribution costs have been falling as a share of the U.S. economy because of less warehousing (as well as deregulation of trucking). This change has uncoupled warehouse construction from retail growth; once they moved in lockstep. Greater efficiency has reduced the amount of truck traffic needed for each dollar of the economy, a clear benefit for the environment in terms of pollution and wasted energy.[10] The chart shows how freight ton-miles have dropped significantly in the last two decades in the United States. During this same period, the average efficiency of trucks (which account for virtually all traffic to and from retail stores) rose from less than eight miles per gallon to nearly eleven miles per gallon.

Fewer truck trips, plus more efficient trucks, add up to a cleaner environment. This is what sustainable development is all about.

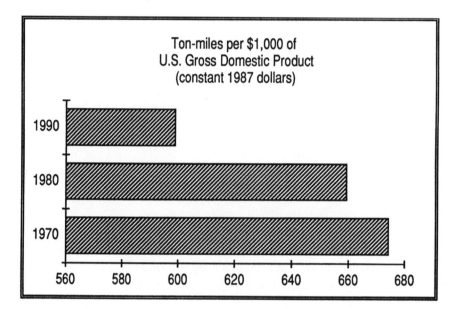

Ton-miles per $1,000 of U.S. Gross Domestic Product (constant 1987 dollars)

SEARS YESTERDAY, WAL-MART TODAY, HOME SHOPPING NETWORK TOMORROW

Falling transportation costs in the late nineteenth century built the Sears Roebuck mail-order empire. With cheap parcel-post rates, Sears could undercut the prices of every general store in America with a range of goods never before seen. Railroads delivered these parcels and also made possible the great department stores of the early twentieth century. Transportation costs continued to fall, placing cars within the reach of all middle-class Americans after the Second World War. Ubiquitous interstate highways opened up the entire country to cheap truck transport. First came the suburban supermarkets and shopping centers, then the discounters.

The arrival of Wal-Mart was different. Wal-Mart's empire is

not built on cheap transportation, but on falling information costs that obviate the need for handling and storage. This substitution of information for natural resources, however good for the environment, affects the lives of millions of people. Main Street retailers cry foul every time a new Wal-Mart opens (just as they did 100 years ago when the big Sears catalog reached every mailbox in America). Wholesalers wail when Wal-Mart negotiates directly with manufacturers to cut out the middlemen and manufacturers' reps who traditionally brokered information and goods between retailers and their suppliers. Unions trying to organize the company maintain that Wal-Mart associates are underpaid (although many built small fortunes in Wal-Mart stock). Environmentalists pronounce that Wal-Mart is helping to destroy the American landscape and reinforcing the country's dependence on the car. There don't seem to be any complaints from truckers, perhaps the biggest losers from Wal-Mart's methods, who quite literally don't know what they are missing.

In turn, Wal-Mart's time may pass. Wal-Mart rode the falling information-cost curve to dominate retailing in America. Eventually, falling information prices will in turn allow others to displace Wal-Mart, further substituting information for transportation. Most intriguing is the development of home shopping television, still in its infancy. In five years, the combined U.S. sales of QVC and Home Shopping Network topped $3 billion, about the size of Wal-Mart in 1983. In 1994, sales from infomercials, those late-night hard-sell pitches, topped $1 billion. Experimentation is taking these shopping channels in many new directions, from erotica to cosmetics and beyond.[11] And all this comes with the most limited use of technology: you watch on TV, then telephone to order.

Cable companies are experimenting with interactive shopping, like Time Warner's Full Service Network, which offers tens of thousands of items that can be examined and ordered right over the cable. Others, including PC software giant Microsoft, are developing shopping capabilities for computer and cable TV networks. On-line PC services like Prodigy, Compuserve, and

America Online already sell electronically everything from travel services to music CDs.

The phenomenal growth of catalog shopping during the 1980s demonstrated that many people consider shopping nothing but a chore. Department stores tried to revive sales by making shopping an "experience," a cross between fashion and theater. But with most adults now working, there simply isn't the huge pool of people with nothing to do but cruise the malls. Others, like Wal-Mart, just make shopping easy, fast, and cheap. Electronic services, particularly when combined with virtual reality to allow a hammer to be held in your hand or a dress to be tried on, may eliminate the need to go shopping at all.

Environmentally, the significance of electronic shopping will be profound. Merchandise can be shipped but once, from manufacturer to customer, saving energy now burned up by trucks on expressways moving goods from one place to the next before consumers carry them home by car. Stores don't need to be built, catalogs printed, shipping cartons folded.

In the United States alone, one out of four Americans is employed moving or selling goods today. Electronic retailing could reduce this number by three-quarters, or more. One hundred years ago, more Americans were farmers than anything else, and domestic help was one of the biggest categories of employment off the farm. Today 3 percent of Americans are farmers, and domestic help is barely a category. The falling cost of information will have the same effect on retailing worldwide. This shift will take the global economy a long way toward sustainable development. Wealth in the future will be created from information, in cyberspace, not from natural resources or manufacturing.

THE LESSONS

In a decade, Wal-Mart went from the minor leagues to the top of the charts. In the process, the company revolutionized how goods are delivered to market. By substituting knowledge in the form of smarter management and better information technology, Wal-Mart pared its costs to the bone, knocking enormous, well-entrenched competitors out of the way. At the same, Wal-Mart significantly reduced the amount of pollution and energy it takes to retail merchandise. There are several lessons to be learned:

Ask, Why are we doing this? Wal-Mart's success, and its environmental contribution, is based on what it cut out of its operations that was expensive and unnecessary.

Look for what does the most damage. Wal-Mart's biggest opportunities for savings were in distribution, not in its stores; what you see when you walk into a Wal-Mart is just the tip of the iceberg. The real money, and the real environmental damage, was in endless truck trips.

Use green marketing judiciously. Many of Wal-Mart's in-store environmental activities save money, and they also raise the company's green profile.

Apply information technology wisely. Wal-Mart's success is based on better management most of all, but the company used the intensive application of information technology to cut waste in a big way.

LUFTHANSA AIRLINES WORKS SMARTER

PASSENGER SATISFACTION FIRST AND FOREMOST

During the 1990s, one big company after another has been blind-sided as the rules of the game change. One day, companies are unassailable market leaders; the next day, they are on the ropes. The causes are varied: deregulation, technology shift, globalization, multilayered management, a CEO who's lost the leadership drive that got him to the top in the first place. The results are the same: loss of innovation and direction; red ink; layoffs; and re-trenchment. As often as not, those at the top eventually get the ax, after a prolonged period of denial, indecision, and in many cases outright panic. Ultimately new management finally accepts that costs are completely out of line with those of competitors, often upstarts. For each of these hard-hit dinosaurs, survival means greatly improving leadership and efficiency while boosting quality and service. Where to start? Look for the telltale waste stream.

For an American traveler, Lufthansa Flight 4359 from Paris to Hamburg in December 1992 was an eye-opener. The gate area at Charles de Gaulle Airport was uncrowded, a few well-dressed businessmen waiting for the evening flight back to Germany. Airline employees were courteous, well informed, and professional. Without jostling, crying babies, or seared tempers, passengers filed onto the waiting 737 in a leisurely fashion. At 7:55 P.M., the aircraft pulled away from the gate, right on time.

On board, service on the 1½-hour flight was *de grand luxe.* Vintage French wine was served from real wine bottles—no portion-controlled four-ounce bottles of imitation burgundy. The meal that followed, delicious and fresh, was served on real china set on heavy linen tablecloths. Clearly competent in any number of languages, the cabin crew was engaging and efficient at the same time. This flight had more in common with the dining car of a crack express train than with a jammed flight out of La Guardia. We were reminded of the halcyon days of American airline travel in the 1950s and 1960s, before airplanes became buses that sprouted wings.

The airfare for this flight was also reminiscent of the good old days: several times what it would have cost to go a similar distance in the United States, say from New York to Cleveland. Deregulation has turned American air travel into a cramped way to get around, but one that is affordable and accessible. Germans fly only half as often as Americans, even though they are just as rich. At these prices, it's no wonder why.

Changes in European and world markets in the early 1990s hit Lufthansa hard. Engineered for the gentlemanly days of flying when markets were carved up among flag carriers like the spoils of war and prices were fixed to accommodate the least efficient player, Lufthansa found itself holding low cards in a high-stakes game. This reversal was immediately reflected in Lufthansa's financial statements. Despite buoyant growth in revenues, the airline lost DM444 million ($280 million) in 1991, then DM373 million ($240 million) in 1992. After a decade of strong growth and unbroken profitability, Lufthansa was headed for a crash landing.

Lufthansa was the prey, not the predator. Three of the world's largest carriers, American Airlines, British Airways, and United Airlines, were slugging it out for world domination. Survivors of fifteen tough years of deregulation at home, these battle-hardened competitors had slashed costs and were crowding Lufthansa. At the same time, a recession hit Europe particularly hard, with passenger airline traffic declining for the first time in history. Demand fell, capacity increased, and prices plunged. To top it all off, the value of the German mark soared, raising the price of everything Lufthansa bought at home.

Declining prices are nothing new to the airline business. They have been falling in real terms since 1960, when jet aircraft first entered commercial service in large numbers.[1] But this time Lufthansa could not keep up; its expenses were spiraling ahead of ticket prices. With deregulation, the German flag carrier had to compete on price, but it found itself carrying costs up to twice that of its leanest rivals.[2] Wages and benefits were high, productivity was poor, and Lufthansa was flying with too many empty seats. Change exposed Lufthansa to severe pressures. Like a 1950s test plane approaching the sound barrier, the company was ready to burst apart.

Despite all these problems, the fundamentals of the airline business have remained good—perhaps better for Lufthansa than most others. Worldwide passenger traffic grew 6 percent per year in the 1980s, and industry observers expect demand to grow by at least 5 percent per year over the 1990s, more than twice as fast as the economy as a whole.[3] While worldwide traffic dipped in 1991,[4] Lufthansa passenger volumes continued to grow. The collapse of the Soviet Union created enormous opportunities for Lufthansa (and the rest of Germany) as the new gateway to the east.

Lufthansa wanted to be one of the survivors in this business. But in the early 1990s, it was only the eleventh largest airline in the world, and the third largest international carrier. In an industry where half a dozen competitors, at most, will become truly "global," Lufthansa's position was vulnerable. It has a big and rich home market and a strong position on major routes throughout the world. But the outlook in 1991–92 was negative; until it put its house in order, Lufthansa was not going to capitalize on any of the opportunities it enjoyed. Outside Germany, aggressive competitors

—especially the Americans and the British—were slashing prices on Lufthansa's most profitable routes. These gate crashers were grabbing market share, while Lufthansa's financial woes mounted. The airline had lost control of its fate.

ONE HAND TIED

Juergen Weber took over the controls at Lufthansa in May 1991, becoming chairman just when the red ink began to flow. An engineer, previously the airline's chief technical officer, Weber had to slash costs, and fast.

His solution: cut waste. By identifying and eliminating pockets of waste throughout its operations, Weber put Lufthansa back on course. He lowered the airline's operating and capital outlays significantly. At the same time, he improved service by zeroing in on what customers value and shedding the rest.

Weber's plan began to pay dividends almost immediately. Within a year of his appointment, costs per seat-mile fell, while traffic volume went up sharply. By the end of his second year, despite continuing problems in the airline business, Lufthansa turned the corner, showing a profit in the second quarter of 1993. For the whole of 1993, losses were cut by two-thirds.[5] Even more impressive was the company's environmental performance, in terms of fuel consumption, noise pollution, emissions, and waste of all kinds. For Lufthansa, efficiency and profit, environmental and financial performance, became inextricably linked.

In many ways Juergen Weber's hands were tied. Germany is a big market, but it is not an easy place to do business. For a company like Lufthansa, the government sets the rules, lots of them, and tough ones. Increasingly, successful Germans are finding this environment oppressive, and a steady stream of big companies are packing their bags. Among car companies, Volkswagen is shifting production to Spain, while BMW and Mercedes are opening new plants in the United States. And while German manufacturers are moving abroad to deal with high costs, Lufthansa is stuck at home. Service providers, like airlines, must make locally what they sell. Weber could not cut and run. He had to be creative.

Weber told an interviewer that 80 percent of Lufthansa's costs were out of the company's control, including fuel costs, airport charges, and interest payments for its fleet. He added that he had the most control over personnel and capacity utilization.[6] Yet, in the short term, Lufthansa's power to affect even these— particularly labor costs, which alone account for one-third of the airline's expenses—was severely circumscribed.

Government-mandated benefits in Germany are generous, and labor unions are notoriously militant. Germans enjoy the highest wages in the world—and the longest vacations. Massive layoffs, so readily employed by American managers, don't play well in Germany, to say the least. Layoffs are unusual and extremely costly. Partially privatized in the early 1980s (the government retained just over half its shares), Lufthansa receives no public subsidies. Government-mandated benefits must be covered from cash flow.

Lufthansa's—and Germany's—prospects looked bad enough that the company cut some 8,000 positions over two years, about 15% of the total.[7] Wages were frozen for one year, and productivity concessions were granted by the unions. In short, Lufthansa got its employees to work more for less money, which is almost unheard of in Germany. Nevertheless, there was a limit to how much the airline could extract from the unions, particularly if the German economy turned up.

German airport charges (including landing, terminal, and air traffic–control fees) are exorbitant, twice as high in Frankfurt as in Paris, and four times what they are in London.[8] Lufthansa's chairman figured he could save DM500 million ($320 million) in airport charges if he were operating out of the United States.[9] This figure is more than the company's total losses in 1991. In 1992, when Lufthansa was struggling to bring its finances under control, airport charges went up 16 percent. Air traffic–control fees alone jumped 33 percent[10] despite notorious inefficiencies in the European air-traffic system that produces thousands of hours of holding time in the air for Lufthansa every year.[11] Those delays cost the airline hundreds of millions of marks, more than its losses in 1992.[12] Since airport and traffic-control operations are monopolies, Lufthansa had no direct control over this expense, its second largest after wages.

BRINGING COSTS DOWN TO EARTH

Oil prices are entirely out of Lufthansa's hands, but the strengthening of the mark has helped keep fuel costs down, since oil is priced in dollars. In the short term, Lufthansa can only hope that the German-mark price of oil keeps falling. In the long run, however, the airline can have a real impact on its finances by raising the fuel efficiency of its fleet. In 1992, its most critical year, Lufthansa spent DM1.2 billion ($750 million) on jet fuel, 10 percent of its expenses.[13]

New planes can cut fuel costs dramatically. The Airbus A340, the first one of which was bought by Lufthansa in 1993, reduces jet fuel consumption by one-third compared to other long-haul aircraft. For example, on the 2,800-mile flight from Munich to Chicago, an A340 burns an estimated fifty-four tons of fuel, while a DC10-30 with the same number of passengers would consume seventy-four tons of fuel. One-third is a big number: in 1992, Lufthansa's entire loss was less than a third of its fuel bill.

By maintaining one of the youngest fleets in the industry—its average jet is only five years old—Lufthansa boosted fuel efficiency radically. Between 1970 and 1990, the amount of jet fuel it took to transport a passenger one mile fell by half. As the chart shows, Lufthansa made large strides in the 1970s, slowed on by the oil crisis. But then efficiency gains stalled in the 1980s, contributing, perhaps, to the financial crisis that began at the end of that decade.

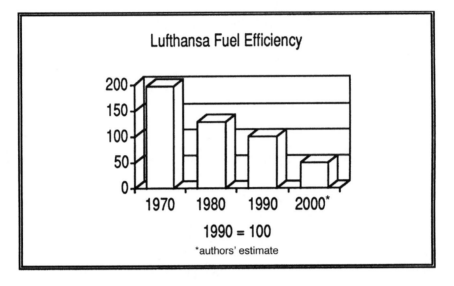

As the performance figures for the A340 demonstrate, there remains considerable scope for further savings. A DM13 billion ($8 billion) fleet modernization plan for the first half of the 1990s[14] reduced operating costs, and the airline grounded or sold the older, inefficient aircraft in its fleet. The savings have gone right to the bottom line, with fuel outlays declining by 5 percent in 1991 and 11 percent in 1992, despite rising traffic. By the end of the decade, Lufthansa expects to burn half as much fuel to transport a passenger one mile it as did in 1990. Without any other changes, this course alone would put Lufthansa solidly back in the black.

Lower fuel consumption is good for the environment. And so are the noise and emission reductions that come with new equipment. Compared to existing long-distance planes, the new A340s reduce exhaust pollutants up to 85 percent. Noise levels are cut in half, reducing Lufthansa's outlays for airport fees.

Noise pollution is a big problem for Lufthansa. In Germany, landing fees are set as a function of noise levels (the only other country that does so is Sweden). Lufthansa spent DM2.5 billion ($1.6 billion) on airport charges in 1992, even more than on fuel. In 1993, the airline outfitted forty of its Boeing 737-200s with "hush kits" to reduce noise levels by up to 80 percent. The savings are real: 737s with the new hush kits pay only DM805 to land, compared to DM2,415 without them, a savings of two-thirds.[15] New planes like the A340 will reduce landing fees even further.

Germany has one of the toughest environmental regimes in the world. The Green Party, with lots of popular support, keeps the environment on the front burner in Germany. A strict recycling law, for example, requires manufacturers to take back from consumers *all* packaging they use. A company like Lufthansa makes a good target: airplanes are noisy, dirty, and burn lots of fuel. To please its volatile Green voters, the German government is turning the screws on Lufthansa to reduce its impact on the environment. As it happens, this pressure also helps the airline to cut operating costs, despite the need for big up-front capital outlays.

FLYING SMARTER

Lufthansa Technik is the largest third-party aircraft maintenance supplier in the world. At one side of the Hamburg airport, away from the passenger terminals, the Technik center faces a runway crowded with planes from around the world waiting to be serviced. Among the many grimy, sprawling buildings is a spanking new hangar with two enormous bays, big enough to accommodate two jets at the same time. This is the Lufthansa Technik paint shop, completed in 1992, where planes are stripped of old paint and refinished, a process that must be repeated every five or six years. This hangar is part of a DM800 million ($500 million) expansion of the Hamburg overhaul center.

On a cold winter day, we came to these new hangars, where Lufthansa was employing its new "Aquastripping" process to remove old paint. While a lone 737 got a new paint job in one of the cavernous buildings, a Lufthansa technician demonstrated in the other how the new process works. He mounted a platform the size of a large car, suspended from the ceiling. From a computer console, the technician controlled a large nozzle as it felt its way along one section of an airplane fuselage.

Aquastripping lessened the environmental damage caused by the Hamburg paint shop by several orders of magnitude. In the past, teams of workers applied 2.5 tons of chemical strippers to each plane. These solvents were dangerous: to apply the stuff, workers had to wear what looked like space suits. Contaminated work clothes, along with the used stripper and the 7.5 tons of water per plane that was needed for the process, all had to be treated as hazardous material. Disposal costs were rising quickly.

By contrast, Aquastripping relied on water under high pressure to remove paint. Chemicals were essentially eliminated, while 97 percent of the water was recycled. After extraction from the air and water in the hangar, only the old paint remained, which was incinerated.

The benefits of Aquastripping to Lufthansa were significant. Material and disposal costs were essentially eliminated. Worker safety was enhanced. Quality was better: Aquastripping could take off the outer coat and leave the primer layer, reducing the damage to the metal underneath. Best of all, one man could do the job faster than thirty had before. Since our visit, Lufthansa has introduced a low-pressure water system that is even more economical than Aquastripping.

To regain its competitiveness, Lufthansa needs more efficiency improvements like this, since labor makes up a third of its costs. Lower fuel costs and landing fees will help the bottom line, but will not be enough. Labor productivity must go up.

Lufthansa must also get more from the capital it has invested. The airline spent DM1.6 billion ($1 billion) in 1992 to pay for its jets, in interest charges, lease payments, and depreciation. But there is little point in increasing fuel economy by 50 percent if planes are running half empty, and Lufthansa "load factors" (the proportion of seats filled with paying passengers) have been low.[16] Lufthansa can do more to repair its finances—and the balance sheet—by filling its planes, and flying fewer of them, than by buying more efficient jets.

Better returns from labor and capital require additional investment, to be sure, but most of all, they require better management. The idea here is simple: put on your thinking cap and figure out a way to get your passengers around with fewer planes. Don't just buy better planes; get rid of some planes altogether. This approach is already paying dividends. Lufthansa has eliminated some routes entirely to save cash, but it has also rethought its route structure. Before, the airline used a complex system, with roundabout routes flown by crews based in Frankfurt only. This affected the convenience of Lufthansa's schedule. In addition, crews had to make costlier transfer flights and overnight stays. This approach, poorly adapted to the German market, has been replaced by direct flights with smaller planes.[17] In just one quarter, such changes helped the airline carry 7 percent more passengers with 3 percent fewer flights. The company had been trying to build market share by adding flights—and flying them with empty planes.

Lufthansa can substitute information for planes and improve service to customers at the same time. Everyone prefers relaxing on a nonstop flight to sprinting between gates at a hub. The bottom line and environmental benefits are large. Sometimes these changes result from nothing more than better thinking—in this case better route planning. Other times, they require additional investment in computers.

Lufthansa developed an onboard system that monitors aircraft performance (including exhaust, fuel consumption, and temperature). Data is recorded on a cassette, then run through a computer on the ground, providing feedback for maintenance crews. For example, the system might tell workers that the third engine should be looked at because that engine is using 4 percent more fuel than necessary. With the new A340, the system will maintain contact with computers on the ground throughout flight. In future, the system will provide in-flight feedback to the pilots, helping safety and lowering fuel consumption.

Lufthansa's flight-monitoring system—the first to be developed and perfected—helps its planes operate more safely and inexpensively than before. But the airline also needs to fill up its planes. The simplest way is to discount fares across the board, but that's a tough game, as airline failures like Laker and People Express show. For high-cost players like Lufthansa, discounting alone is not a viable option. A better approach is to charge full fare when you can (for business travel), then selectively discount seats that would otherwise be empty.

American Airlines wrote the book on "yield management systems," which generate the highest ticket price possible for each available seat, during the rough-and-tumble 1980s, when deregulation swept the U.S. airline industry. Its reservations system has become one of the most profitable operations at American Airlines.[18] Moreover, this computer network has probably done more to reduce aviation energy consumption than any other innovation, by filling seats and eliminating the need for extra airplanes and the fuel they burn.

Lufthansa brought such a system on-line in 1993. Considering that a new jet like the A340 costs $100 million, the potential savings are enormous. In the first quarter of 1993, Lufthansa's load factors rose by six percentage points, after languishing for years. With more than 230 jets in its fleet, a sustained 6 percent increase in capacity utilization could obviate the need for fourteen aircraft. That's a lot of money—and natural resources—that could be saved.

To eliminate short-hop flights with poor profit potential, Lufthansa has experimented with rail service within Germany. One train, introduced in 1982, ran from Frankfurt to Dusseldorf via Bonn and Cologne. Another, started in 1990, connects Frankfurt and Stuttgart. These trains, outfitted like a First Class airplane compartment, have not made money, largely because of the high rent charged by the Bundesbahn, Germany's national railway. In 1993, the *Airport Express* to Dusseldorf was replaced by Bundesbahn-operated service. Lufthansa still maintains that flights of less than 2½ hours—essentially all domestic flights—are better served by train. Short flights are hard to fill, and short-haul planes have the poorest fuel economy. Cooperation with the German railways will save money and cut pollution and energy consumption.

Further integration of Lufthansa's flight schedule with the rail network, however, will be some time off since Frankfurt is the only German airport with its own train station.

Environmental changes can benefit worker safety, ultimately lowering costs even further. Aquastripping, as we have seen, reduced exposure to caustic substances in that area to zero. In another case, maintenance workers were using volatile solvents to clean parts, so Lufthansa developed a closed-loop system that covered the solvent baths, to prevent evaporation. Since this substance was linked to cancer, Lufthansa improved job safety into the bargain. For an airline, of course, safety always comes first, particularly in the air. Lufthansa has reduced its use of ozone-depleting chemicals to zero, eliminating them from maintenance operations (like parts cleaning). But the U.S. Federal Aviation Administration still requires Halon fire extinguishers (with ozone-depleting chemicals) on all planes flying in the United States, even though the EPA is trying to end CFC production.

Whatever it does to remain competitive, Lufthansa can't compromise customer service. If service is lacking, travelers can always find a cheaper alternative. Airline seats are essentially a commodity—one is just like another. Of course prices must be competitive, but few airlines discount their way to success. With its inherently expensive operating structure, Lufthansa must try to differentiate itself based on service. Lufthansa must deliver what the Japanese call *anshinkan,* or peace of mind, and do so at a competitive price.

When asked by one interviewer how his workers maintain service levels during cutbacks, CEO Weber responded bluntly, "We told them if we did not improve vis-à-vis our competitors . . . they would lose their jobs."[19] But a heavy-handed approach will not deliver the consistent quality and large cost savings the carrier needs, year in, year out. Only better productivity can do that. If service starts to slide, the game is over.

Lufthansa managed to maintain, if not improve, customer satisfaction during its retrenchment. Polls consistently rank Lufthansa among the top five carriers, and among international business travelers, the German airline comes out on top.[20] With many of its environmental initiatives, Lufthansa has not only cut costs directly, but also improved service. By rethinking what service really means, the airline has focused better on what customers really want.

For some domestic flights, Lufthansa serves what it calls "Gate Buffets." At the departure gate, passengers can put together their own snack bag to take on the plane, choosing from small sandwiches, cold cuts, fresh fruit, yogurt, baked goods, and candies. This new service has a number of benefits. Flight crews no longer need to serve meals, only beverages. Less food is needed, since not everyone eats. Less food is wasted: before, for example, every packaged snack tray had yogurt, only 40 percent of which were eaten. Less garbage is produced—1,700 tons a year less, representing 7 percent of the company's solid waste.

The Gate Buffet requires somewhat more labor and more complicated logistics compared to having people put everything in plastic trays at the caterer's. Nevertheless, in total, the Gate Buffet has lowered expenses. Best of all, customers love it. They prefer choosing their own meals. One manager told us, "Now, they take handfuls of candy bars for their kids—the cheapest thing we offer. Yogurt and little sandwiches are much more expensive, but people take fewer of them."

To further reduce its volume of garbage, Lufthansa looked at every single item on its aircraft to see what could be eliminated, repackaged, or reused. There are 5,000 in-flight service items on a 747, ranging from aspirins to toothbrushes. Changes resulted in thirty tons less plastic waste alone per year. Reusable coffee mugs and real china were introduced for cabin service (first in Business Class, then in Coach), reducing garbage by 700 tons per year. Single-serving bottles for drinks were replaced by full-size ones, which are easier to recycle. The company may even introduce soda fountains onboard for soft drinks. Glass and aluminum, which accounted for half of in-flight garbage, are separated in the galley for recycling on the ground.

Lufthansa has already broken even on these in-flight changes, so the company is happy. More important is better service. Real china is a nice touch. As for the full-sized wine bottles, our very unscientific customer survey (of two opinionated frequent flyers) revealed a very positive response.

EURO-BLUES

Better service, lower costs, and environmentally correct. This sounds like a winning combination, one that may help solve the perennial European competitiveness problem. Recession in the early 1990s exposed the high cost structure of many European companies, like Lufthansa, that were forced to compete on world markets. During the booming 1980s, Europeans felt like they had a tiger by the tail. The building of the single European market and the fall of the Soviet Union added to the euphoria. But the mood turned sour once the recession of the early 1990s arrived. Many reports showed that Europe had lost its edge, that Europeans could not turn good ideas into profit, that costs were too high. As if to prove the point, many national champions, particularly in high-tech, were looking for the exits. Suddenly the safety net that Europeans took for granted seemed to drop away.

As unemployment lines lengthened, Europeans realized that something had to give. High-profile layoffs (like Lufthansa's) showed that there was a simple, if harsh, way to bring costs back in line with those of American and Japanese competitors. But many Europeans are searching for a third way, one that preserves Europe's highly developed—and expensive—social net. They don't need pantomimes of American and Japanese solutions that probably wouldn't work in Europe anyway.

European manufacturers have been exposed to fierce competition from the United States and Asia for some time, but service industries, like the airlines, went relatively unscathed until the 1990s. In the airline business, as we have seen, the walls of protection finally came down. For Lufthansa, and its continental European rivals, the threat comes primarily from the United States and Britain. But matching these competitors was not enough. With higher wage rates and benefits, Europeans are unlikely to win discounting wars in the airline business (or any other). Rather, to succeed, European companies need to change the rules themselves, to turn the tables on their challengers.

After a decade of brutal price wars, the big U.S. airlines turned to cost reduction in the late 1980s, particularly in the area of wages.[21] Despite well-publicized fights with their unions, these airlines have been able to extract give-backs (like lower wage rates for new workers and longer work hours) on top of big layoffs. This approach does slash expenses at a stroke, but the ultimate effect on service and profits is dubious. Ask anyone who flew Eastern Airlines or Pan Am in the final days.

Certainly there was overmanning at Lufthansa, and at other European airlines, particularly on the ground and in management positions. But lasting efficiency improvements that do not undermine service will come from boosting productivity, not bashing labor. In the first few years after it sank into the red, Lufthansa successfully used its environmental program to flag pockets of cost that could be eliminated, raising the productivity of both labor and capital. This could be the third way, an approach that allows Europe to be competitive with its rivals without abandoning its social contract. A better way? Perhaps. An easy way? Not at all. Restructuring is never easy.

Lufthansa's green flags have helped the company identify waste. But its environmental initiatives also ease competitive pressures in other ways. The best thing that could happen to Lufthansa would be for the price of jet fuel to quadruple, or for every country to base landing fees on noise levels. Strict environmental regulation makes a great barrier to entry for foreigners eyeing Lufthansa's home turf. Environmental regulation in Germany is tough, and consumer awareness of green issues is even tougher. This climate has forced Lufthansa to get ahead of the compliance curve. As one manager said, "We must be active; we can't wait for laws." As other countries catch up with Germany in this area, Lufthansa's edge will increase.

Turning its green program into a marketing advantage is another story. Selling environmental correctness is tough. Ironically, despite its achievements, Lufthansa has a relatively poor environmental image at home. As one airline manager summed it up for us, "Environmental responsibility is not easy for an airline. Lufthansa can't be a 'green' company—airplanes are not environmental, they pollute." In an environmental survey of the German public taken a few years ago, Lufthansa compared well with other airlines, but not so well with companies from other industries; since then, Lufthansa has closed the gap, according to more recent surveys. Green marketing has risks anywhere. If you advertise your achievements, people hold you to a higher standard.

THE GREATEST FORCE IN THE UNIVERSE

Pushing through environmentally driven efficiency improvements has not been easy. Lufthansa has had to fight inertia among its employees and suppliers.

When the airline introduced its Gate Buffet service, according to one manager, "people got hysterical about the whole thing, making this kind of change. When we asked the catering company to switch from plastic to paper bags, there was real drama. People thought there would be thousands of suits ruined." Of course, in any organization, the naysayers will outnumber those advocating change. Nevertheless, going green appeals to many employees. Lufthansa maintains that its environmental programs are not driven from the top. For example, five employees spearheaded the program to eliminate unnecessary supplies from Lufthansa's planes, with unexpectedly large results. The airline has a suggestion program to encourage such good ideas—one employee received DM30,000 ($19,000).

"Responsibility for the environment is part of our culture," we were told by one Lufthansa employee. But ultimately Lufthansa's ability to effect productivity improvements will require new thinking among its employees. Here the Germans should have a real advantage with their highly developed apprenticeship system. Germany has the infrastructure needed to train and retrain its people to get a better return from natural resources, labor, and capital.

Visitors to Lufthansa's giant Technik hangars in Hamburg cannot help but be impressed by the professionalism and assurance of its workforce. With its sophisticated stripping methods, Lufthansa gets more out of its workers, but each operator now needs much more training and has much more responsibility. When the Aquastripping process increased their output by a factor of thirty, the Lufthansa technicians affected were retrained, either to operate the new equipment or for other tasks.

Environmental change also requires an effective organization. At Lufthansa, environmental staff report through the line groups, and there are not separate budgets (which become easy targets when budgets are tight). At the corporate level, there is a commissioner for environmental issues, but each department has its own environmental staff function that reports to line management. The commissioner has no direct authority over employees; he can only persuade. One manager from the environmental department told us how a purchasing agent decided to buy paper at a discount from a Finnish mill, which was trying to dump its inventory of chlorinated paper on the market. The environmental department, worried about bad publicity, stopped the purchase.

Gaining an edge is not easy when technology is a commodity. All airlines buy their planes off the shelf: one 747-400 is the same as another. But by working closely with airframe and engine suppliers during the aircraft-development stage, Lufthansa has managed to maintain a technological and environmental lead over many of its competitors. Lufthansa was the first customer for the Boeing 737, the mainstay of its short-haul fleet, and it has close ties with Airbus. Lufthansa helped design the A340, a long-range aircraft first put into service by Lufthansa. Since efficiency depends as much on the engines as the airframes, Lufthansa has told engine manufacturers that they must improve emission standards and fuel consumption if they want Lufthansa's business. As we have seen, the results have been dramatic.

Suppliers are not always cooperative. As the eleventh largest carrier, Lufthansa can only throw so much weight around. One manager told us, "Boeing has a real attitude; we ask our regional salesmen for things, and they just say no." He gave a recent example: "We asked Boeing and Airbus to give us separate trolleys for sorting garbage. They didn't have them. We said to Boeing, 'What are you going to do about onboard waste management?' and they replied, 'Onboard waste what?' " Lufthansa had to develop its own special trolleys for sorting trash in its galleys, and then find a supplier. To increase its pull, it has worked with other European carriers to twist arms.

Unlike many other airlines, Lufthansa spends its own R&D money on aircraft development. The company put 30,000 man-hours into the A340, submitting 400 design-change suggestions to Airbus (more than half of which were accepted). The reward was an airplane tailored to Lufthansa's needs, particularly its noise, emissions, and fuel-economy requirements. Other projects, some of which are quite exotic, may pay off in the long term. In one case, Lufthansa engineers are developing a new aircraft finish with the texture of sharkskin. Sharks pass through water with very little turbulence, conserving energy. Lufthansa may give new meaning to the phrase "swimming with the sharks."

THE LESSONS

Turning around a company the size of Lufthansa takes many years. The airline skillfully cut much of the fat from its bloated operations by using environmental telltales to flag waste. All Lufthansa environmental activities save money, lift service levels, or both. The German carrier has also sidestepped many potentially expensive environmental problems while minimizing the need to lay off people, its most valuable asset. There are several lessons companies can learn from Lufthansa's experience:

Spend money to save money. By exploiting the latest technology for aircraft, Lufthansa has steadily reduced its fuel bill, one of its largest budget items. Competitors could do this, but don't.

Focus on real customer needs. Lufthansa has made the environment a service issue by eliminating activities that customers don't care about.

Substitute information for natural resources, capital, and labor. Lufthansa has reduced the need for workers, money, aircraft, and fuel with better reservation, yield-management, and flight-planning systems. Software is cheaper than planes—and more environmentally friendly.

Integrate environmental activities. Lufthansa made the environment a mainstream activity. Only when waste is eliminated from line functions are the cost and environmental benefits significant. Staff budgets for environmental programs are easy targets for cuts when times are tough or priorities change.

Turn regulation to advantage. The German government raised the environmental stakes for Lufthansa; Lufthansa turned Germany's tough environmental regime into an opportunity to reduce operating expenses. Once Lufthansa realized that its environmental investments could turn a profit, the company was able to get ahead of the lawmakers.

Don't count on suppliers. They work to their own agenda. Unless they are forced by you or somebody else, they don't care about the environment any more than they do about your customers. Lufthansa has been twisting arms every step of the way.

Don't count on recycling alone. This is a high-profile, low-value activity. Lufthansa's experience (for example, with real china on its flights) shows that the benefit comes from eliminating the activity that generates trash that needs to be recycled in the first place.

HITACHI PREACHES THE GREEN GOSPEL

MANAGING EFFICIENCY FROM TOASTERS TO TURBINES

*Hitachi, Ltd. makes everything from toasters to computer termi-
nals to electric turbines, selling its broad range of products
around the world. Like many other Japanese companies, Hitachi's
success was built on nonstop product development, cost reduction,
and quality improvement. For decades, this formula worked like a
dream, increasing sales and profits year in, year out. Then for
Hitachi, as for Japan, the dream turned to nightmare in the early
1990s when growth ceased and profits collapsed. Only innovation—bold technological strokes—can renew Hitachi, according to
its leaders, engineers to a man. And bold environmental goals
drive innovation at this company. Unlike Japan's other export
champions, Hitachi has committed itself to an extraordinarily aggressive environmental plan.*

Hitachi means "rising sun" in Japanese, and rise this company
has. Hitachi is the fifth largest company in the world, and the
largest electrical and electronics manufacturer, bigger than both
IBM and General Electric. From relative obscurity in Japan,
Hitachi quadrupled in size in the decade to 1975, and in the next

95

fifteen years quadrupled again. Then, rapid appreciation of the yen combined with the collapse of the Japanese "bubble" economy to bring Hitachi's growth to a halt. After peaking at about $65 billion in 1990, revenues started to slide; profits dropped like a rock.

While economic troubles outside its control were the primary cause of its reversals, Hitachi had been riding against the tide for some time. Competition, largely from Japan, had already forced its European and American counterparts like Philips and General Electric to go on crash diets, spinning off peripheral activities and excess staff in order to survive. All of America's once sprawling conglomerates had already narrowed their focus, some dramatically. ITT, for example, was the ultimate conglomerate, much akin to Japan's big *keiretsu*. But this strategy came unraveled. In the late 1970s and early 1980s, ITT sold off many divisions, greatly reducing its size. Today, ITT is a shadow of its former self.

Where others hunker down, Hitachi stands fast. Hitachi, Ltd. encompasses 700 subsidiaries and 330,000 employees, manufacturing over 20,000 products designed in 35 research labs around the world. These labs are the true heart of Hitachi. Here, the company believes, the power of innovation can overcome the centrifugal force pulling the company in 20,000 different directions. Here ideas can be transformed into future sales.

Hitachi needs good ideas—lots of them—because it is being torn by powerful forces: falling prices, rising energy efficiency, and expanding environmental regulation.

A decade or two ago, low prices launched Hitachi overseas. Today, however, competition from Korea and Taiwan can always undercut Hitachi on the price of everything it makes, from VCRs to memory chips. Hitachi must offer its customer more than low prices. According to the Hitachi gospel, R&D will unlock the potential added value in its products.

Something else is tearing at the core of Hitachi's existence. Since everything the company sells consumes energy in one form or another, Hitachi is vulnerable to competitors that can leapfrog it with higher energy efficiency, offering customers more productive use of capital and labor. With ambitious efficiency goals driving new product development, Hitachi must push its technology to the limit.

Regulations by governments everywhere are raising the environmental hurdles for Hitachi and, more importantly, for its customers. Hitachi is working toward an aggressive set of internal efficiency targets in order to stay well ahead of regulators. And the company wants to do the same for its customers: deliver products for which pollution is no longer an issue, and efficiency is without parallel.

INNOVATION AND TECHNOLOGY

Japan has earned a premier reputation for R&D excellence. By many measures, Japan does some of the best research in the world. Japan's enormous investment in semiconductor technology bought it top billing on the world stage, for example. Japanese corporate R&D expenditures as a percent of sales rose steadily during the 1970s and 1980s, producing a growing share of the world's patents. U.S. performance by these measures has declined, particularly when government R&D outlays are factored out. Many take this as a sign of Western industrial decline: they say Japan invests for the future while Americans and Europeans eat their seed corn.

Despite its accomplishments, Japan Inc. is dogged by its reputation as a pirate of foreign ideas. Americans and Europeans frequently complain that their Japanese competitors pilfer their best ideas, then reexport them. According to this view, the Japanese get these good ideas "unfairly": hiring Western scientists at high salaries, buying small high-tech start-ups (especially in America), or locking unwary partners into lopsided technology transfers. In fact, the technological tide has turned, and more good ideas now flow out of Japan than in. Still, where are today's new blockbuster inventions from Japan?

To do more for its customers, Hitachi is looking beyond *kaizen,* Japan's process of incremental improvement, for raising quality and lowering costs. Peter Drucker makes the distinction between *productivity,* which he defines as the application of knowledge to existing products, services, and processes, and *innovation,* the application of knowledge to new ideas. Drucker, believed by many to be the father of modern management and the intellectual leader of Japan's postwar wunderkinder, says Japan excels at productivity but lags in innovation. To make matters worse for Japan Inc., many of its competitors in the Third World have also boosted productivity.

To stay ahead of its low-cost rivals, Hitachi wants to become a master of innovation, to think big. Hitachi's core business is electricity. Power systems for utilities and industries alone account for a third of its sales. Consequently, Hitachi is looking for breakthroughs in clean, efficient power generation. Most energy today is made from oil, coal, and gas, and burning these hydrocarbons produces many pollutants, including carbon dioxide, the cause of global warning. Cleaner, more efficient products will result in less emissions and lower costs for customers.

To a great extent, reducing energy consumption and emissions depends on incremental improvements. But Hitachi wants to leap ahead, lowering them dramatically. Cutting CO_2 production is perhaps the toughest challenge of all. This is a basic scientific barrier: when you burn things, carbon dioxide is a by-product. For many of its ideas, Hitachi can get inspiration from outside Japan, but for CO_2 and other areas of energy efficiency and pollution control there is no one to turn to. Hitachi must establish a proprietary edge.

If innovation is its goal, Hitachi provides the right environment. Founded in 1910, the company is not the offspring of one of the great prewar combines, or *zaibatsu,* like rivals NEC and Toshiba. There is an "outsider" tradition here. Company folklore favors tales of lone scientists advancing their ideas against all odds. At the labs, "skunkworks" are part of the culture. With this approach to product development, small teams focus intense effort on a single project. In many ways, Hitachi has already positioned itself as the world's preeminent high-tech company: the labs, the scientists, the funding are all in place. Perhaps most important of

all, Hitachi has a mountain of cash (and virtually no debt) to keep
its idea mills running for a long time. Still, Hitachi needs results
from its labs now more than ever. For the company as a whole,
sales per employee, the simplest measure of productivity, have
been flat for a decade.

THE LABS

An hour and a half from Tokyo's busy Ueno Station by *Super
Hitachi* express lie the Hitachi Research Labs (HRL), on several
hundred beautifully landscaped acres overlooking the Pacific
Ocean. Here 1,000 scientists and engineers in a dozen departments
research everything from the practical to the abstract, a world
away from the crowded, hyperactive, strictly business atmosphere
of central Tokyo.

Among the many surprises at the labs is an enormous log
cabin brought from Canada, a reminder to all of Hitachi's relationship with the environment (and a modest attempt to redress the
balance of trade). Here, in these unexpected surroundings, we discussed over lunch the company's research philosophy with a group
of Hitachi managers. One of our hosts explained that Hitachi is
"good at muscle, not at thinking." He added that management told
them that "we need to be more creative. We need breakthroughs
to reduce costs and meet our environmental goals. We need technology to get breakthroughs."

Technology covers a lot of ground at Hitachi. The company
has six labs outside Japan, doing basic research in Europe and applications work in the United States. But it is at HRL, Hitachi's
largest and oldest R&D center, that Hitachi does its most valuable
research. Here scientists develop new materials like superconduc-
tors and ceramics from the molecular level on up. Designers experiment with electric cars, high-speed elevators, magnetically
levitated bullet trains. Engineers built exotic power systems like
fuel cells and nuclear fusion devices. Computer scientists program
all manner of systems for controlling Hitachi's many products still

on the drawing boards. A visitor feels like he has discovered one of the great centers of learning, like the library at Alexandria.

This kind of fundamental research has become rare in the industrial labs of America and Europe. The great corporate research centers like those at IBM and AT&T's Bell Labs have been forced by competitive realities to abandon much of their theoretical work in favor of projects that will produce commercial returns quickly. If a customer is not asking for it now, an idea is not worth anything. Of course Hitachi expects results, and its line divisions direct development from R&D to market. Indeed, at HRL 60 percent of research is product related. Nevertheless, there is a sense of long-term commitment to the advancement of science.

At HRL, we saw one particularly exotic experiment. A municipal water company was worried that it could not spot minute quantities of pollutants in its water supply; without a good early warning system, it could only respond to problems after they occurred. Hitachi discovered that fish react more quickly to pollutants in water than any man-made sensing devices. Researchers tracked the behavior of their fish when they were exposed to pollutants, developing a "fuzzy logic" software program to detect irregular behavior patterns that indicated rising levels of pollutants. They combined their fish tank with a proprietary Hitachi imaging computer to build an early warning system for the utility.

At the GREEN Center, a three-story building at one end of the lab grounds, thirty researchers concentrate on the environmental performance of Hitachi's energy generation systems. At any given time, some three or four dozen projects are underway. The GREEN (Global Resources, Environment & ENergy) Center's mandate covers two major environmental problems: acid rain and global warming.

Hydrocarbon combustion, in power plants and automobiles, produces nitrogen-oxygen and sulfur-oxygen compounds that contribute directly to acid rain. At the GREEN Center, Hitachi is changing the way its products work to remove NOx and SOx from emissions, and to prevent them from being formed in the first place. According to GREEN Center manager Dr. Hiroshi

Miyadera, "We've proved successful in this area and are now exporting our technology to Europe."[1] When we visited, one of the GREEN Center projects was to reduce emissions from gas turbines, an important concern of electric utilities. At that time, Hitachi's turbines were producing 40–50 parts per million of NOx; their short-term goal was to reduce this by half. While making this improvement in cleanliness, the engineers were hoping to increase turbine fuel efficiency at the same time.

Global warming, caused by carbon dioxide emissions, is a thornier problem. For the long term, Hitachi is developing advanced systems, like fuel cells that produce electricity from natural gas without burning it. GREEN Center researchers are also studying ways to "fix" CO_2, much as trees take CO_2 out of the air and lock it into wood. In the short term, Hitachi wants to reduce carbon dioxide emissions by raising the energy efficiency of its products. The idea is simple: if you don't use the energy in the first place, there's less CO_2 to worry about.

Several advanced energy-supply programs are running concurrently; all reduce CO_2 emissions while improving energy efficiency dramatically. Conventional power plants recover only about 35 to 40 percent of the energy potential of coal, oil, and natural gas. Working with the Japanese government, Hitachi is developing combined-cycle and fuel-cell technologies. Like cogeneration systems, combined-cycle turbines reuse heat that would otherwise be wasted. Fuel cells turn gas directly into electricity without burning it. These programs will raise energy use into the 50 to 60 percent range while cutting CO_2 emissions by half.

Although it is linked to global warming, CO_2 is not a direct risk to health like many other pollutants. Preventing global warming, the serious consequences of which are some time off, may be expensive. Hitachi is betting that the commitment made by governments around the world in Rio de Janeiro in 1992 to lower carbon dioxide emissions by the end of the decade will be kept. Backsliding caused by more pressing concerns could undermine the potential of some Hitachi research. On the other hand, Hitachi could add some profitable new products to its portfolio, and boost the performance of ones already there. Environmental concerns ebb and flow, but people always like to save money.

Japan supports a wide range of environmental research projects like new clean-energy technologies. In order to jump-start commercial production of hydrogen fuel cells, for example, the government subsidizes utility purchases.[2] And the private sector is headed in the same direction. A survey of R&D specialists indicated that two of the top five research goals in Japanese industry today are environmental.[3] An island nation without natural resources, Japan is particularly concerned about secure sources of energy. Hitachi's renewed commitment to the environment is also well timed for its Japanese customers. In 1993, Japan's new Basic Environmental Law came into effect, tightening standards and raising the stakes for industry.

Many utilities around the world experimented with alternate energy like solar cells and wind turbines after the oil shocks of the 1970s. Then these programs fell by the wayside as the price of oil crashed in the 1980s. One thing remains constant, however: Hitachi's utility customers don't want to run afoul of environmental laws. Pressure to reduce emissions, both in Japan and elsewhere, has been maintained by government regulators. Utilities may not want to hear about wind farms anymore, but any supplier that can keep them ahead of the compliance curve by lowering emissions is in business. If they can lower fuel costs at the same time, so much the better.

ENVIRONMENTAL PLANNING OFFICE

Tetsuro Fukushima is a man with a mission. Middle-aged, earnest, and low-key in the manner of many Japanese salarymen, Fukushima comes to life on the subject of the environment. He is quite convincing when he says that Hitachi wants to make the world a better place, not simply cash in on the Green Wave. We visited Fukushima, general manager of Hitachi's Global Environment Protection Center, in his cramped quarters at the Environment Policy Office in the New Marunouchi Building, a few steps from the beautiful grounds of the Imperial Palace in central Tokyo. "I sometimes feel like a high priest," Fukushima said, "I have a mission. And that mission is to educate all of our employees about cleaning up the environment."[4]

To survive long term, Hitachi must reposition itself further down the Green Wave than any of its competitors. Fukushima's job at the EPO is to make sure the whole company, each of its divisions, gets there together.

Along with some two dozen fellow employees at the Environmental Protection Office, Fukushima plans, coordinates, and monitors Hitachi's environmental progress. The EPO does some allocation of funds for special projects, but most money is budgeted and spent by the lines. Factory people charged with carrying out the company's environmental projects do not report to the EPO but to line management. The EPO's primary job is to keep score, since Hitachi is liable for what happens at all its facilities. Like other companies in this book with operations around the world, Hitachi operates to the highest environmental standards everywhere.

Fukushima's benchmark for measuring the company's progress is four bold goals set in 1991 for the year 2000. These targets relate to ozone layer protection, global warming, industrial waste reduction, and recycling. According to Fukushima, "This is the first time a Japanese company has announced such goals publicly."[5] We asked him what the competitive response had been. He answered, "Very strong. . . . It is unusual for a Japanese company to set specific goals in this area."

As a result of these commitments, Hitachi's investment in environmental projects jumped in the early 1990s, from 5 percent of total investment in 1990 to 12 percent in 1992. Environmental budgets kept rising even though sales flattened out. EPO managers admit that they must sometimes do some arm-twisting to get the line divisions to go along, but as Fukushima explains, "The EPO is a very powerful office. . . . It has to be done." He added that as the head of the EPO, "Dr. Sonoyama is the number-three boss in the company; he's watching everyone. . . . Dr. Sonoyama is very powerful." That helps.

It also helps when real savings result from environmental improvement. Fukushima went to great lengths to impress upon us that Hitachi's motives were pure. Nevertheless, when we asked if management thought of the environmental program as an opportunity to reduce costs, his response was unequivocal: "Yes." Nothing impure about helping the environment *and* making money.

In response to the Montreal Protocol, Hitachi's first goal was to eliminate in two steps the use of chemicals that damage the ozone layer: to stop using chlorofluorocarbons (CFCs) as cleaning agents by the end of 1993, and to take all CFCs out of its products by the end of 1995. Like its competitors, Hitachi used CFCs as a solvent, particularly to clean electronic components. CFCs were also widely used by Hitachi and others as a refrigerant and for foam-making.

Hitachi decided to phase out CFCs as fast as possible, rather than leave the decision to each factory, in order to beat the schedule to which Japan was committed by its treaty obligations. The company spent ¥23 billion ($200 million) to replace 600 machines that used CFCs to clean electronic components. While the primary concern of the EPO was environmental, there have been other benefits. The new machines lower operating costs and, in some cases, produce parts of better quality. Hitachi's goal was the same or better quality after the switch.

A second generation of CFCs, called HCFCs, was developed to reduce ozone layer damage. But, as it turns out, HCFCs also hurt the ozone layer, although not as much as CFCs, and the Montreal Protocol calls for their elimination by 2020. DuPont, the chemical company, will stop HCFC production by 2005. Hitachi will eliminate HCFCs from its products and production processes by 1997. Hitachi also decided to stop using methyl chloroform, another ozone-depleting chemical, by the end of 1994, well ahead of the Montreal Protocol deadline of January 1, 1996. By working quickly, Hitachi thinks it will have a competitive advantage if the phase-out schedule is moved up, as it was once already in 1990 when scientists said the damage to the ozone layer was occurring more quickly than previously thought.

Hitachi's ozone layer protection plan required a specific, one-time change. The company's second goal affects every nook and cranny of its operations, on an ongoing basis: to minimize global warming by lowering the energy consumed per unit of sales 35 percent between 1990 and 2000. The most direct way to avoid global warming is by burning less fossil fuels, the source of 85 percent of Japan's energy. Although CO_2 emissions are low in Japan compared to other industrialized countries, they have nevertheless grown by 25 percent in the past two decades. Fukushima estimates that Hitachi and all its affiliates will spend up to ¥100 billion ($1 billion) to purchase more energy-efficient air conditioners, electric motors, and trucks for its operations.

Hitachi's second goal was to improve the energy efficiency of its own operations. The chart shows an index of Hitachi's energy intensity between 1970 and 2000.

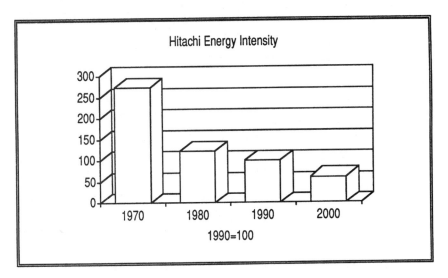

In the decade after the first oil crisis in 1972, Hitachi radically reduced energy waste. Between 1972 and 1976, energy use per unit of sale fell by 19 percent per year; between 1976 and

1981, by 15 percent per year. During this period, the *total* amount of energy used by Hitachi stayed the same at about 30 million liters of oil (including the oil equivalent of electricity and gas consumed) per month while sales rose severalfold. Then, during the 1980s, as oil prices plunged, Hitachi slacked off: energy intensity remained constant at about 150 liters of oil per ¥1 million in sales; total energy consumption rose by about 6 percent per year. Energy consumption by Hitachi's information and electronics divisions grew most quickly in the 1980s.

For the 1990s, the company has recommitted itself to better efficiency: energy use per ¥1 million in sales is to drop to 100 liters by the year 2000, one-third less than in 1990. If these goals are met, total energy use will fall, despite a forecasted increase in total revenues. For the entire period from 1970 to 2000, energy use per unit of sales will have declined by 75 percent. We can vouch for the seam of energy waste that Hitachi can still tap for savings: we sat uncomfortably for several hours one cold January day in a Hitachi office where an air conditioner ran full blast right above a steaming-hot radiator.

During the 1980s, backsliding was caused by more than low oil prices. Hitachi raised its dependence on electricity, from 60 percent of total energy used in 1978 to 80 percent in 1992, Fukushima explained to us. Electricity is a convenient form of energy, but a low-efficiency one; energy is lost when electricity is made, transmitted, and consumed. In Japan, 65 percent of electricity is oil fired and only 39 percent of the oil's original energy potential reaches the consumer. To offset these huge efficiency losses, Hitachi is switching to gas cogenerators, with which electricity and heat are produced at the same time on-site. Gas generators can be used at factories, for example, to produce the electricity needed to run machines; the exhaust heat given off by the generator also heats the building. These cogenerators can recover a very high percentage of the energy in fuel. By experimenting with them at its own facilities, Hitachi can reduce energy consumption while improving these systems for sale to customers.

Other savings result from housekeeping improvements. The company is switching from inefficient electric furnaces to gas ones. For some products, Hitachi is buying precoated sheet metal instead of painting and drying the surfaces itself. Nippon Steel, the company's supplier, can paint metal more efficiently than Hitachi. In other cases, it will simply stop painting metal altogether. This and other changes will cut energy use by 35 percent. Such a big reduction in energy expenditures means real savings for Hitachi.

Hitachi's third goal was to reduce the amount of trash it landfills to 25 percent less than 1991 by 1995 and 60 percent less by 2000. Hitachi will do this in several ways. By decade's end, 85 percent of its waste will be recycled, up from 70 percent in 1995 and 57 percent in 1991. By 2000, Hitachi will use incineration to "recycle" 32,000 tons of trash—almost as much as it landfills—into energy. The company will in fact produce slightly more waste in total, but less will be hauled off to the dump. The EPO estimates that Hitachi's trash volume would grow twice as fast during the 1990s without its program to reduce waste at the source. This requires designing waste out of its production processes in the first place.

These measures will help Hitachi control waste-disposal costs. Fukushima explained how waste reduction pays: "We don't have a lot of landfill space in Japan, so it's expensive. We pay sixty thousand yen [$600] per ton to landfill plastic. The cost is going up quickly." But as with its other environmental goals, Hitachi sees market opportunities in staying ahead of the compliance curve.

The company may build a plant for industrial waste treatment, since dwindling availability of sites will eventually force landfill dumping fees way up, particularly for toxic materials. Fukushima further explained that there was little plastic recycling in Japan. So Hitachi tested several pilot plants to see if it was feasible to extract hydrocarbons, like gasoline, from liquified plastic. The EPO's goal is an eighty-ton full-scale system. Hitachi needs an outlet for its plastic to achieve its recycling goals. When the program began in 1991, the company was recycling 99 percent of its steel, nearly half of its wood and paper, but less than 15 percent of its plastic.

Hitachi's fourth environmental goal called for improving the ability of its customers to recycle Hitachi's own products. This is called "design for disassembly," which first received wide publicity when the German government announced in 1992 that automobile manufacturers would be required to take back their cars for recycling. Hitachi's range of electrical products is vast, and includes home electronics (like stereos, TVs, and VCRs), appliances (like air conditioners, refrigerators, and vacuum cleaners), and office machines (like faxes, PCs, and printers). All these devices are made from many different types of materials, are difficult to take apart, and end up in landfills when they are discarded. Plastic is especially hard to recycle when different types of plastic are mixed together. For many years, Hitachi has been substituting plastics for other materials like metal and glass.

Hitachi's product recycling goals consisted of three parts:

- Reduce disassembly time by half (between 1992 and 1995)
- Recycle 30 percent more of its office products and household appliances (1992–1995)
- Cut polystyrene packaging by half (1990–1995)

Fukushima gave us several examples of projects underway. With a new vacuum cleaner, Hitachi's designers wanted to reduce the number of plastics used in the sweeper and the hose. In the process, they figured out a way to have the sweeper rotate with just air flow, eliminating the need for a motor and the power cord. In total the number of parts was reduced by nearly 40 percent (from 209 to 132). More to the point, said Fukushima, "it cleans better and it's cheaper!"

For a new-model washing machine, designers changed the drum from plastic to stainless steel to make it easier to recycle the product. The old baskets Hitachi used had too many types of plastic to recycle economically. With the switch to stainless steel, costs increased by 10 percent, but the washing load capacity is bigger and cleaning is easier. What's more, because steel can rotate faster than plastic, clothes dry faster. This new machine is very popular in Japan, but it has been hard to raise the price even with all these benefits. In Germany or the United States, Fukushima sighed, "they might pay ten percent more," but not in Japan. For another part of the washing machine, designers specified a polypropylene that is easy to recycle, and, as it turned out, easier to color for improved appearance.

Redesign started with the simplest devices, like rice cookers, and moved up the product chain to more complex ones like refrigerators. The EPO had to prod designers to change, since they did not think recycling was their concern before Hitachi's environmental goals were set. Fukushima encouraged competition between divisions: when the home-appliance designers made changes quickly, the office-automation people raced to catch up.

The marketing benefits Hitachi gets from products that are easy to recycle are limited. Few consumers think about the final resting ground to which their PCs and VCRs are destined. But there are other, real benefits for the company. "We make twenty thousand products, so how we design products is critical. . . . We need a breakthrough concept for designing products; I tell the designers this will help them find a breakthrough," said Fukushima. The pressure to simplify design results in lower costs and higher quality. A 40 percent reduction in the number of parts makes any product faster to assemble, less likely to break, and easier to use. If it's easier to recycle as well, so much the better. Furthermore, Hitachi will be prepared for the kind of laws already enacted in Germany, requiring manufacturers to take their products back. Others will be caught flat-footed.

THE PLANT

It's one thing to issue environmental edicts from headquarters, quite another to translate them into action, particularly while running a factory at the same time. We visited Hitachi's Musashi Works, an hour and a half by train from Tokyo. Here the company makes integrated circuits (i.e., computer chips), an unforgiving market to say the least. And not a business that will survive too much tinkering by idealists with pure motives and no common sense. Of its four bold goals, the most pressing for Hitachi has been the elimination of CFCs from manufacturing. This had the shortest deadline, and the only one imposed from outside the company.

At the Musashi Works, CFCs were used for many purposes, including cleaning, etching, and cooling. But cleaning was the most important application of CFCs in semiconductor production. For ICs (integrated circuits) to meet extremely high tolerances, assembly equipment must be exceptionally clean. And the ICs themselves must be cleaned thoroughly at every step of the way, from wafer fabrication through final assembly. CFCs did the job very well.

The boom came down on the Musashi Works in several steps. In 1989, the director of Hitachi's semiconductor division said that CFC use had to be cut 70 percent. At first managers at the plant thought it would be easy to reduce CFC use by half. One commented, "Suppliers told us it was okay; not to worry." But the company said that 50 percent was not enough, so they set up committees to work on the problem. Each step of the manufacturing process had to be reexamined. "We really had to work at it to get CFCs out," this manager added. Much of Musashi's equipment had to be replaced earlier than would otherwise have been done. But the EPO turned the screws, and the change worked. At least, one manager said, the "target was zero, so that made it easier."

Hitachi had to involve suppliers, because some parts go out to subcontractors and then come back for final assembly. Many alternatives had environmental problems of their own. When the company switched to a cleaning solvent that was flammable (unlike CFCs), fire-code complications arose. Hitachi substituted water cleaning in some cases, and eliminated cleaning altogether in others. Instead of etching the ICs with CFCs, Musashi now marks them with laser, which is simpler, and done in one step. To eliminate cleaning after wire bonding, engineers made the production room cleaner. Now the whole fabrication area is cleaner, essential in an IC plant, so Musashi gets better quality. Under the old system, parts would still be a little bit dirty even after CFC cleaning. Musashi's managers told us that the change reduced their running costs, but required a big investment. They added, "The cost of cleaning is not that large. When you think about how large our capital expenditures are for our IC business, it's just not that big." Perhaps more important, they said, was that they got ahead of regulations; they no longer had to worry about the government looking over their shoulders.

The Musashi Works' environmental program neither began nor ended with CFC elimination. The plant recycles 60 to 70 percent of the water it uses, including 100 percent of what it uses for cooling. Even the water from its toilets is recycled. This first-generation environmental action began twenty years ago when Japan, like other industrial nations, responded to ecological damage.

Reducing industrial waste from the Musashi Works has not been easy. IC production takes low volumes of many kinds of chemicals. Hitachi is looking for several ways to dispose of its IC-production wastes. First, some can be used as inputs by the hundreds of Hitachi affiliate companies. Second, Hitachi wants all the IC companies in Japan to get together and see what the possibilities are for recycling. We asked one manager if it was possible to reduce waste to zero. He answered, that "it was impossible to go to zero, but you can get very close." Hitachi believes it can reduce what it landfills to zero, and incinerate the rest.

THE LESSONS

Hitachi set challenging environmental goals for itself, well beyond what its competitors were doing or what Japan's government regulators required. There are several lessons:

Connect your environmental plan with your core business. At a time when energy costs were falling, Hitachi set out to reduce its energy use substantially. This makes sense, since Hitachi's business is products that generate and consume electricity.

Drive innovation. Environmental goals that seem impossible at the start can produce unexpected innovations; breakthrough ideas result not from incremental improvement but from challenges that galvanize the imaginations of managers, designers, and engineers.

Go public. By committing itself publicly to its environmental goals, Hitachi put the pressure of public opinion to work. In some circumstances this might look like a public relations ploy to be superseded by the next publicity stunt; in Japan, however, "losing face" is a real force, and Hitachi will be held to its public statements.

Don't sell green. Green marketing has little or nothing to do with Hitachi's environmental program. Rather, its efforts produced results that appeal to all consumers, like lower costs and better reliability.

Get beyond compliance. Hitachi got the regulatory monkey off its back by reaching well beyond what the law required. At that place on the other side of the compliance curve, Hitachi found the financial rewards from its environmental program.

ALCATEL TELECOM SENDS A MESSAGE

GO WHERE THE MONEY IS

Survival in high tech may not depend on low wages, but it does depend on low costs. Many electronics manufacturers have shifted production to the Third World to regain their competitive edge, yet some of the world's high-tech leaders keep production at home despite the high wages they must pay. By exploiting to the fullest the skills of its well-educated workers, Alcatel, France's high-tech jewel, has maintained leadership in one of the world's most hotly contested markets. At the same time, Alcatel has kept production in high-wage countries like France, Germany, and the United States. Waste reduction has been key to boosting productivity to levels that can support the good wages paid in these places. At Alcatel, waste reduction depends directly on workers on the shop floor.

Many see France as fine wine, great cheese, and haute couture. Alcatel N.V. represents another kind of France: an industrial export powerhouse. Amid all the bad news about Europe's decline, this success story goes largely untold outside Europe. Alcatel, the largest telecommunications equipment manufacturer in the world, is a subsidiary of Alcatel Alsthom, a $30 billion diversified electric combine headquartered in Paris.

Telecom, accounting for two-thirds of Alcatel Alsthom's sales, is a business cobbled together a decade ago from the remains of France's nationalized telecom sector and the telecom operations of ITT. ITT itself had been created out of the overseas operations of AT&T in 1926, when the U.S. government forced the first breakup of that company. Alcatel was privatized in 1987, and soon after surpassed AT&T as top telecom supplier.

Customers outside of France generate *three-quarters* of Alcatel's sales. For all we read about the export prowess of Japan's electronics giants, none can top this performance. Alcatel is the largest supplier of telephone exchanges and cables in the world, and the second largest supplier of transmission equipment, business communications systems, and telephone sets. The company's telecom technology is second to none, and many consider Alcatel the best-run company in France. To underscore its international outlook, a few years ago management decreed that English, the lingua franca of business, was to be used at Alcatel's headquarters in Paris. That's quite a statement in France, where "franglais" isn't just bad form—it's illegal.

No industry has brighter prospects than telecommunications. In the first century after its invention, telephony evolved into a utility not much different from electricity, gas, and water. Then deregulation unleashed powerful market forces. Beginning in the United States, then spreading around the world, deregulation turned telecom into the go-go industry of the 1990s. Convergence of telephone communications with entertainment and computers further stoked the flames. By the year 2000, telecom will be a trillion-dollar business, bigger than the entire economy of the United States in 1975. Some call it the biggest growth market in history. And Alcatel, France's telecom champion, sits in the front car as this *train à grande vitesse* rocks down the power curve.

NASTY BUSINESS

From the Gare de l'Est in Paris, the sleek *Trans-European Express* transports us in about two hours to Strasbourg, near the German border in northeast France. A city of history, Strasbourg embodies all that visitors from the New World hope to experience in the Old. Strasbourg appears as it has long been, a medieval market town. At its heart is the magnificent Gothic cathedral of Notre Dame, dating from the year 1015, surrounded by ancient buildings overhanging narrow streets and lanes. At any one of dozens of down-to-earth brasseries, a visitor can sample the hearty Alsatian cuisine and exceptional beer that tell of Strasbourg's German past. Founded by the Romans, fought over by the French and Germans for centuries, Strasbourg is now home to the European Union parliament. Pedestrians can wander freely around the city center, an island formed by the Ill River (a tributary of the Rhine), which is closed to car traffic and served by a brand-new tram system.

A short drive from Strasbourg, out toward the airport on a flat expanse of farmland to the west, is a small town called Illkirch. Here, in a beautifully landscaped industrial park on forty acres adjacent to the tree-lined Rhine-Rhone Canal, is the flagship factory of Alcatel Business Systems (ABS). At the brand-new, state-of-the-art Illkirch facility, Alcatel designs and manufactures computerized telephone systems for business applications. Looking nothing like a factory, but more like a large, attractive college library, Illkirch is an expanse of glass and light dominated by an enormous central corridor (nearly two football fields long) called *la rue,* literally "the street." Off *la rue* are assembly and design facilities, in total some three-quarters of a million square feet. While ABS has been in Strasbourg since 1919, the Illkirch plant did not open until 1988.

With the languid Rhine-Rhone Canal and nearby Strasbourg as a backdrop, Alcatel's Illkirch plant is unusual. But in many other ways it is much like the modern research and production facilities of Alcatel's competitors in California and Tokyo. There are no belching smokestacks, no parking lots piled high with rusting fifty-five-gallon drums and ringed with razor wire. Telecom, like computers, is a semiconductor-based business, the kind of clean, light manufacturing that every industrial development agency lusts after.

But there is nothing inherently "clean" about making integrated circuits, printed circuit boards, computers, or telephone systems. In fact, there are some very nasty chemicals involved in every process along the way, from concept to loading dock. In the early 1990s, there was a scare that some chemicals used in semiconductor production were causing miscarriages among female workers.[1] In a number of high-profile cases, chip and computer makers were pumping heavy metals, dangerous acids, and contaminated water into the ground. In the United States, for example, there are more toxic Superfund sites in Silicon Valley than anywhere else.[2]

Indeed, one consultant who sold surplus computer factories in Silicon Valley told us some real horror stories. At a number of sites, companies had simply drilled well holes in the factory floor for dumping toxic wastes. In others, they had dug ponds out back for holding toxic liquids. He had seen one pond in which a heavy-metal soup was simply covered up with tarps. From the outside these facilities looked "clean" and "modern." But no one knows what damage these conditions caused for workers. Nearby farmers drilling irrigation wells into the same water tables also got some nasty surprises, to say nothing of what this dumping did to local drinking water. It's no wonder that many companies have moved semiconductor and PCB production offshore in recent years to avoid liability and tightening regulations.

At Illkirch, Alcatel took a completely different approach. This site is as clean on the inside as it appears on the outside. By wringing the waste out of production, the company has dramatically reduced emissions, and at the same time, lowered its costs.

WATCH THE CENTIMES AND THE FRANCS WILL TAKE CARE OF THEMSELVES

Maurice Kretz is manager of environmental affairs at Illkirch, where he has worked for a decade. He explained to us that ABS has "had an environmental manager for twelve years, before it was fashionable." Heat and energy waste were his first priorities, but now his responsibilities extend to other environmental problems as well.

Kretz is a down-to-earth guy, with a very clear idea of his mission: reduce waste and save money (not necessarily in that order). And while his efforts at Alcatel help the environment, Kretz is not ashamed that his MO is strictly business. In surveying his domain, he told us, "The environmentalists talk a lot, but this is the real thing." Speaking of himself and others like him in the trenches, he said, "We are the unsung heroes of the environmental movement." Amen.

Kretz has to keep his eye on the bottom line, because Alcatel is in a very tough business. Consider the market into which Alcatel sells its computerized communications systems. By the mid-1990s, the costs of telephone switching and transmission equipment had fallen 80 to 90 percent from what they were in the early 1980s. Suppliers like Alcatel, slashing prices year in, year out, make ubiquitous communications possible, forming the vanguard of the information revolution.

True, the cost of some key electronic components Alcatel purchases from others, like microprocessors and memory chips, is falling quickly, too. But most costs, especially wages, are rising, particularly in Europe. France is an expensive place to do business, to say the least. Factory wages (including benefits) are higher in France than in Japan or the United States. Taxes are especially high, 50 percent higher than in Japan or the United States, higher even than in Germany.[3] High taxes are reflected in the prices of everything that manufacturers like Alcatel must purchase, from energy to water.

Unlike competitors elsewhere, Alcatel can't just lay off thousands of employees every time it has a bad quarter. In France, unions are strong and the government makes layoffs extremely costly. In the United States, since the breakup of the Bell System in 1984, a quarter of a million telecom jobs have been lost. No doubt, these layoffs cut costs in a big way for many American companies. But life is not so simple for Alcatel, which must look harder for ways to save money. Alcatel must raise the productivity of its workers, not ax them. And the company must squeeze every last bit of waste out of its manufacturing processes.

Water was Kretz's first target. Water pollution is the greatest source of environmental damage from an electronics facility; all those Superfund sites in Silicon Valley are caused by groundwater contamination. In Illkirch, the water table is about 1½ feet below the surface in most places, and in some spots only 1 foot. Consequently, nothing can be spilled at the plant without causing serious damage. What's more, everyone who works here knows that the plant is only a few hundred yards upstream from the town's main source of drinking water. The water table runs right under the plant to the local wells. Furthermore, the facility is adjacent to the canal, and right in the middle of a pleasant residential area. Not much room for error here.

The easiest way to reduce the risk of water pollution is to reduce the amount of water needed. In 1982, ABS used 2,000 liters of water for each square meter of printed circuit board produced; Kretz and his team have reduced this to 50 liters/m^2, a reduction of 97.5 percent. With this and other changes, the plant cut total water consumption by a factor of six in ten years, while doubling production. During the past five years, the plant's water bill dropped by nearly half, and was about a quarter of what it would have been if water consumption had grown as fast as PCB output. This change produced savings of some 2 million francs per year ($350,000). Wastewater, after purification on-site, is tested fifteen times per day. In this way, according to Kretz, "we are transparent to the local authorities." Environment officials only test the water four times per year.

Such vigilance is not limited to the Illkirch site. The manager at another Alcatel facility said the company's goal was zero discharge, closing the loop with treatment and reuse of water. Such improvements require investment in equipment, and product redesign in some cases. To eliminate cyanide from metal plating, for example, the company switched to more benign zinc-oxide and zinc-chloride processes.

Kretz's next target at Illkirch was energy costs. Alcatel must pay as much as 60 to 85 centimes (11 to 16 cents) per kilowatt-hour (kwh) to Électricité de France, the government-owned power company, depending on the time of day and time of year. But Kretz realized that the company could produce power for 40 centimes per kilowatt-hour with its own generators, half that if waste heat was captured. He switched over from EDF to superefficient, on-site gas cogenerators in 1989–1990, lowering the plant's electric bill by nearly half, and its total energy bill by one-third. Unit energy costs fell even faster, since plant output has increased. Several million dollars have been saved, not insignificant for a company whose survival depends on shaving costs every day. And by combining electric and heat generation, the company has reduced its total annual energy consumption by the equivalent of 250 tons of oil.

Like others, Alcatel must observe Montreal Protocol by eliminating emissions of ozone-damaging chemicals, particularly CFC like Freon, by the year 2000. At Illkirch, Alcatel was releasing fifty-five pounds of CFCs per hour when they first started to grapple with the problem. Kretz and his team considered a carbon treatment system to capture and filter CFC releases, but this approach was impractical and expensive. Then, as a stopgap measure, they decided to switch to a process that used CFCs more efficiently, reducing emissions by 88 percent.

Finally, Alcatel's engineers decided to eliminate CFCs altogether by changing their production processes, obviating the need for cleaning with CFCs or anything else. CFC emissions were reduced to zero at Illkirch in 1993. According to a manager at another Alcatel site in the United States, The company also tried some old water-cleaning processes, abandoned twenty years ago, as well as some high-tech alternatives to CFCs. But the company does not want to substitute one problem for another. Instead, engineers designed the problem out of Alcatel's products, using, for example, surface mounting. With this technique, components are glued, not soldered, to printed circuit boards. In the United States, where the government slapped a tax on CFCs that goes up every year, eliminating CFCs cut Alcatel's PCB production costs by 30 to 40 percent.

Other air emissions have been cut dramatically as well. By modifying production techniques and by adding a condensation system, Illkirch has cut total atmospheric emissions of solvents by 80 percent in four years. A staggering 50,000 cubic meters of air are cleaned every hour.

One Alcatel manager told us, "Sixty-five percent of product cost is purchased materials, so if we can reduce waste, we reduce costs." By reducing scrap, plant managers can reduce material-purchasing requirements and disposal costs. The easiest way to do this is to avoid creating waste in the first place. For example, Illkirch takes back packaging material and pallets for reuse. At another site, an engineer described his plant's recycling program and switch to nonhazardous materials. He added, "The idea is to have products that can be disposed of easily; for example, some copper alloys are dangerous to throw out, so we are using more benign battery technologies." But, he concluded, "the end of the tunnel is zero discharge."

NO UMBRELLAS HERE

To make environmentalism pay, Alcatel has integrated environmental control with its other activities. Maurice Kretz described three stages that Illkirch went through to reduce water consumption. At first, one part of the organization created wastewater, then another treated it. Dirty water flowed from the production line to the water treatment area. There was little or no communication between the two groups, and pollution problems were dealt with in isolation, after they occurred. The next step was to close the loop, with treated water returning to the production line after it had been cleaned. This helped, but there was still a time lag between when pollution occurred and production was affected.

The third, and most critical step, was to integrate treatment with the production process. Water treatment takes place at the same machine where the water is used in the first place. By integrating water treatment into each production stage, consumption was minimized—and the production team had an interest in keeping it that way. At each machine there is an operator responsible for water consumption and treatment; if water treatment fails, the whole line fails. If a machine breaks, it must be fixed right away. Furthermore, the cost of water treatment is amortized with production equipment, not separately. In short, those on the line could no longer say, "That's not my job." Illkirch adopted this approach in 1987, which resulted in a big drop in water use at first, followed by steady reduction since then.

Before, environmental problems could be ignored because they were dealt with by another part of the organization. Transforming production this way was no mean task: Illkirch produces more than 100,000 circuit boards per month. And there are some 400 different types of boards, with 2 new kinds created every day.

By dealing with waste and pollution as close to the source as possible, Kretz told us, "nothing is hidden." He encouraged us to look in every nook and cranny of his plant, with a disparaging remark about his competitors: "Elsewhere it is very clean on the production line; then when you go down in the basement, you have to put on your boots and open up you umbrella." He concluded, "Our philosophy is to make waste transparent; if you don't hide the problems, you have to deal with them."

Illkirch now requires all its production equipment to integrate environmental controls, and Kretz concedes that this puts the company at the mercy of suppliers to some extent. If it only looks to the production line for improvement, Alcatel will have to wait for a shift in manufacturing technology to get big reductions in waste.

Instead, he said that the company must redesign products so they are inherently less wasteful. This was the next step for ABS. And, he added, "the more we do now, the more complex it becomes."

As another manager put it, "We want to design-in green manufacturing." Alcatel has made big strides away from end-of-pipe environmental management, but opportunities for waste reduction, and cost savings, remain. At Illkirch, since R&D is done right at the plant, redesigning Alcatel's product line will be easier than at other telecom companies, where research is normally kept separate from production.

While a number of managers we spoke to at Alcatel said zero emissions was the ultimate goal, Maurice Kretz keeps his eye on the bottom line. He maintained, for example, that solid waste was not a big problem at Illkirch. By recycling and reducing packaging waste, the plant has indeed reduced solid waste dramatically, but Kretz's goal is not to go to zero waste anytime soon. It's simply too costly to go that last few percentage points to zero—with little environmental benefit.

Maurice Kretz and other environmental engineers at plants around the world have considerable authority over day-to-day management. Alcatel N.V.'s parent company, Alcatel Alsthom, views environmental compliance as a problem of risk management. The director of environmental affairs in Paris, for example, reports through Alcatel's head of insurance to the CFO. Since Alcatel Alsthom is a holding company, one manager told us, "We must protect the value of our assets." He added, "We do risk management for the company; we are learning to help anticipate problems before they occur."

Individual divisions, like ABS, set their own environmental policies, and their own budgets (French manufacturers like Alcatel can also tap a government fund financed by pollution fines). Operations in First World countries (like France and the United States) "manage up," telling headquarters what local environmental laws are and how they intend to comply. For Alcatel divisions in countries where standards may be lax, headquarters will impose environmental requirements up to the level mandated in France, or even higher.

Corporate-level responsibility also extends to site remediation, which can be an expensive proposition beyond the means of individual organizations, and to legal and engineering audits of new properties. Paris is also trying to influence new legislation, like packaging laws, which are an especially hot issue in Europe, and carbon taxes, which continue to be mooted around the world.

LA CULTURE DE MOUVEMENT

Telecom, like computers, changes by the day. Technology continuously makes old products obsolete. A generation ago, an Alcatel telephone exchange had a product life of fifteen or twenty years. Today, products must be updated annually, if not faster. Where a single product once served everyone's needs, today dozens of systems are tailored for selected customers. What's more, the telecom market has been flooded with new competitors and wrenched by a multitude of new distribution channels. In short, this is an industry that has gone through the wringer in the past decade, and this is nothing compared to the multimedia hurricane that is about to make landfall. To maintain its leadership, Alcatel must adapt rapidly, while operating in eighty countries around the globe.

Alcatel managers like to talk about the company's *"culture de mouvement,"* which allows it to adapt rapidly to new developments, driving quality, but permitting flexibility. This pitch sounds like one of Charles de Gaulle's famous lectures at Saint Cyr after the First World War (ignored by the French general staff) about the army's need for a flexible response to the threat from Germany. And, in fact, Alcatel has created a remarkably flexible and efficient system for managing its environmental responsibility, which changes all the time. The job has been turned over to those on the production line.

At Illkirch, there is no separate organization to clean up environmental messes. Production workers are charged with doing it right the first time. That goes for quality as well: workers are responsible for the quality of their own output. By taking this approach, Alcatel saves a lot of money: three jobs—production, quality control, and environmental management—are done by one person. These same workers must also help reduce inventory of parts and work-in-progress, the key to lower costs in a business in which purchases make up two-thirds of all expenses. This additional goal brings them back to quality and the environment: less waste means lower emissions and fewer defects.

Employees with this kind of responsibility have to be well trained, well educated, and well paid. These skills don't come cheap: Alcatel's workers in France are among the best paid in the world—and the best educated. At ABS in 1970, a newly hired production worker needed an eighth-grade education—in those days Alcatel's products were reprogrammed with a screwdriver and a wrench. By 1980, Alcatel workers needed a high-school diploma; now, at least two years of college. And at Illkirch, there are as many engineers and programmers as factory workers. Yet despite its high wages, Alcatel can remain competitive because its people are productive.

At Illkirch, in particular, Alcatel integrated the environment, in the largest sense, into manufacturing. This is a new plant, built from the ground up, to expose, not conceal, pollution problems. But this is an extraordinary working environment as well. According to one manager, "We put a lot of energy into developing a good environment for the workers, to make it nonhierarchical." Despite the fast pace of production, the place is quiet, airy, and bathed in natural light. From almost any point in the facility, the green landscape is visible, a subtle reminder to all of what can be spoiled through carelessness. Of the many other factories we have visited, most, even new ones, were loud, hectic, and closed to the outside world.

Alcatel has a small corporate environmental staff organization, no press-release mill, no "save-the-planet" drumbeat. At its plants, there is a no-nonsense, roll-up-your-sleeves approach to reducing waste. Alcatel's environment strategy is in stark contrast to that of some competitors. At one large telecom equipment supplier in the United States with a very high profile environmentally, we were stunned by what we heard when we spoke to environmental officials. From the VP of environmental affairs at the company's head office and from the environmental manager at one of the company's big plants, we heard two very different stories. The VP went on and on about good citizenship, sustainable development, and environmentalism as an extension of quality. Meanwhile, the engineer at the plant told us that there were so many problems with toxic substances that worker safety was her first concern. She said that her goal was to get the site into compliance with the law, adding that they were lucky they weren't getting fined by the EPA. At this facility, "sustainable development" was some time off, to say the least.

Managers at the Illkirch plant were quick to attribute their environmental success to the Alsace region's unique culture, both German and French. They told us, "Germans are naturally more concerned with the environment than are the French. It comes naturally to the people here—most of our people speak German at home—to be more concerned than anyone else in France with the environment. . . . They have the German *l'amour de nature.*" As a result, employees are open to new ideas and often put forward suggestions of their own. Many of the ideas for environmental improvement come from the ranks, not from above. Since 20 percent of voters in the area cast their ballots for the Green Party, a radical environmental group, management must assume that at least the same proportion of workers feels strongly about the environment. Management also explained that workers in Alsace were not as unionized or militant as in other parts of France, but they added that "as a result of German culture, they follow rules, they conform, but the demand for green changes comes from below. . . . The German culture of our people makes them naturally concerned with ensuring that everything works and that there are no spills."

THE LESSONS

In a business in which every penny counts, Alcatel has dramatically reduced the environmental impact of its manufacturing plants while reducing costs. Others can learn several important lessons from this company's success:

Go where the money is. Alcatel identified the pockets of waste that represented significant potential manufacturing savings.

Integrate environmental management. Alcatel designed its plant at Illkirch from the people up, building the environment into everything that they do. By combining environmental and other functions, end-of-pipe surprises are all but eliminated; if environmental standards slip, the consequences are immediately reflected in production.

Charge everyone with improvement. Since everyone is *individually* responsible for their workplace (and, because of the high water table, for their own drinking water as well), no one can blame it on the big bad company if something goes wrong. There an individual is fully accountable to community, co-workers, and customers; no one can say, "I was only taking orders."

Keep it practical. Without fanfare or flurry of press releases, Alcatel has produced steady improvement, with large performance gains over time. The philosophizing is left to others, while Alcatel gets on with the job.

HOWE SOUND
PULP AND
PAPER

SMELLING LIKE A ROSE

Pulp and paper is one of the most brutally competitive businesses on the planet and one of the most filthy. Plagued by wild imbalances of supply and demand, producers face the constant threat of collapsing prices, currency gyrations, plant closures, and sudden shifts in demand—all of which wreak havoc on their income statements. Under these circumstances there seems to be little incentive to go "green." Why add risk to an already immensely risky business? The answer is simple: The mills best able to handle the vagaries of the pulp and paper market are also the cleanest.

Anyone who has ever lived within fifteen or twenty miles of a pulp mill knows what "environmental impact" means. Pulp mills are notorious polluters, usually emitting furans, sulfides, and dioxin, to name but a few of their by-products. Mills are disgusting. Their waterborne pollutants, like dioxin, are silent killers. Their evil-smelling airborne pollutants turn even the strongest stomachs. Perhaps the only less pleasant neighbor is a high-security prison with a serious labor-relations problem. There are plenty who would take the prison.

A few years ago, Howe Sound Pulp and Paper fit the profile of a typical mill. Located at Port Mellon, deep in Howe Sound, a beautiful West Coast fjord, this company was long one of Canada's worst polluters. Plagued since its founding in 1909 with repeated bankruptcies, plant closings, and changes of ownership, Port Mellon was an environmental disaster and a quality nightmare. The mill—the oldest on the British Columbia coast—was small, filthy, and uneconomical. Pulp quality was poor. One manager frankly remarked, "You had a mill making probably the poorest quality pulp on the B.C. Coast at a cost per ton higher than anyone else, so when the recession came in 1982, nobody took our pulp."[1] At Japanese plants like Oji's Tomakomai mill, newsprint machines ran with one or two paper breaks a month. Port Mellon was getting three breaks a day. The mill's future was doubtful.

To residents of adjacent coastal towns, *Port Mellon* (as the mill is called) was a dirty word. The place stank. It polluted their waters, killed off a once thriving Howe Sound prawn fishery,[2] chased away vacationers, and threatened to push local unemployment rates through the roof. Howe Sound may have looked picture perfect, but its waters were dying, and when the winds were onshore, especially at night, the air reeked of sulfide emissions.

By 1985, the combined effects of pollution, inefficiency, and a prolonged recession had taken a high toll on the Port Mellon area. Every other house was for sale in nearby Gibson's Landing, where people depended on the mill for jobs and all the other things that Port Mellon was killing off, like fishing and tourism. There was no question that the mill was on its way out. Merchants were closing up. The town looked doomed.

During the long 1982–85 Canadian recession, Canada Forest Products (Canfor), owners of the Port Mellon mill, lost C$200 million. Moreover, environmental fines were mounting up. The place was bleeding money along with its stinking effluents. When mill pollution finally closed the Howe Sound crab fishery, a local fisherman sued for C$20 million in damages. The provincial Supreme Court dismissed the case, but Canfor already had the message: Clean up or close down.

As early as 1978, now retired mill manager Bill Hughes had begun to plan a turnaround. But the combined impact of the prolonged recession, large losses, and a dismal market for pulp put his plans on hold. Then, in the late eighties, Japanese paper companies came to Canada looking for joint-venture opportunities. Hughes had one for them.

His idea was simple: rebuild the mill from scratch, using the latest environmental technology to maximize output and raise quality and productivity to the highest levels in the world. He would double output[3] and bring onstream a state-of-the-art newsprint line capable of serving the exceptionally demanding Japanese market. Meet and then beat Japanese quality requirements, he reasoned, and Howe Sound can beat anyone in the world.

Hughes won over Japan's Oji Paper, which ponied up C$308 million in cash in 1988 for 50 percent of Howe Sound Pulp and Paper. The makeover of Port Mellon was on. Today, C$1.3 billion later, Howe Sound Pulp and Paper is a clean money-spinner, one of the world's largest and cleanest pulp and paper mills. And one of the very, very few making money.

Testifying to the exceptional quality of Port Mellon paper, 80 percent of its newsprint goes to Japan, where it is used for Japan's leading business daily, the *Nihon Keizei Shimbum,* among other papers. Not only is Port Mellon quality good enough for the Japanese, but praise has come from around the globe. When Canfor invited Dr. Egon Klepsch, president of the European Parliament, to tour its Howe Sound Pulp and Paper facilities, Klepsch went home and told the *Financial Times* that he had become "an advocate for Canadian forestry. Canada is a model for all of us."[4] In large, quality-conscious markets like Europe, no amount of advertising could match these few words.

Howe Sound Pulp and Paper had broken the mold. This company is not competitive in spite of the environmental cleanup there, but *because* of it.

THE INDUSTRY THAT CANADA LOVES TO HATE

Pollution brought Howe Sound Pulp and Paper into conflict with just about all the powers that be in the province of British Columbia. Howe Sound is one of Canada's great beauty spots. Here the majestic Rocky Mountains that stretch hundreds of miles west from the prairies of Alberta to the Coastal Mountains of British Columbia plunge into the sea. Spoiling this place was guaranteed to raise the ire of British Columbians justifiably proud of the stunning magnificence of their province—and well aware of the tourist dollars that its magnificence brings them.

More important, just across the sound lies Vancouver, one of Canada's largest and fastest-growing cities. The communities surrounding the sound, including the islands of Bowen, Gambier, and Keats, have long been handy vacation spots for Vancouverites. And as Vancouver has grown, commuters have moved west over the sound to Gibson's Landing. They must cross Howe Sound every day by car ferry to reach the city. Each day, twice a day, they sailed past the mill's stinking by-products. Vancouver, it should also be noted, is home to Greenpeace, the polluter's worst nightmare.

Port Mellon was a classic example of the conflict between profit and pollution. Mills employ many of the people who live in towns like Gibson's Landing in high-paying, union jobs. These communities rise and fall on the fortunes of the mills they were created to serve. But the better the mills do, and the more people they employ, the worse the environment gets. For residents there seems to be no way out. Either they work, or they don't. The price of employment seems high, but the alternative is far worse.

The situation in Port Mellon was far from unique. Wherever there are pulp mills, people are confronted with the same hard choice between jobs and the environment. In 1992, for example, Wallace, Louisiana, a small town in a state hard hit by declining employment, made front-page news when it lost 1,800 high-paying jobs. A Taiwanese company, Formosa Plastics, dropped plans to build a $700 million pulp mill there when it failed to win the support of the local community.[5]

The Formosa mill would have been the world's largest wood-pulp and rayon plant. But the plant would have spilled 16 billion gallons of chemical effluents into the Mississippi River every year—very bad news for people downstream in New Orleans. Formosa's plans were stopped by a coalition of local interests, environmentalists, neighbors, and the EPA. The fight split Wallace into warring factions. One landowner felt so threatened by the new plant he told the *New York Times* that he "had reached the point where I was willing to lose my property in the defense of it."[6] Those are bitter words. Others saw the hard economics of losing a major employer. One resident told the *Times*, "Young people are not going to get jobs. Formosa was to many people here a dream come true."

Pulp and paper is big business. In Canada—the world's top paper and paperboard exporter—forestry is the nation's largest manufacturing industry, employing over 1 million people. That's about 7 percent of all employment, and nearly 9 percent of Canada's GNP.[7] Pulp and paper alone accounts for 150,000 jobs.[8] In the United States, forest products are worth $190 billion a year to the economy, about 4 percent of U.S. GNP.[9] In other areas like Scandinavia, South America, and Southeast Asia, forest products are also central to economic survival.

Even if they are willing to accept pollution, however, Howe Sound residents were not guaranteed jobs—not by a long shot. Port Mellon was like most Canadian mills: small, outdated, and inefficient, requiring twice as many workers per ton of output as newer mills elsewhere.[10]

As if poor productivity was not enough, wages are high in Canada, and so is the cost of raw materials. Canadian wood remains desirable, prized for its grain and for the long, strong fibers that make the very finest papers. But many Canadian papers can also be made from faster-growing trees in the warmer climates of the southern United States, Brazil, and Indonesia. A eucalyptus planted in Brazil can be harvested in just 8 years. Canadian softwoods, by contrast, can take 60 to 100 years, giving Brazilian paper-makers an enormous cost advantage.

Adding to Howe Sound's woes, the world pulp market has been plagued with overcapacity since the mid-1980s, depressing prices. Worldwide demand has been running at about 28 million tons a year. But, by the early 1990s, capacity had reached 33 million tons, and another 4 million tons was to come onstream by mid-decade. That's an incredible twenty-eight Port Mellons in excess capacity, mostly in the Third World, which has no trouble undercutting Canada on price.

Demand for new pulp produced at mills like Port Mellon was further depressed by recycling. Dr. Jan Remröd, director general of the Swedish Pulp and Paper Association, says that "the fastest-growing 'forests' are in the cities of Europe."[11] In the United States, 52 percent of all newsprint is now being recovered for recycling.[12] Japan recycles 50 percent of its paper and board, and Weyerhaeuser has a Washington state pulp mill that uses 85 percent recycled paper.[13] Recycling has introduced ever greater imbalances between demand and supply into an already overburdened industry. Canadian mills had failed to catch this recycling wave and were vulnerable.

Canadian mills have been hard hit as a result, and capacity is being slashed like so many clear-cut forests. In 1989, the last good year, Canada's big forest-products companies recorded a profit of C$2.4 billion. But pulp and paper has always been highly cyclical—this is not an industry for the faint-hearted. So when the recession throttled demand just as all those new mills were being completed, forestry fell with a mighty crash. Two short years later, the industry racked up a combined loss of C$2.5 billion.[14] It seemed like economics would do what Greenpeace could not: close down Port Mellon once and for all.

THE PROBLEM WITH PAPER

Paper is a classic "green" problem: people hate to see the trees cut down and they can't stand the smell of the mills. Still, people use more and more paper every year. And they're not too worried about what they do with the stuff after they use it. This attitude drives the industry nuts. It's almost as if people's appetite for steak increased *after* an afternoon at the abattoir. And then they vote for laws that promote animal rights.

The most visible problem with paper is the trash it produces. Paper is commonly thought of as biodegradable. Well, it is. And it isn't. Researchers made news when they found legible copies of twenty-five-year old newspapers mummified deep in virtually air-tight landfills. The problem with all this paper is that economic prosperity and paper use go hand in hand. In low-income countries, paper accounts for only 2 percent of solid waste. In high-income countries, like Canada and the United States, it is the single largest component, accounting for 31 percent of waste.[15] Newspapers are the biggest single type of garbage in U.S. landfills, accounting for a constant 18 percent of volume for the last thirty years.[16] Recycling can help with the trash mountain, but there are bigger, more serious problems with this industry.

Paper is made in a chemical soup. These chemicals are nasty, and they end up in the environment in a variety of ways: up the smokestack, down the drain, or in the paper products the mills ship to their customers. One of the toughest chemicals to get out of paper production is chlorine, which Greenpeace has made number one on its chemicals-to-hate list. Chlorine may purify our drinking water, but Greenpeace leaflets ask bluntly: "What do famine, sterility, and disease have in common?" Answer: chlorine.[17]

Chlorinated products read like a list of the green movement's most wanted: DDT, PCB, CFCs, and dioxin. Through CFCs, chlorine has been implicated in ozone depletion and skin cancer. Chlorine has a big, bad image problem that extends far beyond pulp mills. Nevertheless, paper products consume some 11 percent of chlorine globally, making this the second most chlorine-intensive industry after plastics.[18] Once Greenpeace targeted chlorine, mills like Port Mellon were sitting ducks.

Perhaps the nastiest pulp mill by-product is dioxin, one of the deadliest substances known to man. While some scientists and industry officials believe that the risks of dioxin have been overstated, an independent panel set up by the U.S. Environmental Protection Agency says that dioxin risks may be much greater than assumed.[19]

The U.S. pulp and paper industry has already spent about $1 billion to cut its use of chlorine. But, taken as a group, these mills still don't meet the EPA's standards for dioxin emissions. So the industry wants to prove that there is a threshold below which dioxin won't hurt the environment, or people. In Canada, it's the same story. At one pulp mill we saw in British Columbia, the tour guide, a mill chemist, handed out leaflets that said that dioxin is "no more risky than spending a week sunbathing." This is a little bit like trying to persuade someone that the Black Death is no big deal if you use the right sunblock lotion.

When the Canadian province Ontario introduced new emissions legislation for its Kraft pulp mills, the Ontario Forest Industries Association said simply that the industry didn't support the legislation because studies hadn't found any link between the chlorinated compounds found in mill effluent and abnormalities in fish.[20] This is the argument cigarette companies used for decades against the antismoking lobby to ward off liability suits. But it has done nothing for the cigarette market, which has collapsed.

Others invoke a technological force majeure, throwing up their hands and saying simply that if man were meant to fly, well, he would have grown wings. One of Canada's premier forestry producers said, for example, that "as technology is not currently available to meet these requirements, the economic consequences of these laws cannot be determined."[21] Another player, a big European paper company, laid it on the line in a similar way: "We are in a position to slow down our environmental expenditure—and that suits us just fine."[22]

THE LONG ROAD BACK

Most people in British Columbia recognize the cloud hanging over forestry. Provincial Forestry Minister Dan Miller conceded to an interviewer that British Columbia no longer set the pace in the industry, but simply took whatever price it could get for its products on world markets.[23] One analyst told the *Financial Times* that it would take British Columbia's pulp and paper industry ten to twenty years to get back on track.[24] In a world built on thirty-, sixty-, and ninety-day sales targets, that is a long, long time.

Bill Hughes, and others like him at Port Mellon, knew that Howe Sound Pulp and Paper could not afford ten years. So, while many in the industry planned to stonewall environmental regulation while waiting out the world recession, Howe Sound moved early to get control of its own fate. Management decided to look at this problem differently. Where others saw an excuse for inaction, Howe Sound Pulp and Paper saw an opportunity to move forward, leapfrogging the competition in quality and productivity. The firm took bold action that dramatically cut the risks to its business and made it one of the cleanest pulp mills in the world today.

The rebuilding of Port Mellon took four years and 1,800 workers at its peak and cost C$1.3 billion. But just putting a lot of workers on-site with a fistful of dollars cannot remake a company's relationship with its suppliers, its customers, the communities in which it operates, and, of course, the environment.

For many of Howe Sound's competitors, throwing money at the problem has not worked. At one mill on nearby Vancouver Island, management poured in hundreds of millions of dollars during the early 1990s to upgrade its facility and clean up the environment, only to face market exit again a few years later. In the United States, giant Boise Cascade spent $2.2 billion on its paper-making operations after the industry hit the skids in 1989. The company then found itself on the hot seat before its biggest investor, the California Public Employee Retirement System.[25] If CALPERS runs out of patience before the market recovers, somebody at Boise Cascade will be looking for another line of work.

Where others stumbled, Howe Sound succeeded. The company began with something rare in this, or any other, business: a strategic plan designed from the start to make money from environmental expenditures. Management looked at all the problems in the industry, the future of paper, the needs of its customers, employees, and neighbors. The solutions would involve everything from managing feed-stocks to delivery and customer service. Many thousands of people inside and outside the company would be affected. To focus their efforts, the company reformulated its mission statement:

We will be a highly successful competitor in the global forest products industry, managing with integrity the resources entrusted to our care. We will be guided by the core values of integrity, trust, openness and respect for people.

This simple message clearly integrates competitive success—and jobs—with resource management. A nice start, but a lot more had to be done before the first newsprint went on the reel. To integrate the environment into its productivity plans, Howe Sound had to rethink the way wood pulp was made. Management's objective was to design a plant and to select equipment to meet the requirements of the "receiving" environment of Howe Sound.[26] Furthermore, the company decided that the mill should use waste by-products for its raw materials. It should be self-sufficient in energy, and have zero emissions.

The results speak for themselves. Between 1989, when the renovation of the mill began, and the end of 1992, when it was largely completed, Howe Sound's discharge of all chemical waste dropped dramatically, in most cases by more than 80 percent (see chart). Port Mellon uses less than 24 million gallons of water a day. Another modernized (but less profitable) mill we saw in British Columbia, with one-third the output, uses 50 million gallons a day.

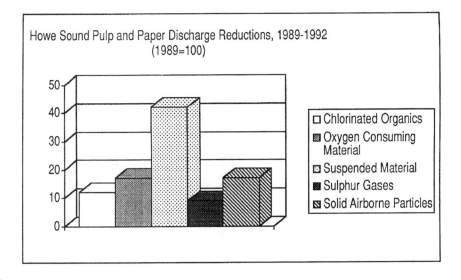

Howe Sound Pulp and Paper Discharge Reductions, 1989-1992 (1989=100)

- Chlorinated Organics
- Oxygen Consuming Material
- Suspended Material
- Sulphur Gases
- Solid Airborne Particles

Howe Sound Pulp and Paper exceeds government-mandated emission levels, often by several orders of magnitude. The company has put itself ahead of the compliance curve so it can focus on its customer needs instead of slugging it out with the government. For others, the regulatory noose keeps tightening. The federal government was satisfied with emissions of 2.5 kilograms of chlorinated organic compounds per tonne of effluent in 1994, but British Columbia wanted to see only 1.5 kilograms per tonne in 1995 and none at all by 2002.[27] While the rest of the industry in British Columbia is resisting, Howe Sound is ready. Dioxin and furan emissions are down 99.9 percent from 1,340 parts per quadrillion to 0.8 part per quadrillion. At the same time, the mill is producing, on a gigantic scale, some of the finest Kraft and newsprint products in the world. And doing so at exceptional levels of productivity.

Dave Sellors worked for four years on the rebuilding of Port

Mellon. A steamfitter by training, Sellors is immensely proud of the improvements in the mill. As we walk through the plant, up and down through a maze of pipes and valves around the six-story high-power boiler, we find the place spotless. Unlike other mills we have seen, this one has no rags wrapped around ill-fitting joints in the piping. Nor are there pools of water or leaking steam. At another mill we visited, we were sprayed with liquid Kraft pulp slurry as we dodged pipes, steam, and pools of water. Scraps of paper and pulp were everywhere. Containers around the plant marked for recycling of metals and newsprint were filled with coffee cups, soda cans, and bags of garbage. It was more like a descent into Hades than a plant tour. Port Mellon, safely on this side of the River Stix, is clean and well laid out, efficient, and profitable.

Port Mellon cogenerates 70 percent of its own energy needs. A 238-foot Babcock and Wilcox recovery boiler, where Sellors did a lot of his work, was built to refire wood waste called "black liquor," generating enough steam to run a Mitsubishi extraction back-pressure turbine and a sixty-three-megawatt Alcatel Alsthom generator. This supplies all the heat for chip cooking, pulp drying, and pulp bleaching. For the rest of the mill's power needs, Sellors and his co-workers installed a fifty-megawatt Babcock and Wilcox boiler powered by hog fuel—bark and sawdust from Vancouver area sawmills that would otherwise go into landfills—and solids removed from the mill's own effluents. This boiler will drive a fifty-megawatt Mitsubishi turbogenerator. One of the proudest achievements of workers like Sellors is that they did all this while maintaining existing production.

Things have changed since Howe Sound shut down its old digesters, huge vats where a witches' brew of chemicals turned wood chips into paper fibers. Back then a coven of workers in cat-walks overhead fed the digesters and controlled the process in large batches, to pretty wide tolerances. Now the new fiber line is run on an Asea Brown Boverei–designed computer system that monitors, graphically on large color screens, every aspect of pulp manufacturing operations. Operators in a safe control room can immediately see where problems exist, and only then do they venture out onto the shop floor. As a result, Port Mellon eerily appears almost devoid of people.

Today the plant lives largely off recycling. Its raw materials are the wood chip by-products of one industry: lumbering. And it reuses almost all of its own by-products to make other paper products and to fire its generators, although natural gas is burned in the lime kiln and some gas is burned in the power boiler.

To cut out particle emissions, Howe Sound has large Flakt electrostatic precipitators that use electrically charged plates to capture 99.7 percent of the particles that are suspended in flue gases and would otherwise go straight up the chimney.

Management chose new suppliers to minimize costs and maximize customer service. Long-term contracts allow these suppliers to think less about price and more about how they can contribute to Howe Sound's productivity improvement program.

For example, Canfor could not ship newsprint to Japan rolled onto cores having the wrong moisture content. Howe Sound uses 260,000 of these cardboard cores (which are like big toilet-paper rolls) a year, and their moisture content must be just slightly less than that of the newsprint they carry. Moisture levels that are too high or too low cause malfunctions in the press rooms of Oji's Japanese customers. To get this just right, the core supplier, Sonoco, built its facility on-site and uses recycled plant materials. Sonoco is not only providing a quality product, but also using some of Howe Sound's own waste.

Similarly, Canfor and Oji cut a ten-year deal with Gearbulk Shipping, a Norwegian company, to design, build, and operate three new vessels. These can load and unload newsprint rolls completely under cover, and transport them halfway around the world in a climate-controlled environment.[28] This way quality isn't something that ends at the loading dock in Port Mellon; it reaches right into the printing presses of Howe Sound customers anywhere in the world.

Canfor's goal was to ensure that the experience of its customers with Canfor pulp and paper products was better than anything that customers could expect. The company soon realized that sloppy—and polluting—production processes were inconsistent with quality products and service.

To make sure they saw how to do things the right way, Howe Sound sent its senior managers and equipment operators to spend several weeks at Oji's superefficient Tomakomai plant in Japan. There they received intensive training in Japanese quality methods. By the time the mill opened, many employees had spent a full year in school, relearning the business of paper-making. This was perhaps the most important element in the success at Howe Sound.

Forestry workers have never been the best-educated people in the world. Stories abound of workers damaging yellow cedar logs worth $40,000 each because they don't know how to handle them properly, of truck drivers casually lopping the end of a yellow cedar log, literally cutting its value in half.[29] Traditionally, cutting trees and making paper was reserved for those with the least education. As every Canadian knows, logging hard and drinking hard just go together. This had to change for Howe Sound's C$1.3 billion investment to pay off.

It did change, as did the very nature of work at the plant. At other mills, gangs of pipe fitters and metalworkers roam around trying to keep the machinery running. These craftsmen are much like those in a 1930s steam locomotive workshop, machining parts on the spot, jerry-rigging equipment, massaging a few more weeks out of fully depreciated plant. These workers are responding to problems, not anticipating them. Quality is extremely difficult to maintain under such circumstances. At Howe Sound, continuous monitoring of production processes allows workers to prevent downtime before it occurs.

Across the industry many workers and managers continue to view environmental regulations as a burden, despite clear evidence that green processes can improve quality and lower costs. Many mills have been forced by customers to raise environmental standards, because customers now view quality differently. At these paper companies, the employees have not been shown the connection between quality and the environment.

In one mill, we saw a rough square of cardboard tacked up next to a vat of Kraft pulp, hand-lettered with the words: *No plastic in pulp; spoiled Kraft means lost customers.* Clearly, workers who must be reminded not to pitch their garbage into the pulp vats are not tuned in to what is going on. Employees must be taught about quality, they must be trained to be part of the team. Howe Sound has made this transition.

Better training is reflected in productivity. Before the makeover, Port Mellon produced 200,000 tons of pulp a year, and no newsprint at all. Today the mill produces 300,000 tons of Kraft pulp and 180,000 tons of newsprint a year. Employment will stabilize at 620 people, up from the 500 that worked in the old plant. One nearby competitor (which also upgraded its facilities at great expense) gets one-third less output from twice as many workers. Port Mellon is several times as productive. This is how good blue-collar jobs are made.

The workers have gotten the message. One spokesman at the Canadian branch of the International Woodworkers of America, for example, told the press recently, "You have to increase productivity to survive in world markets." To protect jobs, the IWA now insists on the productivity improvements demanded by management.[30]

It is a measure of the strength of public pressure in British Columbia—including that of the workers themselves—that only one of the province's twenty-two pulp mills said it would not be able to comply with a 1994 federal government requirement that mills have no measurable dioxin or furan output. In Quebec, by contrast, thirty-seven out of thirty-nine mills said that they could not comply.[31] In the short run, those mills in Quebec may avoid big capital expenditures. But in the long run, they are forsaking the productivity gains and quality leadership that mean jobs.

YUPPIES, TREE HUGGERS,
AND OTHER ANIMALS

The journey from Vancouver to Port Mellon is short and pleasant. Get off the Langdale car ferry thirty minutes from Vancouver's Horseshoe Bay terminal, turn right, and drive about ten miles on forest roads into the upper reaches of Howe Sound. Here the annual rainfall is three times what it is at the ferry terminal. The ocean-borne clouds climb into the mountains just at this point, giving Port Mellon the kind of pure runoff and clear streams it needs to produce clean paper.

Jennifer Earwaker greets us at the tour center. Port Mellon has been the butt of so much bad press for so many years that we expect her to be at least a bit defensive. With surprising self-assurance—gained from hosting Japanese and European customers and politicians almost weekly—she skips the environment and goes straight to the heart of the problem. The plant was old and decrepit. So we tore it down and built another one. Only by setting the highest possible quality goals from the outset, however, could we meet the standards of our customers and, by the way, virtually eliminate pollution and pioneer development of chlorine-free pulp.

As she takes us through the operation, we begin to see why. The place is like a ghost town. An immense site, today there are only a few hundred people working here in three shifts. Because the plant is highly automated, most of these are in control rooms far removed from the mill itself. The air is clear and there is only a slight sulfur odor.

Canfor is using pollution to flag management and quality problems. As a result, managers can evaluate their progress at Howe Sound by simply opening the windows, and by measuring the impact of the mill on the surrounding environment. Stinking air or fouled waters would tell them that they are off track. At Howe Sound, Canfor has integrated the "receiving environment" into its quality management process.

As Canfor knows well, British Columbians like to compare

their forests to Europe's great cathedrals. Indeed, one of the province's primary tourist attractions, a breathtaking stand of primeval cedars on Vancouver Island, is actually called Cathedral Grove. British Columbia Environment Minister John Cashmore said simply that the province's ecosystem is "a heritage which should be protected."[32]

To protect this heritage, British Columbia has plenty of leverage. It owns 90 percent of the province's forests and plans to double the size of park lands and wilderness areas from 6 percent to 12 percent over the next ten years.[33] While timber cutting in Canada has increased fivefold since the 1920s, the use of Canada's forests by holiday makers has risen 100 times. And in the United States, congressional studies show that recreation now accounts for two-fifths of the value of America's forests.[34]

Canada has a history of forestry management that aggravates an already difficult situation. Vacationers could not miss seeing the damage to their blighted country when, by 1991, for example, more than a quarter of the timberland harvested during the years 1985 and 1986 had not yet been replanted. The drive from Cathedral Grove to Long Beach on the west coast of Vancouver Island can be particularly unpleasant. Where Sweden spends 40 percent of its forestry budget on intensive forestry management, Canada spends less than 3 percent.

There are now tree-cutting moratoria in a few places and some, like much-televised Clayoquot Sound on scenic Vancouver Island, have become major battlegrounds between voters and the forestry industry. Government waffling in an attempt to please everybody only makes the problem worse. There is a price to pay, of course, and partly as a result Canadian harvests appear to have peaked in 1987.[35] All the while the industry loses precious credibility that it cannot afford.

In this climate, the public-relations front cannot be ignored. Howe Sound appears to have won the battle. Its community relations are unusually sophisticated for a company this size. After the renovations of the mill started, management initiated Saturday morning meetings with the nearby community of Gibson's Landing. To ensure that mill workers, many of whom commuted to Port Mellon by ferry, didn't crowd out other commuters, Howe Sound moved shift changes around to off-peak ferry runs. Carefully avoiding large public forums that could quickly become confrontational, management went on the road, taking slide shows and videos to Vancouver high schools, for example, to show teachers and students what the company was planning to do and the results it expected to get. This was a calculated risk. If the Howe Sound project had failed to deliver on its environmental promises, everyone would know. In short, Canfor turned the entire province of British Columbia into its quality control department. By making the public so aware of what it was doing, Canfor upped the ante for its own people: they simply could not afford to fail.

Perhaps Canfor could have kept the regulators at bay. British Columbia has a limited industrial base. "When it gets down to it," Vancouver tax lawyer Rick Bennet told us, speaking of his customers, "everyone out here is connected one way or another with the natural resource business." Politicians cannot place too much pressure on the forestry industry without costing constituents jobs. The trick for them is to strike the right balance between loud noises and inaction.

Appeasing the neighbors is one thing. Customers are quite another story. Canadians have learned the hard way that when the public turns against your product, watch out. The European market for Canadian furs evaporated when pictures of baby seals being clubbed to death killed demand almost overnight. Europe buys about 15 percent of Canadian pulp products, about C$2.5 billion worth a year.[36]

The environmental movement knows a weakness like this and how to leverage it. In the early 1990s, Greenpeace was turning up the heat. In Germany, Greenpeace published *Der Plagiat,* a takeoff of the popular German magazine *Der Spiegel* intended to stop German paper-makers from buying British Columbia pulp because of its chlorine content. This was followed by a TV program on British Columbia forestry called "Paradise Spoiled."[37] Howe

Sound officials saw bloodied seal pups all over again. They acted not a moment too soon.

One of Canfor's wisest moves, according to Bill Hughes, was offering Greenpeace a seminar on pulp and paper done the Port Mellon way. This encouraged Greenpeace to see Port Mellon as more of a benchmark rather than as a lightning rod for attacks. And it substantially eliminated an issue Greenpeace needs to mobilize the public and raise the funds it needs to keep going, forcing it to move on to other issues.[38]

Nevertheless, Greenpeace's propaganda campaign has killed the market for chlorine-bleached paper in Europe. In the United States, the same shift in preferences is underway. Greenpeace threatened *Time* magazine over the issue. Then an unholy alliance of environmental groups and paper companies tried to get the U.S. government to buy chlorine-free paper. No matter how much the paper industry objects, customers have been persuaded that chlorine-free paper is better. Environmentalism has gone beyond public relations; green credentials are necessary to clinch the sale. And when the market shifted, Port Mellon was ahead of the competition with the most important by-product of its new plant: chlorine-free paper.

A VIEW FROM THE BOTTOM OF HOWE SOUND

The best way to see how well the mill at Port Mellon achieved its goals is to go with Bill Sluis to the bottom of Howe Sound. Sluis teaches high school physical education in Gibson's Landing. While his big-city colleagues work the sweaty confines of the high school gym, every year Sluis uses the abundance of nature on his doorstep to plan imaginative field trips for his students.

He spots a good site years in advance. Once he decides on a trip, his classes spend their whole year raising money and planning for the outing. The Sluis field trip is a major event in Gibson's and it sets his class apart. He wants his classes to look back for years afterwards at these field trips as "defining moments" in their lives. He usually succeeds.

For his next trip, Sluis was considering an open-water dive in the luxuriant waters of the nearby Georgia Strait. Today, on a trial run, we are diving about ten miles from Port Mellon, near where Howe Sound empties into the Georgia Strait and on into the Pacific. Fisheries have been closed here for years, fouled to extinction by the mill. As we prepare to dive, checking our equipment carefully, he talks about what to expect. Not much. Life, it seems, is not what experienced divers like Sluis look forward to when they plumb the depths of Howe Sound. Indeed, he hasn't been here for a while because there isn't much to see. But, for his students, the location is manageable: a small cove, not too deep, and with minimal tidal complications. If Sluis is going to introduce students to open-water diving, this may be the best place around to do it.

After a brief trip to the bottom, Bill Sluis surfaces ecstatic. Pulling his regulator out of his mouth, he exults, "There's life down there!" Life in Howe Sound means that something is changing for the good at Port Mellon. It is also a certain indication that the people of Gibson's Landing will get their jobs and a safe environment. The hard choice between employment and the environment does not have to be made here.

While the rest of North America was mired in the recession of the early nineties, Gibson's Landing had its biggest boom ever. The tourists returned, real estate prices rose, a large mall opened, along with several new restaurants, and even a new yacht club. And, the biggest surprise of all, *Port Mellon* is no longer a dirty word. Mill workers who used to be afraid to be seen with their mill jackets on now sport them proudly. Port Mellon's neighbors brag about the place. Many of them directly attribute their improved circumstances to changes at the mill. So they should. Port Mellon injects millions into the local economy each year.

THE LESSONS

In four years, Howe Sound Pulp and Paper went from loser to winner. Competitors continue to see their business eroded by over-capacity, falling prices, and Third World competitors. Some rivals spent billions to upgrade their operations without achieving Howe Sound's success. There are several lessons to be learned from Canfor's experience:

Get into the education business. Your workforce is the cutting edge of your competitive capability. Going green means adding value by replacing mechanical work with knowledge. Make sure all your employees, from the executive suite to the shop floor, are the most knowledgeable, articulate, and competent in your industry.

Don't accept conventional wisdom. Howe Sound set goals for itself, like zero emissions and energy self-sufficiency, that seemed ridiculous when they were set, then went on to meet them.

Let your environmental goals drive quality. Use pollution as a flag for quality and other management problems; eliminate the pollution and the other problems will go away, too. You are kidding yourself to think you can be sloppy in one area and not in another.

Integrate the "receiving" environment into your production process. Let your receiving environment tell you what is right and wrong about what you are doing. Measure yourself by the air and water in which you operate, and your quality will be unbeatable.

Turn the public into your quality control department. There is no better quality control department than the public. So force the pace. Set real goals that people can understand and measure for themselves. Then get senior management out to local schools and community centers. Talk about what you intend to do and how you expect everyone to benefit. Let the public tell you what is right and wrong with your goals, your methods. Deal with objections quickly and let the public verify that you have met, indeed exceeded, those objections.

BLACK PHOTO

DEVELOPING A
POLLUTION-FREE ENVIRONMENT

When Black Photo's executives looked into their crystal ball, they saw that the time was coming when they would no longer be able to dump hundreds of thousands of gallons of chemical-contaminated water into the sewer every day. So they decided to do a preemptive strike on the regulators: eliminate all discharge of photographic chemicals from their operations. The results surprised even Black Photo, the largest chain of photo-processing labs in Canada. The lessons for marketers and advertising companies the world over are profound and could revolutionize the way they position their clients.

Toronto is loved by tourists, especially Americans, who return home raving about its down-home goodness, cleanliness, and, above all else, its safety. It's no wonder: more people are murdered in New York in two weeks than in Toronto in an entire year.[1] Canada's craving for "peace, order, and good government"[2] is, after its mountains, forests, and lakes, its primary tourist attraction. But Toronto is not a beautiful city; it lacks the grace and sophistication of Paris, the hustle and bustle of Tokyo, the sheer majesty of Vancouver. Actor Peter Ustinov once called Toronto a New York run by the Swiss, if you can imagine that.

This is the world in which Black Photo Corporation, Canada's largest photofinisher, operates. Black's customers are dominated by an overwhelming Canadian desire for cleanliness and order. Moreover, in this kind of market, there is always an activist ready to bring down any company that gets too arrogant or that takes the environment for granted. Canadians are deeply aware that they have the world's second largest land mass and that it is full of exploitable minerals, forests, and waters that could make them fabulously wealthy. But they are equally determined not to become fabulously wealthy—something disparaged among Canadians in conversation as the "American model"—and to keep their minerals and waters just where they are, in the ground. Nothing gets a Canadian's back up faster than talk of spoiling Canada's pristine wilderness for corporate profit. And, unlike Americans, they are not afraid to invoke "good government" to drive down any business that doesn't behave.

On the face of it, none of this should trouble a photofinisher like Black Photo. They are, after all, just those nice people who send you back the great pictures you took of the kids last summer canoeing in the Haliburtons or lunching at picturesque Chaffeys Locks. But that's not what the people at Black Photo saw when they looked into their crystal ball.

WE DON'T CARE ABOUT WHAT WE DON'T SEE

In our increasingly convenience-driven, high-tech age, dropping off our film at the local drugstore or minilab for immediate development is something we simply take for granted. We rush in, drop our pictures, and leave, fully expecting a result when we return. Naturally we blame the photofinishers if our snaps don't turn out right and we rarely, if ever, give a thought to the environmental impact of what we are doing. We want our pictures and we get our pictures and that's all there is to it.

Well, as the people at Black Photo know better than anyone else, that is not all there is to it. Photofinishers pollute, big time. Developing photographs means using enormous amounts of water. Every year North America's photofinishers dump several hundred million gallons of developers, fixers, and bleaches down the drain. Moreover, some 60 percent of all silver mined in North America goes into the photography industry, and each liter of dumped fixer contains between 1.5 and 4.0 grams of it.[3] In most places, photofinishers simply dilute their chemicals with the prodigious amounts of water they take from the mains and flush the lot down the drain. No fuss, no muss, and lots of polluted wastewater. Most sewage treatment plants can't handle the stuff, and it goes straight back into our rivers and lakes, ready for drinking through the next intake valve. When nobody sees, nobody cares.

The saving grace for photofinishers, for the moment at least, is that this pollution is quiet. The public's attention is fixed on more obvious culprits like pulp mills and oil refineries. But all it would take is one cub reporter looking for a big story to break the bad news about photofinishing into every home in Canada.

This news would soon be followed by draconian legislation. Indeed, by 1989, the government of Ontario was already starting to make noises.[4]

The way the media work, this story could break anywhere in the world, not just at home in Toronto. It could break on TV, in a newspaper, or, more likely with breaking news these days, on an electronic network of personal computers, like Compuserve. Black Photo had no way of knowing when this story would come out or where. All it knew for sure is that break it would and when it did, Black Photo, as Canada's premier photofinisher, would be painted as a master polluter. After decades of extremely careful positioning, its name would be blackened, literally. Its shareholders might never recover.

To any sentient being looking at this problem, pollution presented Black Photo with two threats: one to its major source of business, photofinishing; and another—potentially more damaging —to the company's brand, a valuable property in its own right.

The killing off of the Black brand name would destroy any opportunities the company might want to exploit outside photofinishing. Because electronic cameras may kill off photofinishing the same way camcorders killed home movies, the destruction of its brand would eliminate Black Photo's exit strategy. It was something Black Photo could not take lightly.

Many businesses face the same problem Black Photo faces. Few companies are more easily tarred with the opprobrium of pollution than oil companies. Exxon, for example, has been through the miseries of the *Exxon Valdez* oil spill in Alaska's beautiful Prince William Sound. But Exxon still has to protect its valuable brand name in order to sell gasoline to consumers. The *Exxon Valdez* incident threatened to lumber Exxon with high cleanup costs certainly, but more importantly, it threatened Exxon's brand.

This chapter is about turning a potential environmental and business nightmare to strategic and profitable advantage.

THE CANADIAN MANIA FOR FRESH WATER

For Black Photo, the pollution issue is twofold: water consumption and water pollution. In some places, like California and New York City, excessive water consumption has long been a big problem. There are simply too many people and not enough water for them to drink and meet local agricultural and industrial needs. Canadians know that Canada has the lion's share of the continent's fresh water. Because of this accident of geography you might think that spending cheap and plentiful water is not a national priority. Quite the contrary. Their national terror is that pressure from thirsty New Yorkers and Californians will drive Americans someday to cross the border and take it. This may sound startlingly irrational to Asians and Europeans used to thinking of North America as one big, happy place. But Canada owes its very existence to the successful repulsion of American invasions in 1775–1776 and 1812–1814 and to deft political maneuvering to parry threats to invade again in the 1840s and 1860s. Indeed, while Americans celebrate their first 100 years as a century of unchecked expansion and growth, Canadians look back on the same period as one long, tough grind keeping American expansionists, who outnumbered them enormously, in check. Their major source of national pride is that they succeeded where none of the major powers of the day, including France, Spain, and Russia, could.

Canadians look at it this way: if the United States can send a 500,000-man military expedition halfway around the globe for Kuwaiti oil, what might it do for all the water right next door?

Combining Canada's mania for fresh water with its penchant for tough regulation, management at Black Photo did not take long to realize that they faced a regulatory nightmare. A household brand name that took years to build would collapse. And Black Photo's current and future opportunities would vanish.

To avoid this calamity, Black Photo obviously had to deal with the immediate problem of pollution. But more importantly, it had to preserve, indeed reinforce if possible, the Black brand without which the company has no future in digital photography.

What started out as an environmental question quickly became a question of brand management.

To solve the pollution problem, Black Photo had to reinvent completely the way pictures are developed, virtually eliminating byproducts and slashing water use to a fraction of what it had been. In doing this, the company has slam-dunked competitors not prepared to clean up. In fact, the industry has closed ranks, labeling Black's new pollution-free process as "unfair competition."

To solve the branding problem, Black has rebuilt the relationship between the environment and consumer loyalty in mass marketing, a complex and difficult step that Japanese companies like Hitachi (see chapter "Hitachi Preaches the Green Gospel") and American companies like Texaco have been struggling with for some time. Today Black's rebranding has positioned the company to move freely into the business of computerized pictures, something few of its competitors are ready to do.

There have been numerous additional benefits. The company had spent years differentiating itself on product and service. This strategy had run its full course and offered few new opportunities. By breaking with the past, management gained real focus. The firm turned a commodity—film developing—into a premium product and learned how to launch products and services completely unrelated to photofinishing—all without letting the whole company spin out of control.

"WE MAKE MEMORIES"

Black Photo director of public relations, Rob Buschelt, says simply that the company's mission is to "make memories." This fundamental recognition of what the company does provided the firm a coherent basis for understanding the rebranding process. For example, technology allows consumers to make, manage, preserve, and transmit "memories" in dozens of ways. Photofinishing is just one of them. And it may not be the biggest or the fastest-growing method. Positioning itself as a maker of memories allows Black Photo to offer a full range of these services.

At the same time, Black Photo's mission to "make memories" is part of a carefully crafted image designed to set it apart from competitors that also turn around pictures fast. The idea is to build consumer loyalty for the long haul, bringing customers back time and again over their entire lives to have their memories carefully recorded and thoughtfully preserved at Black's. If its customers truly believe that Black is the keeper of their fondest memories— holidays, weddings, vacations, honeymoons, graduations, and so on—they will turn to Black forever. This kind of franchise is invaluable.

Black works at building consumer loyalty with great care. Company marketing features constant refrains like "making memories for Christmas morning," and that Black's is "ready to capture it all," or "ready to capture Christmas morning." This repetition drives home the idea that Black and only Black can "capture" and "make" your most cherished memories. In effect, Black Photo has created a memories environment that captures everything its customers cherish most.

Black serves Canada from some 209 retail outlets located in malls and shopping centers coast to coast. Each outlet is carefully designed to enhance Black's memory-preservation image. Outlets sell film, of course, but they also sell a broad range of cameras, camera accessories, binoculars, camcorders and accessories, albums, frames and a wide variety of picture mounts, and can print pictures on cups, mugs, T-shirts, plates, even on Christmas tree decorations. Black Photo advertising offers a full range of image creation (cameras) and image enhancement and preservation (film processing and picture mounting) products and services. In stores, everything is laid out to reinforce the central theme of making memories. These stores have a certain atmosphere, not unlike Ralph Lauren's clothing stores, and are heavily decorated to sell commodity products that might otherwise be indistinguishable from those of the competition.

Black Photo encourages employees to use the products and services they sell. Corporate office hallways and company stores all feature photographs snapped by employees on standard thirty-five-millimeter film. Many of these pictures are mounted on Black's twenty-inch-by-thirty-inch gallery mounts. Blown up this large, they reveal every possible flaw in the picture and the development process.

Black wants customers to see themselves in these displays, so they are composed simply. No trick photos, just well-taken happy snaps that anybody could shoot with an inexpensive autofocus. In short, the company is careful not to overplay its memory image. Every picture in its stores, offices, and advertising is clearly one that anyone can take unaided by strobe lights, expensive lenses, filters, and other dauntingly complex and costly equipment.

To further reinforce this image of simplicity, company advertising, promotional material, and newspaper and magazine inserts not only feature pictures by employees, but pictures *of* employees and their families as well. The message is that the once mysterious and complex art of taking a good picture—setting f-stops and shutter speeds and calculating exposure equivalents—is now accessible and easy, with Black's help, of course.

At the same time, however, making photography accessible to consumers means leaving Black wide open for blame if anything goes wrong. Take Black's suggestion that customers use their firm to "make beautiful pictures into great gifts." This is fine, but no man, for example, wants to admit to his wife that his disastrous Christmas pics of their just-born baby are the result of his own complete incompetence! It must be the camera (perhaps not; she gave it to him last Christmas for just this purpose). Better to blame the developer.

To succeed selling memories, Black has to be blame-free. Black's promises "big beautiful prints . . . guaranteed." Quality is inherent in the brand; a small failure in photo processing is a complete, and gigantic, failure for a customer.

A franchise like this takes decades to build and can be lost in a second. Says Alan Henkelman, Black's director of photo-processing operations, "What happens if our customers open their shoe boxes, even one hundred years from now, and they don't have any pictures left? Whatever we do, it *cannot* affect the product." The quality of the preserved memory—the images Black Photo sells—must be superior. If it isn't, Black's reputation, at its very best, is no better than the least quality-driven competitor. And since Black's reputation will have fallen from such a great height of consumer expectation, it could be even worse. Indeed, a quality problem could simply kill their business.

Finally, the biggest threat to Black Photo is weak advertising. Advertising not only has to convince the public of the value of the Black Photo brand, but also has to make that brand strong enough to carry Black Photo into the post-photo-processing business. A poor campaign now could kill Black's future opportunities. So, if Black Photo was to go to the public with a new message about "green" photo processing, the message had better be good. This made the choice of ad campaigns critical.

Moreover, what little is known about consumer buying habits and "green" products shows that consumers will not pay a premium for something that is environmentally clean. So a marketing strategy that is obviously green is a nonstarter.

"WE HAVE TO BE FIRST
IN EVERYTHING WE DO"

Compounding Black Photo's positioning problem and the makeup of its advertising campaign, the company's main strategy has long been to be "first in everything we do."[5] Black Photo has led the Canadian market in several innovations in the past, like oversized prints. The problem with being first is that risk—and reward—is always greater than for followers.

Consumer markets change fast. The competition is always ready to beat you to the punch and often does. Unless you are at the top of your game and know how to stay there, maintaining a "first" ranking in consumer markets is very tough indeed. Moreover, you not only have to be first, but you also have to be first in the mind of your customer, which is quite another thing.

Wherever technology is involved, as in photo processing and consumer electronics, there is the additional risk of someone obsoleting your process and introducing something twice as effective to the market at half the price. Black Photo had to be ahead of this curve. So whatever it did had to keep it well in front of the competition both in process technology and in perceived value for its customers.

While it is easy to think of photography as an old technology—it has been around for 150 years—it is always new. The pictures themselves are always changing, as do the people and things being photographed. But so do the cameras. The old 120-millimeter Kodak Brownies, still popular in the early 1960s, have been replaced by 35-millimeter infrared autofocus and programmable cameras. The resulting leap in picture quality—and customer quality expectations—has been quantum. In addition, we are now on the verge of a new world of digital photography and multimedia, the blending of sound and man-made computer art with still and moving pictures. Soon your kids will send these mini "shows" to Grandma over the cable TV network or even your phone lines. Black Photo wants to be at the center of all these opportunities. But it will be the center of absolutely nothing if its image is ruined by some breaking press story about Black Photo polluting the water you drink at home.

So Black Photo decided to combine the two problems into one new positioning strategy: they would use an advertising campaign about their preemptive first strike to preserve the environment to reinforce, indeed rebuild, their brand from the ground up. If they succeeded, they knew that they would have turned a chemistry problem into an advertising masterstroke.

If they failed, on the other hand, their customers would walk. In this age of consumer empowerment,[6] there is simply nothing, absolutely nothing, to prevent customers from leaving Black high and dry. The days when a company could lock its customers in and expect them to stay for the rest of their lives ("My mother always said, 'Use Tide.' And today my children . . .") are long gone. Consumers no longer attach the same value they once did to well-known brands; few will pay a premium to buy "brand name" anymore. So-called "ghost" brands like Brylcreem, Lavoris, and Lifebuoy have lost their position. They have been superseded by new products, new technologies, and by brand owners who have simply lost interest in them.[7] Some of the world's most savvy consumer marketers, like Procter & Gamble, are killing moribund brands quickly to clear the decks for new products. Black Photo definitely did not want to be consigned to the ash heap of brand history.

Today marketers have to lock in customer loyalty with something new. Brand alone won't do it anymore. In automobiles, first Volkswagen, then the Japanese, broke the stranglehold of Detroit's careful brand management by selling lifestyle. To reposition itself Black Photo decided to use the environment.

Black's biggest brag is that "Black *Is* Photography." Their goal is to convince consumers that there is a photograph, and then there is a Black's photograph. Everything else is off-brand and probably of questionable quality. Black sells photofinishing the way Kodak sells film, Procter & Gamble sells baby diapers, and IBM used to sell computers. Theirs is the premier product. If you don't send your pictures to Black, their marketing seems to say, it's a wonder that you'll get them back at all!

This constant harping on their quality and reliability is essential to Black's promotion of its brand. "Anything we have to do to enhance the brand, we will do," says Henkelman. Buschelt agrees: "We want to be first in a broad range of photofinishing products, processes, and advertising." So, when confronted with new environmental legislation that might be enforced, the firm made up its mind: "We had to go first."

A being-first-in-everything mantra sounds great, but doing it in a synchronized way isn't so easy. Most businesses lack the focus to get the job done.

So when Black Photo first faced its environmental problems, the firm had a lot at risk. Being the first to come up with a green process is one thing, but making sure that doing so did not inadvertently and adversely affect the quality and durability of its customers' memories is quite another.

THE QUALITY PROBLEM:
MAKING THOSE MEMORIES LAST

The first questions the company asked itself was how far to go. Should it meet existing legislative limits? Or should it do something that would meet legislative limits forever? "Most consultants tell you to go to the existing limits and no further," says Henkelman. "But this means reengineering every time the government changes legislation. And we had to provide for ten different provinces with ten different standards." Not to mention the federal government and municipalities. Discussion on this point was serious and drawn out. But the sheer number of jurisdictions and the unpredictability of future government action made Black's choice inevitable. "We decided," Henkelman said, "to go for a closed loop." With nowhere to go, a closed loop ensures zero emissions. This in turn means nothing to regulate.

At the same time, making memories means making them last. Simply eliminating dirty water isn't enough. Memory is only as good as its clarity—crystal clarity. And, as Director of Photoprocessing Operations Alan Henkelman had said, nothing Black undertook could affect what its customers put in their photo albums and up on the walls. At the very least quality had to remain the same. Ideally, it should improve. And because photofinishing is brutally competitive, nothing Black did could push up prices. Indeed, if everything worked perfectly, whatever Black came up with should cut costs. Finally, Black Photo had to be seen as the only purveyor of clear memories, regardless of medium.

RETHINKING HOW PICTURES ARE MADE AND PROCESSED

Until recently, no one thought that there was much you could do about photographs. The basic principles of picture developing were established long ago and seemed immutable. If you wanted photographs, you had to live with pollution.

To create a closed-loop system with zero emissions, Black had to rethink the way pictures are made from the ground up. Says Henkelman, "Early on in the process my favorite question was, How much water does it take to make a print? The textbook answer is that it takes a lot. So I started asking, How little can we use and still make it work right?"

By asking fundamental questions about the process of film developing, Black began to find ways of using much less water than before. Then the company began asking other questions, like, How clear does the water have to be to ensure fine-quality prints? The answers to these questions changed the way the company thought about what it was doing and how it managed what it was doing.

After three years and 1 million Canadian dollars, Black's was able to announce that it had cut its annual water use of 60 million liters to less than 2 million, a cutback of 97 percent. The discharge of wastewater and chemicals into the municipal sewer system had been virtually eliminated. Today this process is used in the company's main photofinishing locations in Toronto, Calgary, and Vancouver. Soon it will be available for all of the firm's 171 minilabs as well. All this is available at no charge to customers and with product quality that meets or exceeds Black's standards, thus protecting its franchise.

Black calls its new process System Crystal, a name designed to be easily recognized and to reflect the crystal-clear quality of the photographic memories Black's is selling.

Almost immediately after Black Photo launched System Crystal—a name that suggests the exact opposite of its own—the company began to attract investors interested in participating in the benefits of the new process.

Here again, Black Photo was able to turn its green campaign into tangible shareholder value: because Black leapfrogged the competition on so many fronts at once—technology, process, advertising, positioning, and brand maintenance—companies interested in buying Black Photo started to show up. Moreover, where in the past they would have been buying a chain of camera and photo-processing outlets, now they would be looking at a more valuable property capable of leading a revolution in consumer electronics.

SYSTEM CRYSTAL EVOLUTION

A closed loop like System Crystal is comprehensive: it may be designed to eliminate one type of problem—in this case water pollution—but deals effectively with several others like air pollution and solid-waste management. This makes the process inherently more manageable. Any kind of waste or leakage indicates a faulty process and quality failure. Management can focus directly on these and expect to get significant improvements. Being comprehensive, a closed loop also eliminates dozens of regulatory headaches at once, lowering compliance costs dramatically.

The company's goals for System Crystal were sixfold. Black Photo wanted to:

- Ensure that products and services are safe for employees, customers, and the environment
- Reduce, and even eliminate, the environmental impact of products, services, and packaging
- Meet or exceed the standards of environmental laws and regulations
- Continually improve all environmental processes
- Keep customers and employees up to date on System Crystal progress
- Ensure that every employee is responsible and accountable for the integrity of company environmental processes

Only one of these goals—the second—is really "environmental." The rest are designed to cut costs, improve marketing and employee accountability, and introduce a Japanese process of continuous improvement, or *kaizen* (literally "change that is good"). This is important: Black Photo recognized right from the beginning that System Crystal would be more than just nice words about regulatory compliance; it would be a fundamental change in Black's way of doing business.

System Crystal is built around three processes: Aqua-Flo, a continuous-cycle water reuse and purification system; Chemcharge, for reusing and regenerating the more than forty different chemicals used in photo processing; and Chemnet, for gathering and disposing the few remaining wastes in an environmentally safe manner.

In Aqua-Flo wash water is purified and reused. Water usage is cut to the small amount—3 percent—lost through evaporation. Water flows through three stages as pressures increase from 225 pounds per square inch to 400. In the first stage, ultraviolet radiation cuts bacterial impurities. In the second stage, called nanofiltration, the water is passed through microscopic filters. After a final process of reverse osmosis, water leaves Aqua-Flo with 150 parts per million dissolved solids. In the Toronto suburb of Markham where Black Photo operates, regular tap water contains more than twice as much, 370 parts per million.[8] Aqua-Flo water is therefore more than clean enough to be discharged—a distinct quality advantage—but is instead recycled into the photofinishing process.

Chemcharge returns all partially spent chemicals back to one location, where the silver thiosulfate used in making pictures is removed by electrolysis. The 10 percent that cannot be recovered is sent to Chemnet. What remains is recharged with new chemicals and stored until it begins the cycle all over again.

The used chemicals from Chemcharge still contain about 90 percent water. These are sent to Chemnet, where they are distilled and passed through an activated carbon filter to remove all remaining organic compounds and then through ion-exchange columns to remove ammonia. This water then goes back into Aqua-Flo. Chemnet's small remaining chemical output is mixed with other liquid wastes, neutralized, stabilized, and incinerated.[9] The ash goes to a landfill or can be used as fertilizer.[10]

Black Photo is extending the reach of System Crystal to its minilabs across the country. Previously, Black Photo shipped their minilabs chemicals that lab employees had to open, mix manually with water, and eventually flush down the drains. This exposed them to hazards and required them to use protective clothing. Black Photo now ships chemicals in reusable containers. Minilab employees no longer have to mix the contents and they can send used chemicals back to the main labs in the same containers in which they arrived. Minilabs no longer need local water and don't discharge into local drains. Working conditions are safe and Black Photo cuts back on plastic and paper packaging costs and wastes.

Indeed, working conditions are one of the most obvious improvements in Black Photo's Markham labs. Gone is the almost overwhelming smell of photofinishing chemicals that permeates most labs. The nature of chemical and water reuse means that seals and gaskets are tight: there is no slop running over tanks, through joints, and all over the floor. Quality is easier to manage and easier to achieve.

When its original plant was built, Black Photo had drains cut into the floors to take chemical runoff directly from the processing tanks to the Markham sewers and straight into Lake Ontario. The stench must have been unbearable. Today these drains are dry. Employees benefit greatly from this and so, naturally, do customers, who get higher quality when employees are happier.

THE GREEN GHETTO

The same upstanding citizen who will donate to a Greenpeace volunteer knocking at the front door will casually drive to the mall to buy consumer disposables like film without the slightest thought to environmental impact.

This trend has been well tracked by market researchers. Typically, they find that half the consumers surveyed will say that they buy "green" when no more than 6 percent of the products they purchased are "green."[11] Indeed, this trend is so disturbing that many green marketers fear being locked into the "green ghetto," a narrow market niche of specialty catalogs, health/natural-products stores, and earth stores. The green ghetto may draw highly motivated consumers, but not enough of them to support a company like Black's. As a result this submarket is populated by tiny businesses, many of which never break through the "green ceiling."

The Green Ghetto is death to major market producers. On the other hand, few seem to have figured out how to turn the consumer's well-documented green-product recognition into a profitable business strategy.

BRANDING AND ENVIRONMENTAL PROCESS

In its public relations literature, Black Photo tallies the impact on its bottom line ($35,000 less in water costs per year), as well the savings enjoyed by taxpayers ($20,000 the public no longer has to pay to subsidize water delivery).[12] Of course, Black discloses some information on System Crystal's technical merits. But all this is what you would expect from any green initiative. What is of supreme importance to managers everywhere is Black's ability to brand System Crystal.

This Branding ability has a lot to do with the name of the process itself, System Crystal. Black could have called this process FBWE 2 Super (Feed-back and Water Eliminator 2 Super) or something else just as incomprehensible. And the firm could simply have buried the thing in the plant and never spoken a word on the subject. Instead, the company chose a name it thought its customers would understand and then went public. More important, in System Crystal ads, the environmental aspect is oblique; it is a catalyst for Black Photo's rebranding strategy.

There are huge risks in doing something like this. The public likes green and can be counted on to vote for it. Being green is like motherhood: it's something that only a fool criticizes. At the same time, however, the public is nervous about new things. Will it work? How will it affect me? How much will it cost? And, Why can't I just stick with the old way that I know so well? All these questions were exaggerated by the sensitive nature of Black's products, the memories it sells.

Black Photo has increased the degree of risk by doing far more than announcing a new process with a readily understandable name. They hired Martin Shore, a well-known Canadian comic actor, to launch a national advertising campaign on television. Shot against a bright turquoise background, the commercial has Shore holding a fishbowl containing a bright orange goldfish in one hand and a picture of the fish, bowl, and background in the other. The high contrast between the goldfish and the turquoise works well on television and speaks to the obvious crystal clarity. The photographs speak to Black's equally obvious ability to replicate this crystal-clear image, hence "System Crystal." Consumers are assured through this careful balancing of images that whatever Shore says, it will reinforce Black's ability to preserve their memories.

But "Crystal" implies more than image clarity. Black Photo seems to be saying that, like a crystal ball, System Crystal lets us see the past again, certainly, and also into the future. System Crystal is the Black Photo commitment to all our tomorrows as well as to our yesterdays.

Then there is the use of water. Shore's goldfish is named Sparkle, another reference to crystal clarity. Sparkle talks back to Shore, enhancing the comic relief. But the message is clear: Sparkle lives in water and for him to survive, that water has to be very, very clean. If Sparkle doesn't like his watery home, Shore is sure to hear about it. In one commercial Sparkle even gives Shore an eyeful of water. By using System Crystal, Black is saying, we are giving Sparkle a home. And if Sparkle can live in it, we can drink it. This is high-risk advertising. If for any reason someone should discover that Black's water is, well, black, the company would pay a very high price.

In the Black's commercials, Shore urges consumers to "protect the purity of the water" by insisting on System Crystal for their picture developing. So not only are consumers doing themselves a big favor by getting crystal-clear memories, they are doing their friends and neighbors a big favor too by giving Sparkle a home. Meaning, of course, that when they turn the tap for some water to drink, it doesn't come out smelling of developer.

The commercials have been successful enough that Black has taken the next step: it is selling products and services under the System Crystal brand name. The Crystal 48 is a disposable flash camera packaged with processing and two sets of prints. The trick here, of course, is that Black gets the camera back for recycling. And you get System Crystal clear memories. There is also the Crystal Card, a program that offers anyone spending $25.00 or more a 25-percent discount on any purchase for a year.

One can see the way this could go. In a few years, Black Photo could reconstitute itself as System Crystal. Thus, Black has used a "green" process essentially to re-create the company both operationally and in the eyes of its customers. The central identity of the product has been strongly reinforced and a strong bond forged between Black Photo's self-interest and the self-interest of its customers. Played out right, this allows the firm many new opportunities, hopefully profitable ones.

SLAM-DUNKING THE COMPETITION

When Black Photo announced System Crystal, it found itself glorified by environmentalists and vilified by competitors. Instantly, its pollution-free System Crystal process developed broad brand recognition. Meanwhile, the photofinishing trade association denounced Black's action as "unfair competition" that brought unwanted attention to its still-polluting rivals scrambling to catch up. Best of all, Black's new process costs only two cents more a roll than the old,[13] and none of this has been passed on to consumers.

Competitors were caught flat-footed: they were not ready for the pollution-free technology, they were not ready for a powerful new brand, and they certainly were not ready for the storm kicked up by regulators now alerted by Black Photo to the pollution generated by photofinishing. After the System Crystal campaign began, Ontario threatened to force industrial water users to pay the full costs of the water treatment,[14] leaving Black Photo with significant cost advantages over its competition. With zero emissions, Black's water bill goes down, and so does the compliance burden: fewer filings on metering, water recycling, wastewater reclamation.

The not-so-subtle message in Black Photo's TV campaign is that others just can't do what Black Photo can. That message got competitors screaming. The photofinishing industry association's self-serving position (i.e., that discharges of formaldehyde, chlorides, amines, carbonate, and sulfate are no hazard to the public) has been completely undermined.[15] Now that Black Photo has demonstrated that these discharges are unnecessary and that preventing them costs consumers nothing, other photofinishers are taking some hard hits.

Municipalities and governments everywhere from Toronto to Hong Kong can now demand that all photofinishers meet Black's standards. Because few are able to do so, Black Photo has an inherent advantage. Others will have to raise their prices or go out of business. And the genius of Black's branding is that it cannot be emulated simply, *even if you had access to the identical technology*. The company has positioned itself years ahead of its competitors.

Not only was Black Photo's move preemptive, but it also raised questions about the industry that no one else had thought to raise. Many began to complain that Black Photo was being unfair, or that pouring polluted water into the public drains isn't so bad for you. Indeed, Black Photo had struck so hard and so deep that even the biggest players, like Kodak and Fuji Film, began to take notice. Small players—especially storefront minilabs with no thoughts about pollution abatement and none of the muscle to pay for it—were left howling in pain. Worse, the more loudly the competition screamed, the more they reinforced the System Crystal brand.

Thus, Black Photo has raised important barriers in front of any challengers with an eye on its market. Throwing a minilab into a mall won't be so easy anymore. The impact will not be regional, or even national. It will be global. Government environmental protection agencies the world over will have defacto standards to lay down. Hard-pressed regulators in Hong Kong and Singapore, for example, are certain to jump on the bandwagon. If one company can do it in water-sensitive Canada, they will say, so can you all. Building inspectors everywhere will have more stringent measures to impose, and will. No wonder the competition is upset.

These same barriers to entry are also barriers to exit. Companies will not be able to exit the business simply because they find photo-processing unprofitable. System Crystal has raised the question of cleanup. If what has been going on all these years has been dirty, how will suppliers ensure that when they leave they leave the site clean? Whether or not cleanup costs are high, those exiting the market will have to demonstrate through an endless process of proofs and certifications that the site is indeed pristine.

"YOU CAN'T COMPLAIN ABOUT 100 PERCENT"

One thing System Crystal does do is to get the regulators off Black's back for good. As Henkelman says, "You can't complain about one hundred percent." The firm, he reasons, will be in compliance forever. This gives Black a flexibility many firms simply don't have. While Black is ahead of the compliance curve, the others lag far behind. As Black Photo pushes out the limits of the envelope in branding and packaging, the competition remains weighed down with inflexibility and regulatory issues.

Once raised, the question of quality will be foremost. Consumers always want more for less. When told they can have both, they don't walk, they *run,* to the new supplier. Japan broke the stranglehold of Detroit that way in cars, and until Detroit went through the long (twenty-year) process of learning how to offer more for less, the Japanese kept taking away market share with impunity.

THE LESSONS

Waste is a symptom of a problem. Wherever there is waste there are changes that must be made to make the business more efficient, more profitable. Like a canary in a mine shaft, waste alerts us to mistakes we are making in the way we do things. It flags the areas where you have to act. Dealing with waste also forces decision-making away from management and into the front lines.

The lessons we can learn from Black Photo's success are:

Brand your process. Remember that your good name may be even more important than the business you are now in. If your name is destroyed, you have no future. Use branding to build a platform for future opportunities. Black used green to turn a commodity into a premium product while controlling costs and restructuring without spinning out of control.

Use green to reinforce your image. Don't just say something is "green" and expect good things to happen. Use the qualities built into the "green" way of doing things to build on specific benefits your customers value, like speed of delivery, quality of service, commitment to their future needs, lifestyle choices, and so on.

Use green to pull your company together. Waste covers a lot of mistakes. Use waste elimination to reengineer your business from stem to stern. Use waste elimination to pull the whole company together around the people with the experience to make the right decisions, your front-line employees.

Make educated consumers your best customers. On televisions across the United States, Sy Syms and his daughter Marci love to tell their customers, "An educated consumer is our best customer." They are careful not to insult the intelligence of their customers; in a sixty-second TV spot they show their customers *how* to get the best possible deal at Syms. Educate your customers. Don't just tell them you've got a good "green" deal. Show them how to benefit from their relationship with you.

Lead regulators, don't follow them. If you foresee a risk to your business, don't wait for the regulators to clean your clock. Set the pace. Make sure that you meet standards they haven't even thought of yet. Then push these standards. You could never buy the positive advertising that will result.

Improve shareholder value. Your ultimate goal must be to improve shareholder value. Companies that are forever behind the compliance curve face eroding market valuation: investors will go where there are better returns. Companies with good values and strong brand names are better investments.

Kill the competition. Use green processes to preempt the competition, forcing them to dance to your tune. Do this by coopting regulators: set standards so high that regulators adopt them as their own.

INTER-
CONTINENTAL
HOTELS

GUESTS AND SHAREHOLDERS
GET A GOOD NIGHT'S SLEEP

The impact of service industries on the environment may not be obvious. There are no belching smokestacks over your local Mc-Donald's. What's easier to see is the problem of poor productivity in services. While output per man-hour in manufacturing has risen quickly in the last ten years, the service sector has lagged badly. By some measures, productivity has actually declined. Running a hotel is extremely labor intensive: a hotel is nothing but a building and people—lots of them. And hotels have had another big problem: wild overbuilding in the 1980s kept prices down well into the 1990s. The result has been squeezed margins, and a decade of losses for the industry as a whole. For Inter-Continental Hotels and Resorts, part of the solution has been an innovate green strategy. The benefits are lower operating costs, higher productivity, and better service.

M any industries fell on tough times in the early 1990s, but none more so than travel. While airlines lurching from government bailout to reorganization to bankruptcy court and back again made front-page news, the plight of hotels was less publicized. After a decade-long building binge in the 1980s, global demand turned flat after the Gulf War, saddling the industry with overcapacity that forced down prices. The long-term outlook for hotels (and the travel industry generally) remained good, but the long term doesn't matter when you're facing major deficits now.[1]

One of the world's leading luxury hotel chains, Inter-Continental Hotels, did not escape the worldwide economic downturn in the early 1990s. While the rich may always get richer, they were not spending more of their money on hotels. Those staying at Inter-Continental were suddenly looking for value, just like the vacationing family at Holiday Inn. Many Inter-Continental guests are on expense accounts, but their employers cut travel budgets with a vengeance. With higher prices and costs, five-star hotels like the Inter-Continental had farther to fall than many competitors.

Inter-Continental Hotels operates more than 100 hotels in four dozen countries around the world. Founded by Pan American World Airlines in 1946, the first Inter-Continental Hotels were built along Pan Am's routes in Latin America and other parts of the globe. Several years after Pan Am went bankrupt, Inter-Continental was acquired by its present owners, Saison Group, a Japanese hotel, retailing, and property conglomerate. With headquarters in several cities, Inter-Continental, because of its history and the scope of its operations, is truly a "global" company.

If you think you have problems with your business, consider Edward Andrews, manager of Inter-Continental's flagship hotel in Paris in the early 1990s. Operating in one of the most expensive cities in the world, with a heavily unionized workforce, Andrews was charged with making a profit from this property at a time when his industry was in a tailspin. When we asked Andrews what kept him awake at night, his response was immediate: "Demand for hotel rooms is flat into the foreseeable future. Our labor costs are up, and customer expectations are up. We must get by with less."

Most service companies face the same challenge. Until the 1990s, the service sector seemed immune to the ups and downs of economic cycles. No more. Like their manufacturing counterparts, service providers must also reduce costs fast. In a very tight market, the challenge for Edward Andrews was to increase productivity and save money, and to *improve service at the same time.* And let's face it, Paris is not exactly known for the charm of its service workers. Getting bellmen, waiters, and chambermaids to be polite—helpful even—to the long-suffering foreigners who populate the hotels of Paris is no small job for any manager.

Nevertheless, service—an elusive idea at the best of times—is all that distinguishes Inter-Continental from its innumerable competitors. Any effort to reduce costs that also hurt service would come back to haunt the company many times over. Furthermore, to attract the frequent international business travelers who are its best customers, Inter-Continental must maintain high and predictable service standards across many countries and highly diverse cultures.

A key part of the solution for Inter-Continental Hotels was its environmental program, the most aggressive in the industry. Smart environmental action has improved quality by empowering employees to make continuous service improvements, and reduced costs by eliminating activities the hotel's guests do not demand.

Inter-Continental set high environmental standards as a catalyst for change, tackling the costs-service dilemma head-on. Environmental dividends result from such programs—less energy used, less solid waste dumped, less exposure to toxins, less Freon and other harmful gases released into the atmosphere—but these are gravy. The real benefit is an improved bottom line. For Edward Andrews, the hotel's environmental strategy was a way to redesign management, empower lower-level staff, and gain a competitive edge over his rivals by offering better customer service than any other hotel in Paris. If you can crack French culture, you're on to something.

STAYING FOCUSED ON YOUR MISSION

Half-baked ideas about recycling Coca-Cola cans and turning off lights have little to do with the real problems facing hotel managers, or decision-makers in any industry for that matter. Inter-Continental Hotels' corporate mission, for example, is "to become the leading global hospitality and travel group."[2] In a down market, Inter-Continental could expand only by taking share away from its competitors, not by riding the growth curve. To do so management had to be focused and tough-minded.

There's nothing half-baked about Inter-Continental's environmental initiative. Phase One, started in 1991, focused on waste and pollution. Phase Two, launched in 1992, zeroed in on energy management. Armed with a 200-page manual and a 134-point checklist, one manager at each hotel led the charge. To show that it meant business, the company tied the program to monetary incentives, including bonuses, for compliance. Crews from headquarters audit the performance of each hotel annually. And while objectives were set from above, managers in the field had to figure out the most cost-effective way of executing the plan.[3]

For Andrews, the guidance from headquarters was essential. Like most countries, including the United States, France places the heaviest burden of environment legislation on factories, the traditional source of pollution. Service companies, including hotels, face little regulation. France's *Ecoembalmage* laws require recycling of some product packaging, affecting those at Inter-Continental Hotels like everyone else. But that's about it. We asked Andrews what kind of environmental standards he had to meet in France. The reply: "Absolutely none. We are under no pressure from the government of France. They have some programs, but there is no pressure on us, no regulations or government burden." The City of Paris doesn't make any demands? "Nothing." He went on, "We finally got the city to accept our minibar bottles for recycling—we generate 100,000 a year—but this was a result of our request to the City of Paris, not their pressure on us."

Andrews's counterparts in Germany get plenty of direction from the government, where recycling requirements are unusually intense. Reinhold Faller, manager of the Inter-Continental Hotel in Hamburg, explained, "First, we have our packaging law. We have deposits on plastic bottles of fifty pfennigs [about 30 cents] and on glass of thirty pfennigs [about 20 cents] for one-way bottles, so we are reintroducing reusable bottles. Our suppliers are pushing this too for water and soda bottles. Now eighty percent of our bottles are reusable, up from forty-five percent when we started. Only beer and wine bottles are left." And that's just the beginning, according to Faller. "We have to separate garbage into many containers. Hazardous waste handling is very strict compared to France and the U.K. For example, we have to separate fluorescent bulbs and batteries; dry-cleaning fluid; paint, paintbrushes—even clothes with paint on them." In Hamburg, the hotel installed a device that sucks up compostable waste from the kitchens and puts it into a special container that is collected by a composting firm.

Inter-Continental began its program voluntarily. In most places, there is little or no government pressure to reduce hotel waste. But that may be changing. Clearly in Germany recycling requirements are already extremely onerous. Inter-Continental Hotels has decided to operate to the "highest common denominator," exceeding even German standards everywhere in the world. In future, this company will have nothing to worry about from tougher regulations. Indeed, Inter-Continental welcomes them. Why not? They make life tougher for the competition.

THE BEST IDEAS REDUCE COSTS

Inter-Continental set up environmental committees at each of its hotels to review virtually every aspect of its operations. This forced the hotel to rethink, and in many cases, redefine, what "service" means to a hotel guest. Where others might hire outside consultants or send in teams of heavies from headquarters, Inter-Continental charged local employees to look at every procedure, to tally the environmental impact of each activity.

The first step, according to Edward Andrews, was to organize teams of employees "to go through the hotel and identify *every* item." They identified what could be recycled, instead of thrown out; ways to use recycled materials instead of new ones; more benign materials, like all-natural cleaning fluids, that could be substituted for toxic ones. These kinds of changes might make them feel good about themselves at Inter-Continental, but what about the bottom line?

Direct-costs savings from the Inter-Continental environmental program have been significant. There are many examples:[4]

- In Sydney, Australia, energy savings during the first twelve months totaled A$230,000 ($175,000) as a result of thirty-one changes, mostly at modest cost, like shower-flow restrictors and low-power fluorescent lights.
- In New Orleans, recycling reduced costs by $79,000 in the first year through lower disposal fees, sale of recyclable material, and recovery of supplies like cutlery, plates, and sheets that were thrown out by mistake.
- In London, energy bills were cut by £28,000 ($45,000) in the first year by new air-conditioning controls, with a payback in less than four years.
- In Chicago, annual electric bills were cut by $20,000 by replacing forty-five-watt incandescent bulbs with fifteen-watt fluorescent ones.
- In Hanover, Germany, more efficient ovens and dishwashers in the kitchen saved $13,560 in one year, and will pay for themselves in less than three years.
- In North America at all ten hotels, the switch to environmentally correct bath amenities, like vegetable-based soaps in packages made from recycled soda bottles, saves $300,000 per year.

Sometimes the savings are more symbolic than real. In Paris, the hotel cut office-paper use in half through two-sided copying. Also the hotel gets a credit from the City of Paris for recycling its bottles, which it donates to a cancer-research charity. In Hamburg, used soap is collected and sent to Russia, where such consumer goods are in short supply. In Germany, where the environmental laws are very strict, the hotel must make investments that do not always pay. Separating paint cans, paintbrushes, and clothes with paint on them into three piles is probably pointless.

The biggest savings are for energy, where the connection to environmental performance is direct. Inter-Continental Hotels spends some $50 million per year on energy, and saved over $1 million in the first year of its environmental program.[5] At one London hotel, the energy budget equals revenues from 25,000 room-nights, so this is a big area. In Miami, a $12,000 investment in wiring changes lowered energy consumption by 6 percent, representing some $50,000 per year. These and other savings played an important role in turning around Inter-Continental's Miami property.[6]

Sometimes improvements are cheap and simple, sometimes expensive and high-tech. Changes in attitude can be important. Suzanne Gryner, another manager in Paris, told us, "People around here are trying to save energy . . . habits are changing." In Yokohama, the heat and lights in each room stay off until the key goes into the door. An engineer in Hamburg diverted clean hot water coming out of the hotel's heating and air-conditioning cooling tower for reuse doing laundry. With this hot water, which was previously wasted, the hotel reduced the use of heated fresh water for laundering by 60 to 70 percent. "That's real money," a manager at Hamburg explained to us.

An older hotel like the Inter-Continental in Paris can save 50 percent of its energy bill by updating its mechanical systems. In a city of old hotels like Paris, this kind of investment can give Inter-Continental an enormous cost advantage. Of course, replacing heating and cooling systems is not cheap. Andrews put off implementing the second phase of the Inter-Continental environmental program, which deals with energy savings, because he operates in a 115-year-old building. Instead, management decided to consider a major renovation, which would include updated mechanicals. Energy savings will help pay the freight. This top-to-bottom renovation planned for Paris, a four-year project, will also reduce the consumption of water, an expensive commodity in that city.

Recycling can reduce trash bills: in North America, the chain reduced solid-waste handling costs by 30 percent.[7] But sorting can increase labor costs, too. At the Paris Inter-Continental, they sort trash into twenty containers; even broken glasses are handled separately. The hotel negotiated with its cleaning company to do the sorting at no extra cost. Since times were tough, the hotel cleaners were willing to take on this extra job. Like most of the managers we talked to, however, Andrews did not find his suppliers cooperative as a rule. To implement their environmental initiatives, leaders find themselves twisting arms.

Energy savings can have a visible effect on the bottom line, but require capital outlays. Often, however, the payback can be extremely fast, especially in countries where energy costs are high. Solid-waste reduction can be important when activities are eliminated, but the value of recycling alone is largely symbolic. Unless the sources of trash are eliminated, recycling can increase labor costs more than it lowers disposal fees. And rising labor costs are already the hotel's biggest problem. As with all service industries, hotels find it hard to control wage bills. Improving the productivity of labor is difficult.

Edward Andrews told us his hotel probably has the highest labor costs in the world. He could not afford to have a half dozen highly paid, unionized workers separating wine bottles from Coke cans in the basement. He needed to cut costs; to do so he could not dodge the thorny question of labor productivity. How do you get people to work harder and keep smiling at the same time? Hotel guests will not accept surly service, especially not in a luxury hotel like the Inter-Continental.

EXCEEDING CUSTOMER EXPECTATIONS

The entrance to the Inter-Continental Hotel in Paris is just off Rue de Rivoli at the magnificent Place Vendôme, one of the most exclusive addresses in the world. This is the city of light at its best: across the street is the Louvre museum; down the block, the Tuileries Gardens; and beyond, the broad Champs-Élysées. Opened in 1878, the hotel is large by Paris standards, with 450 rooms, running a full city block. An elegant row of expensive shops faces the hotel's historical neighbors from underneath a two-story arcade. Inside, a large, dramatic courtyard brings natural light to the hotel's sumptuous interior.

When a guest strolls into this setting, he expects something special. Management's biggest challenge is to meet these expectations—exceeding them is extraordinarily difficult. The opportunities for coming up short are innumerable. One small slip and a guest may depart, never to return.

In a five-star hotel like the Inter-Continental in Paris, management cannot make changes that affect service without courting disaster. Hectoring guests to turn off lights, keep showers short, and recycle their champagne bottles will not play. If guests are not happy with environmental initiatives (particularly if they are inconvenient, self-serving, or both), they might not return to the Paris hotel, or any other Inter-Continental property. However, if they are to have a real effect on costs and on the environment, changes must inevitably affect the hotel's guests. Unlike many businesses, you can't hide what goes on in a hotel. Management is exoskeletal; the customer is immersed in the hotel's operations. George Orwell's description of Paris Hotels in *Down and Out in Paris and London* notwithstanding, there is very little that guests do not see, and all their experiences must be positive. Especially when demand is flat and prices are high.

While there is lots of downside risk to trying new ideas, like Inter-Continental's environmental initiative, the upside potential is limited. Perhaps some customers will be drawn to the hotel if it is perceived as "green." During the 1992 political convention in New York for the Democratic Party, for example, the Clinton-Gore entourage stayed at the Inter-Continental Hotel because its green credentials appealed to Al Gore, later vice president of the United States and a well-known environmentalist.[8] But generally, in the hotel business, as in most others, the value of green marketing is limited. In France, Andrews told us, Inter-Continental must be careful with the "green" claims since there is a Green Party and environmental discussions there quickly take on political overtones. The manager of the Inter-Continental in Hamburg told us that the only thing that sells is better service, saying, "This is a luxury hotel. We always worry about what the customer perceives. The environmental marketing is secondary."

With fears of rocking the service boat, management was nervous about making too many environmental changes. There was even some concern about pestering guests with too many questions about what they wanted. Nevertheless, Inter-Continental came to the conclusion that they had to go forward.

In the bathroom, a guest at the Hamburg Inter-Continental finds the following note on the sink:

> *Dear Guest,*
> *Literally, tons of towels are washed daily in hotels all over the world, and tons of washing chemicals are used in the process, polluting our water supply.*
> *Please decide:*
> *Towels in the bath tub means: please exchange.*
> *Towels on the rack means: I will be using them again.*
> *—for the sake of our environment*

Reinhold Faller told us that they received no negative comments regarding this note, and that in fact many guests are happy to reuse their towels. He added, "Our worry was that guests would think, 'I'm paying all this money and so I want fresh towels every morning and evening.' Before it was ridiculous that we changed them so often; at home we don't do this, we use towels for a few days." After agonizing over the wording for the note, they took the plunge.

This bridge successfully crossed, the next challenge was bathroom amenities. As one manager explained, "Our customers want these changes. They pay two hundred to four hundred dollars per night here, and they see us throwing out soap and shampoo. They say to themselves, 'No wonder we pay so much.' I think that we will try pumps on the wall for soap and shampoo; then the customers can have as much as they want without throwing all this stuff away." In a different city, another Inter-Continental manager said, "Doesn't it just drive you crazy when you spend two hundred to three hundred dollars a night and you use a tiny bit of soap or shampoo and they throw it out? You feel that you are paying all this money and these people are wasting it." The next frontier: asking guests whether they want the bedsheets changed every night.

These minor changes may seem trivial, but they illustrate the obsession with service in a luxury hotel. Complexity increases with the cost of a room stay. There are more elements to the "customer experience," and customers expect more.

In luxury hotels, there is much that can go wrong. This is how these hotels differentiate themselves. When you pay fifty dollars to stay at a cheap hotel, you know full well that there is only so much they can do or that it is wise to ask them to do. Luxury hotels love to regale their guests with stories of service above and beyond the call of duty. One manager told us, "I have even heard stories of hoteliers at this level taking customers shopping for the day. I have had them manage entire travel itineraries and know that they offer discreet services of a personal kind to the most precise specification." As a result, luxury hotels are doubly exposed. So much is expected and so much can fall through the cracks. Edward Andrews referred to the "complex" experience at "complex" hotels like his.

Ironically, some budget hotel chains are raising the service stakes. Hampton Inn has a 100 percent satisfaction guarantee: any guests who have problems that are not resolved to their satisfaction by the time they leave get one night's stay free. Everybody—even the post office—offers some kind of "satisfaction guarantee." At Hampton Inn, however, this is not an empty offer. Every hotel employee—bellhop, chambermaid, front-desk clerk, or manager—is authorized "to take whatever action is necessary to keep the customer satisfied." At a Hampton Inn one of us visited (for fifty dollars per night), there was a printed note near the telephone with the office and home number of the manager, to be called if there were any problems whatsoever, at any time, day or night. We've never seen that kind of statement at any other hotel, at any price.

We talked with one frequent traveler, the president of a mortgage bank who can afford to stay at any hotel he wants. Instead, he goes to Hampton Inn, more than 100 times at the latest count. He told us, "Once in a while I'll stay at the Hyatt if I get a fifty-percent-off coupon, but frankly it's still not worth it. Hampton is better. I even stay there when I go on vacation." That's quite a testimonial—and quite a threat to Inter-Continental Hotels.

We asked Edward Andrews if this challenge concerned him. "Yes," he replied, "but the more expensive you are the harder it is to do. It's harder here than at Hampton Inn to meet the customer's expectations; a more expensive hotel like this has more layers, more departments. We are more complex, because we have so many more services." After initial jitters about pushing the environmental message, Andrews realized that the environmental initiative could be used as a tool to push up service levels.

FRONT-LINE EMPLOYEES MAKE IT HAPPEN

At more than 100 locations around the world, Inter-Continental must provide a high and predictable level of customer service. But if customers wanted each hotel stay to be the same, they would go somewhere else. While some are new, many Inter-Continental Hotels are unique landmarks, like the Willard Hotel in Washington, D.C., where President Grant strolled from time to time for an after-dinner cigar. When guests walk through the doors of the

Inter-Continental Hotel in Paris, they want a high level of service, and a uniquely Parisian experience.

Andrews told us, "I've been in some of the best hotels in the world, and none are perfect; sooner or later something goes wrong. I've held my breath for three days, but something always goes wrong. The trick is how you respond to the problem, how you make sure the customer leaves happy despite the problem. . . . If the problem is handled well, they feel even better than if there had been no problem." This is how customers are made to feel at the Inter-Continental in Paris.[9]

The successful hotel—the successful business—must meet customer expectations. But a hotel stay is an intangible experience. Solutions cannot be prescribed from headquarters, even if the level of service can. If expectations are high, they can only be met by front-line employees with great latitude for decision-making. Inter-Continental Hotels cannot produce a manual like McDonald's that results in a uniform level of service everywhere; that's simply not the nature of a hotel stay at a place like the Grand Hotel in Paris.

To make sure that guests don't go away dissatisfied, Inter-Continental must trust its employees with sufficient authority to satisfy customer demands quickly. Employees must find a way to put things right without involving managers in time-consuming solutions. Fixing problems means that employees must have the power to take corrective action on the spot, using their own initiative. As Andrews put it, "If you want to improve service in a hotel like this, you have to start with the employees; how the employees treat the guests determines the level of service, not what management decides. . . . If you want to affect the guest experience, you must go after the hearts and minds of the employees."

The Inter-Continental environmental program turned out to be an effective way to empower employees. While objectives were set centrally, the details were left to local hotel managers. In Paris, they formed teams of front-line employees to review every aspect of the hotel's operations. Every employee was assigned to a committee that met every week or two; each person did research on one environmental subject. Thousands of hours were spent on these reviews. Concern about the environment, shared by almost everyone, galvanized employees in an unprecedented way.

Employee empowerment is the key to service-industry productivity. In manufacturing, every motion every worker makes can be choreographed for maximum efficiency. And while many manufacturers now get more out of their workers by giving them greater command over the production line, there is a degree of control over the entire process that cannot be replicated in the service sector. The person at the front desk of a hotel cannot refer to the manager or a manual that looks like a phone book every time a problem arises. Delays only infuriate customers.

At the same time, service employees with control over their work can ask the most important question of all: Why do we do this? This question is integral to Inter-Continental Hotels' environmental plans; every employee in every hotel was asked to review everything they do. The opportunity for knowledgeable, motivated front-line employees to eliminate unnecessary activities is enormous. This was the very mandate given to the workers in Paris and elsewhere. It is also the key to service-industry productivity.

MAINSTREAMING ENVIRONMENTAL MANAGEMENT

At Inter-Continental Hotels, there is no separate staff organization for environmental affairs. Rather, it involves all employees and is the ultimate responsibility of line managers in the field. At each hotel, one manager, who has other responsibilities, is the point-man for the environment. Performance of all senior managers is measured against six goals, of which one relates to the environment.

When the program was launched in 1991, there was one coordinator at Inter-Continental's corporate office in London, an assistant to the CEO. Subsequently, all authority was dispersed throughout the organization. Only one key function was not devolved to individual hotels: keeping score. A SWAT team from headquarters comes through on a surprise visit once a year to check on progress involving environmental objectives. Each hotel is given a rating, which is used to compute environmental bonuses. The same procedures are used to track service quality. In the first two years after the program started, 62 percent of Inter-Continental's environmental directives had been met worldwide. In Paris, the hotel reached 94 percent. Periodically, managers from around the world meet to review Inter-Continental's environmental progress, and to set new goals for the future. When we spoke to Edward Andrews, a weeklong meeting had recently been held at his hotel.

There are no separate budgets for environmental projects at Inter-Continental Hotels. Any environmental plans must be squared with mainstream objectives. While centrally funded schemes can lead to fast results, high-profile, separate budgets are prime targets for cuts when conditions change or key managers leave. Mainstream activities, particularly those that pay their own way, produce better results in the long term.

At Inter-Continental, any environmental investment has to make sense financially. Even more important, changes cannot hurt service. For example, in Paris, they had a look at the laundry items, like bags and shirt boards, but the cost of going to recycled substitutes was too high. As Reinhold Faller, the manager in Hamburg, put it, "We have to be careful that we don't run away with the idea; we have to do what's possible."

"NOT EVERYBODY WANTS TO BE EMPOWERED"

Designing a program that can be implemented in dozens of countries at the same time is not easy. In France, hotel employees are highly educated; they can be retrained and expected to follow procedures. In many countries, including the United States, hotel workers may be illiterate.

Employees around the world have different ideas about hierarchy and what "empowerment" means. Not everyone wants to be empowered. France, for example, is a hierarchical society, nowhere more so than in its hotels and restaurants. This is the culture that produced the great nineteenth-century chef Georges-Auguste Escoffier. With Escoffier's *brigade de cuisine* system for large restaurants, everyone from the highest chef to lowest potato peeler has an inflexibly defined role. No initiative asked, none given. The French like things done this way. It's traditional. It's comfortable and reassuring. Most important, it's French.

Andrews's job is to undo this frame of mind. For him, success depends on initiative. As one manager in Paris explained to us about empowerment, "Maybe the French will like this in fifteen or twenty years. I'm trying to push down decision-making, but they think, 'This guy is not doing his job.' " There is little of the familiarity in the workplace that exists, for example, in the United States.

Like the Inter-Continental in Paris, any company with a heavily unionized workforce is likely to encounter resistance to empowerment, which is, after all, a way to get more work out of employees. Empowerment can also cut the union out of "collective" decision-making and supplant its monopoly on relations with management. Never mind that it makes jobs more interesting, and ultimately better paid.

Empowerment upsets the order of things, which is why companies do it, of course. In Paris, Inter-Continental found that its environment program allowed the hotel to change France's rigid stratification of job functions without threatening labor. Thus, they were able to break down some of the barriers between management and labor, bringing more decentralization and flexibility to bear on the customer's experience at the hotel. Environmental initiatives, which don't have the appearance of management bias, met with less resistance from employees than the hotel's other customer-service and quality programs. Workers get defensive about service: "Wasn't our service good enough in the past?" By contrast, everybody knows there is room for improvement on the environment. Greening the hotel can also play to the employees' enlightened self-interest. Some changes made life easier for employees, for example, like switching to nontoxic cleaning products. An early priority was to eliminate harsh chemicals, especially in the laundry, where staff had to wear special clothes to protect themselves.

A further challenge to administering any new management idea is cynicism. If the environment is the latest *strategy du jour,* employees will balk. At the first staff meeting to implement the plan in Paris, some fifty people turned up. They were skeptical; they all had other priorities. As Edward Andrews put it, "When we had the first meeting with the department heads, they asked me, 'Is this a one-time deal?' They were concerned that this was just another management initiative."

Ultimately Inter-Continental convinced its employees that it was serious: the program withstood the test of time, producing tangible benefits. Despite changes in the executive suite, a poor economy, and tight budgets, the program survived. It was not the passing fancy of a long-gone CEO.

In Paris in particular, Inter-Continental was dealing with smart people who would have seen right through any cynical publicity ploys. Nevertheless, a strong team spirit developed at the hotel, which is now an environmental leader in France. Many changes were recommended by employees, like the one asking guests if they need their towels changed. Chambermaids recommended switching to products made with recycled materials, from toilet paper to air-conditioner filters. These ideas sound small, but this ongoing, incremental progress the Japanese call *kaizen* is what makes for leadership in any industry. In a labor-intensive service business like hotels, big improvements are rare. Trained, motivated employees who keep their eyes open can make continuous improvement an everyday occurrence.

Identifying these small changes is the essence of Andrews's job. Like other Inter-Continental managers, he lives in his hotel, witnessing for himself every day the experience of his guests. As he put it, "I see what needs changing." He tells his managers to ride the elevators for fifteen minutes a day to hear what the customers are talking about. Andrews added, "We don't have blockbuster improvements in service; you have to like detail to do this job well."

THE LESSONS

Edward Andrews was surprised that we found so much about Inter-Continental's environmental program interesting. "Anyone could make these changes," he observed. Anyone could, but most don't. This isn't rocket science. It's about saving money the old-fashioned way: by reducing waste one dollar at a time. It's about reexamining and rethinking every aspect of your business from the *customer's* point of view. There are several lessons here:

Discover ideas that pay. Virtually every change that Inter-Continental Hotels has made saves money directly. Indirectly, service has been improved; while the judicious application of technology, like new air-conditioning systems, makes sense, the real benefits come from simplified ways of operating.

Pinch pennies. Small, seemingly inconsequential improvements can add up, particularly when many customers are served. In fast-growing markets, lots of problems can be swept under the rug; in slow-growth, competitive ones, success lies in the details.

Keep environmental programs mainstream. Reporting and budgeting must be integral parts of operations, not isolated staff functions. If the environment is a staff responsibility alone, it will fail; it must be a line activity. Environmental programs work only if responsibility for them is dispersed throughout all departments; otherwise, today's bright idea is tomorrow's budget cut.

Trust your employees. By turning over implementation of its environmental program to front-line employees, Inter-Continental tapped a deep well of ideas. As a bonus, this empowerment of workers improved customer service.

Ask, Why are we doing this? Rethink service from the customer's point of view. In all service industries, the productivity of labor is a problem; many activities can be eliminated, but only with the customer's idea of service in mind. Less activity means less waste means less environmental damage.

Set high standards. Even if the government regulation is not there, reaching for environmental goals voluntarily can help channel employee enthusiasm in a profitable direction.

Make it real. Management commitment over many years is necessary to make any environmental program pay.

BUENA VISTA WINERY TAKES THE NEXT STEP

GRAPES GROWN ORGANICALLY

No business can succeed without clear focus. Companies must ask themselves, What is it that we do best? What do our customers value about us most? Answer these questions, and you have identified those activities where you truly add value—in other words, where you can make the most money. While your competitors try to be all things to all people, you must concentrate on one activity where all your energies can be brought to bear. But isolating those core activities is not always easy. Buena Vista, California's oldest premium winery, used organic farming methods as a catalyst to refocus its business for growth and profit.

According to some eighteenth-century French philosophers, manufacturing (to say nothing of trade and finance) added little to the wealth of nations; manufacturers were simply parasites living off the surpluses generated by farming. Even Adam Smith, the first modern economist, conceded to his French contemporaries that "farmers and country laborers, indeed, over and above the stock which maintains and employs them, reproduce annually a neat produce, a free rent to the landlord . . . [their labor] is certainly more productive than that of merchants, artificers and manufacturers."[1]

Today we believe that wealth is generated on and off the land. Nevertheless, agriculture remains one of the largest and most productive industries in the world (a tiny proportion of Americans can feed the whole country and a good part of the rest of the world). One of the most successful agricultural activities of the past generation has been wine-making.

As the French have known for some time, long before they formulated any economic theories, wine-making may be the ultimate business, a kind of alchemy that turns twenty-five cents' worth of grapes into twenty-five dollars' worth of wine. And of course, the French are not alone in believing that good wine cannot be valued in financial terms only. Agriculture is about survival at one level, and good living is survival at another. As an industry, farming is in direct contact with the earth—for good or bad—in a way that is unlike any other. Similarly, the farmer's land is literally his biggest asset. For this asset to show a return, it must be properly maintained. The farmer must in every sense be a steward of his land. Organic farming is one way for the farmer to enhance the value of his biggest asset. But many doubt the commercial potential of organic farming, particularly for large agribusinesses.

Like that other great value-adding activity, which turns sand into semiconductors, the wine industry in the United States is centered in northern California. Less than an hour from downtown San Francisco, across the Golden Gate Bridge, through the suburban sprawl of Marin County, lies California's rich wine country, home to hundreds of vineyards, both large and small. At the southernmost edge of the Sonoma and Napa valleys, on San Pablo Bay directly across from San Francisco, visitors can find the Carneros region, one of California's most fertile grape-growing districts.

Buena Vista Winery, the largest estate winery in Carneros, is located at the end of a long, dusty dirt road, about ten miles from the town of Sonoma. Lined with eucalyptus trees, the road follows the Southern Pacific Railroad tracks along the edge of the low-lying marshland of San Pablo Bay. To the west, a distant ridge is visible; to the east, along the road are sprawling ranches lined with painted white fences that recall the area's sheep-farming past. Hawks slowly circle high above the parched brown land, held aloft by the gentle breezes off the bay.

A few miles on, the neat, well-tended rows of grapevines begin. Each plant is carefully attached to a metal stake; thin, black PCV water lines tied with white ribbons snake between the endless rows of vines. Here and there windmills slowly turn, bringing water to the surface, allowing the vines to defy nature by thriving in earth that has suffered half a decade of drought.

Off to the east, another dusty dirt road leads through the vineyards into the Buena Vista Winery. On one side of a small parking area is an old white clapboard farmhouse surrounded by a dense thicket of trees. On the other sits a cluster of low-lying buildings: the offices, winery, and warehouses of Buena Vista. With brown cedar-shake roofs and earth-tone stucco walls, these buildings are constructed in the mission style (perhaps more "nouveau" mission style), which is well suited to this arid region first developed by the Spanish centuries ago. The office buildings are beautifully landscaped; the nearby farm buildings are well maintained and freshly painted in beige with green trim. There is no one in sight. Amid a half dozen cars, a lone dog barks.

The picture is serene, but the business is serious. Founded in 1857, Buena Vista in its current, prosperous incarnation dates from 1979, when the winery was acquired by the Moller-Rackes, a German wine-making family. Moved in 1984 from the edge of Sonoma to this 1,000-acre estate in Carneros, Buena Vista grows its grapes employing organic methods. Strictly defined by the California Certified Organic Farmers, an independent regulatory group, the rigorous certification process began here in 1989.[2] For Buena Vista, 1992 was the first vintage year the winery could label some of its wines "grown organically."

While one of the most advanced, Buena Vista is by no means the only winery with organically certified vineyards. Only 1 or 2 percent of the wine grapes in California are organically grown, but more than 10 percent of vineyards have some of their acreage organically certified.[3] A few years ago, industry giant Gallo, for example, began experimenting with organic methods on thousands of acres of its vineyards.[4] Medium-sized Fetzer Vineyards had some 500 of its 3,000 acres organically certified when it was acquired in 1992 by Brown-Forman Corporation (maker of Jack Daniel's whiskey).[5] And there are numerous small wineries that specialize in organic wines.

KEEPING YOUR EYES ON THE BALL

Organic methods helped Buena Vista focus on its true mission: to grow good grapes that make good wines. And focused you'd better be to survive in the wine business. There's a popular image of wineries as an expensive pastime for entrepreneurs from nearby Silicon Valley looking for a gentrified way to spend their untold millions. For all its airs, however, wine-making is a cutthroat industry with a long list of problems.

In many ways, wine-making suffered the same fate as personal computers in the late 1980s and early 1990s. After a booming decade, demand started to slack off. Health-conscious Americans were drinking less. In the United States, per capita wine consumption fell by about 10 percent between 1988 and 1993,[6] with no end in sight. Demand measured in dollars continued to grow, however, because wine drinkers switched from cheap "jug" wines to more expensive varietals. This move upmarket saved many American wineries, including Gallo, the world's largest wine producer, which has successfully repositioned itself as a quality leader. Gallo's top-of-the-line Cabernet Sauvignon commands $60 a bottle.[7]

At the same time, a host of new competitors rushed in to get their share of the action. Cheap imports from Australia and Chile began to pour into U.S. wine stores. Many French and other European wineries with deep pockets staked out their claims in northern California, joined by those Silicon Valley tycoons looking for ways to stay busy when they retired. To make matters worse, the best grape-growing areas suffered years of drought. Then the region was rocked by two grapevine diseases that forced the replanting of thousands of acres, a process that will continue until every grapevine in northern California is replaced.[8] Not much room under these circumstances for sloppy management.

It was under such a cloud that Jill Davis, the winemaker at Buena Vista, proposed to go organic. Her idea was to improve vineyard management by going back to basics. As one Buena Vista manager put it, "There's an old saying in the wine business that fine wines start in the vineyards. Good grapes make for good wines. By going organic, we have to focus on the grapes; it makes you a better manager of your vineyards. We can focus more on the vineyards." This change forced Buena Vista to ask, What is it that we do? The answer, deceptively simple, is, Grow grapes for wine.

When the process began in 1989, Buena Vista could not make a compelling business case to management for the change. The company could not point to clear financial benefits, better wine, or even marketing advantages. But Davis did know that organic methods require farmers to pay more attention to their crops and land.

To maximize leverage with customers, successful companies zero in on what they do best. The *Queen Elizabeth II* can't turn on a dime, and neither can any large organization with too much on its plate. Companies without clear focus are frequently driven by the internal political needs of their organization, not by the all-important needs of customers.

Focused companies are often smaller than their less flexible competitors. As the people in Silicon Valley know, the most profitable computer competitors are ones with less than $5 billion in annual sales, making one type of product like disk drives or PC software. Far-flung giants like Fujitsu at $20 billion and IBM at $60 billion are jacks-of-all-trades and masters of none. In the computer industry, focus, not size, is the key to success. Winemaking is no different.

What do we do best? is not an easy question for any business to answer. And customers will invariably have a different answer from managers. Why do customers buy? It sounds silly, but most companies don't have the faintest idea. Knowing what customers value about a firm is the flip side of knowing what customers want. To sell their products, managers must know what customers need. But if they don't know what customers value about them, they will find themselves constantly missing the mark in advertising, new-product development, and strategic direction. Managers who don't know what customers value about them won't know where to focus their energy. Furthermore, what a company does best is also where it makes its highest return. The bean counters may be skeptical at first, but they will like the results. They did at Buena Vista.

LEADING FROM THE FRONT

A. Racke Co., founded in 1855, is an old-line, family-owned German firm that is one of Europe's leading wine and spirits merchants. When Jill Davis proposed to take Buena Vista organic, Racke welcomed her request. In fact, the owners, who believe in organic farming as part of their philosophy, made it a priority.

When Racke took over Buena Vista in 1979, the whole operation was a shambles. Marcus Moller-Racke became chairman of the vineyard in 1982, and in that same year hired Jill Davis as an assistant winemaker. A graduate of the University of California at Davis, the training ground for some of the world's best winemakers, Davis worked at Beringer Vineyards for several years before joining Buena Vista. Three months after she was hired, at the age of twenty-seven, she was made head winemaker. Since then, she has forged a reputation for herself as one of the industry's young stars, winning many awards for the quality of Buena Vista's wines.

Like Jill Davis, Mary Hall has had a stellar rise at Buena Vista. In 1985, two years after she graduated from California State University with a B.S. in Microbiology, she jointed the vineyard as quality control manager. By 1989, she was vineyard manager, directing the conversion to organic farming at Buena Vista.

Management—from the Moller-Rackes at headquarters in Germany to Mary Hall in the vineyards in Carneros—led the switch to organic at Buena Vista. Commitment right from the top down through every level of management helped make this change work. What does not work is the "Gamelin system" of issuing environmental directives from the head office. Field Marshal Gamelin will forever be famous for resisting the German invasion of France in 1940 from the comfort of GHQ near Paris, many hours from the front. Every morning he methodically sent orders by courier to his commanders in the field, who usually received them after they had been overrun. Few recognize, as Buena Vista has, the Green Wave as an opportunity to make sure they don't suffer the same fate that befell France a few decades ago.

When Davis and her team first considered going organic, their bet was by no means a certain one. Traditional accounting and forecasting methods are ill suited to measuring the benefits of process changes. They require a leap of faith by leaders willing to take risks. The Buena Vista team gambled and made the switch on faith. They could not make a dollars-and-cents business case on a computer spreadsheet, but they were confident that it would pay in the long run. Having commitment to this idea at the top, as well as owners with a long-term view, made such a bet possible.

CASH ON THE BARRELHEAD

In many ways, vineyards are well suited to organic farming. Generally, winemakers do not need to worry about the appearance of their grapes. Some fruit, like peaches and table grapes, must look perfect or consumers won't buy them. And compared to other fruit, like pears and apples, grapes have relatively few insect predators. Consequently, growing wine grapes is generally less chemical intensive than other kinds of farming. Nevertheless, Buena

Vista, like other vineyards, used chemicals to deal with a number of problems.

Mold and mildew can spoil grapes while they still are on the vine. To eliminate fungicides, Mary Hall and her vineyard crew changed how they pruned and trellised their plants, and they adjusted the spacing between rows, to allow air to circulate better. By trimming back the vine leaves, they let the wind dry their grapes (and even blow off some insects). Fortunately, the Carneros region, where Buena Vista is located, is well suited to organic farming methods. There are good breezes, which minimizes mildew problems. The shallow clay soil cannot support large-leaf vines that attract many bugs. Other grape-growing regions of California like the San Joaquin Valley and the north coast, have more problems with pests and mold.

Then Buena Vista tried to eliminate pesticides. First, they introduced ladybugs to counter some predators. Then they planted cover crops (like clover, oats, and peas) between the vine rows. These harbor the predator insects that eat the bugs that attack the grapes. Ground covers also add nutrients and keep down weeds, reducing the need for fertilizer and herbicides. Elsewhere in the vineyard, natural landscaping kept undesirable bugs down. A compost mixture of pomace (what's left of the grapes after the juice has been squeezed out) and manure replaced synthetic fertilizer.[9] When necessary, soap-and-water mixtures were used to discourage pests.

All this sounds pretty simple, but organic methods vastly increase labor costs. By the estimate of one vineyard, growing grapes organically costs as much as three times as chemical practices do.[10] At another, hoeing weeds costs two-thirds more per acre than spraying them with herbicides.[11] At Buena Vista, there was more mowing, pruning, and tending the vines, all labor-intensive activities. Before, they just sprayed everything with herbicides and fungicides once a week or once a month. Now daily or weekly tending is necessary.

Other costs rose as well. The vineyard had to purchase new equipment, like tillers and cover-crop seeders.[12] And the cost of organic certification itself is high. Detailed records must be kept, and the certification organization charges a fee and a commission on the value of the crop.[13] Nevertheless, at Buena Vista they concluded that these costs were manageable and were overshadowed by other considerations, like the price per ton of grapes in Carneros, the highest in California. Savings on chemical purchases are large and growing, since government regulation of pesticides has increased their costs dramatically over the past decade. Still, these savings are not enough to offset the increase in labor costs. "So," we asked one Buena Vista manager, "how do you preserve your margins? This is a competitive business." The response: "We have a three- to four-year lead on this, so we can fold it into the overall price. In the long term, we hope to break even."

A number of winemakers believe they can keep their costs competitive while going organic.[14] But not everyone in the wine business is so sanguine. The vineyard manager at one of Buena Vista's competitors told us that he was not seeking organic certification, "but we are reducing chemical inputs; reducing chemical usage can reduce costs—obviously, if you buy less chemicals, you save money. But going organic costs more." He was seeking the minimal level of pesticide use, an economic threshold between pests and chemicals, seeing how little he could spray before mold and insect damage to the crop went too high. He added that certification itself was expensive, and the ongoing process remained so, because of the need for more cultivation and other labor-intensive activities. He concluded, "You are trading off a known fix for an unknown; the long-term costs are unknown."

If the direct costs are a close call at best, indirect benefits made organic farming a winner for Buena Vista. These include better consistency, easier fermentation, improved quality, plus a lower risk of lawsuits from employees exposed to toxic chemicals.

With organic methods, Buena Vista found that the consistency of its crops improved. Here we're talking cash flow. As one Buena Vista manager told us, "A couple of bad years and you're dead in farming." The vines themselves were heartier. In addition, they found that grapes grown organically are easier to ferment.

Fermenting can be tricky; it can halt in the middle of the process, and the winemaker has to get it going again. Organic grapes are cleaner and ferment more smoothly, so wine-making is easier. Smoother operations and better consistency lower costs in the long run, although the change may be difficult to quantify.

The consensus among those growing grapes organically seems to be that costs rise at first but then decline after several years. The spokesman for one vineyard experimenting with organic methods told us, "It is twenty percent more expensive in the beginning, the first couple of years, but after the second or third year, you get more consistent grapes and you have lower input costs." One reason may be that soil gets worn out by chemical farming. Marcus Moller-Racke, Buena Vista's chairman, told *California Farmer,* "In Germany the soils are depleted. Everyone uses synthetic fertilizers. It's almost impossible to grow organic grapes."[15] Healthier soil leads to healthier plants, consistently high yields, better grapes . . . and hopefully, better wines. According to Jill Davis, "Fine wine begins in the vineyard."

Any farming operating using chemical pesticides has to be concerned about liability for the health of its workers. On vineyards that have not gone organic, workers encased in protective clothing look like astronauts in deep space. Even if growers do not get hit with any lawsuits, they must still pay higher workers' compensation, disability, and general-liability insurance premiums to cover their risks.

And of course, any farmer who does not use chemicals avoids lurches in government policy. A few years ago, public outcry caused the EPA to ban the use of Alar, causing havoc for apple farmers. More recently the agency threatened to prohibit all traces of cancer-causing chemicals (which includes most pesticides) from the food supply. Wines would not be spared. In 1992, the EPA called for a ban on methyl bromide, a pesticide widely used by wine-grape growers.[16] In 1991, the government banned procymidone, a fungicide popular among growers in Europe.[17] On the local level, communities have become more concerned about the effects of agricultural chemicals on water suppliers and wetlands, like Pablo Bay, a short distance from Buena Vista's slopes. Organic farmers do not face these problems, or their costs.

THE DOMAINE CHANDON EXPERIENCE

Twenty miles north of Buena Vista in the Napa Valley is the Domaine Chandon champagne winery, an operation that could not be more different from the bucolic serenity of Buena Vista. Domaine Chandon is the Disneyland of California wineries; the whole place is designed for visitors. It is packed with tourists, a hub of activity centered on the wine-making process. One tour after another wends its way through spotless cellars where champagne ferments in enormous tanks, to the fast-paced bottling operation where 7 million bottles of bubbly per year make their way to market. A wine-tasting terrace, three-star restaurant, and a well-stocked gift shop ensure that Domaine Chandon profits even as new champagne-toasting customers are brought into the fold.

The most important differences between Domaine Chandon and Buena Vista are less visible. Buena Vista is primarily a vineyard, producing in one area 80 percent of the grapes that go into its wines (of which 80 to 85 percent are grown organically). Domaine Chandon is more of a winemaker, buying one-third of its grapes from others, growing the rest on its own 1,500 acres in five Napa–Sonoma locations. It is also a larger company; parent Moët & Chandon has wineries around the world—in France, Australia, and South America. Chandon has not gone as far as Buena Vista down the organic road, but their experiences have been similar.

Without pressure from marketing people or from other higher-ups, like the owners, the vineyard staff at Domaine Chandon has pushed organic farming methods forward. Zack Berkowitz, responsible for vineyard operations, told us that the upfront costs are higher, but that in the long term the costs are less, once you reach what he called the "equilibrium stage." In Domaine Chandon's oldest trials, grape production is higher. "If you are patient," Berkowitz told us, "you can reach an equilibrium stage where you are better off."

In Domaine Chandon's experience, avoiding chemicals does not significantly hurt harvests. But improving erosion control is expensive. In the past, farmers kept tilling and tilling to keep down the weeds; now they realize they must maintain the soil. "Better drainage and sediment basins cost real money," Berkowitz said, "and now it's the law in Napa." But even that investment pays in the long run: if you lose topsoil, you have to spend more on chemicals. He added, "I was over at one of our vineyards yesterday where there has been so much tilling that the bedrock is showing in one area." You can't grow grapes on bedrock and you can't buy topsoil. Farmland is ruined and rivers silted up by erosion.

To control insects, Chandon encourages biodiversity, like Buena Vista, creating an attractive environment for predator insects. Cover crops are good for that, especially flowers that bloom late in the season. According to Berkowitz, "If you cultivate early—doing what a 'good' farmer does—there is nothing left, so that the insects have nowhere to go but on the vines." Well-tilled fields may look good, but they require chemicals for insect control.

Another champagne vineyard has gone back to the future, housing its bottles in underground caves to reduce power consumption for cooling. And some vineyards are recycling wastewater from the Sonoma water authority, for both environmental and economic reasons. However, there has been some bad press from this. As one manager explained, "People can see the toilet bowl and the grapes with nothing in between."

None of these changes come easily. There is a learning curve, where the vineyard manager fine-tunes the mix between good and bad bugs, ground covers and weeds. When the equilibrium stage is reached, there can be a dramatic effect on the bottom line. Without cultivation and spraying, the farmer can reduce inputs and reduce costs. There is an investment in some special equipment, but this is offset by the lower costs of chemicals and spraying. Labor costs can also go up, but can be controlled with better management.

Then there is the effect on quality. Ten years ago people

didn't worry about the quality of the grapes: grapes were grapes. Now, some grapes cost more. It's a market reality, especially when demand for grapes is soft, as it is so often now with the rapid increase in the number of vineyards. Farmers who don't have good-quality grapes get a lower price—if they can sell them at all. The attention to details that goes into organic farming produces better grapes. "Besides," Berkowitz added, "nobody wants to be on the front page of the paper after your vineyard slid into the river, and the county writes a new ordinance just to deal with you. There's good publicity from doing it right."

THE BIG PICTURE

The fate of agriculture affects us all. Most directly, we all have to eat. If the food supply is reduced by natural disasters or tainted by pesticides, everyone feels the effects almost immediately. Agricultural employment has fallen steadily since industrialization began in the nineteenth century, but remains a huge business. More than 3 million people still work on America's farms, for example, several times more than in the manufacture of automobiles, electronics, and computers combined.

For the past four decades, agricultural exports have also led America's growth in global markets. The United States is the world's largest exporter of food by far, quite literally feeding the world, including Japan, where some three-quarters of food imports are American. But in the past decade, U.S. farms started to lose their edge. In the late 1970s, the U.S. share of food exports shot up to nearly 30 percent, but then plunged back down to about 20 percent after 1985.[18]

Stiffer competition was the cause. Many other countries began heavily subsidizing food exports. Europe, in particular, poured billions into farm exports, and may soon displace the United States as the world's number-one exporter. In addition, farmers around the world have adopted the high-tech, chemical-based farming practices that built American agriculture. Many countries, including those in the Third World like Mexico and India, went from big customers to tough competitors in a generation. Once the huge farms of eastern Europe and the former Soviet Union hit their stride, the world will be swamped with cheap food that will further erode America's share of the pie.[19]

While Europe has given the United States a run for its money, the fight has taken its toll on European agriculture as well. In Germany, for example, agriculture's share of the GNP has slid from 9.5 percent in 1950 to less than 1.5 percent today. Between 1980 and 1990, full-time agricultural employment fell from 394,000 to 260,000. By 2000, a mere 120,000 Germans may till the soil.[20] Agriculture is under stress throughout the industrialized world.

We all lament the decline of great companies like IBM and Volkswagen, but the fall from grace of agriculture may have a bigger impact on our pocketbooks. This is an industry that needs to be turned around, to be reinvented as the car and computer industries were. Organic farming may be the catalyst for this change.

Throughout the world, consumers are concerned about the quality of the environment and the food they eat. Chemical-based agriculture loses on both counts. Many people think of farming as amber waves of grain and contented cows, but in fact agriculture causes as much or more pollution as any other industry. And in many ways this damage is more insidious since we associate environmental damage with smokestacks and clogged freeways. Farms look environmentally benign, but they are not.

The list of problems caused by modern farming techniques is endless, from the accumulation of pesticides to soil erosion. Continual tilling removes topsoil and silts up nearby rivers. Fertilizers "burn" the soil and cause lakes to be choked with algae. Over the past two decades in the United States, for example, the amount of fertilizer used rose by a third to nearly two tons per square mile of arable land.[21] Pesticides turn underground wells into toxic-waste sites. Irrigation destroys natural water flows. And while we have large surpluses, the quality of our food is in question. Residues of pesticides, fertilizers, and feed additives permeate everything we eat and drink. For many, particularly those with small children, this is alarming.

There is also the bigger question of sustainable agriculture. Farmers are destroying the local ecology in a number of areas. South of San Francisco, in the fertile Salinas Valley, irrigation of fruit and vegetable farms may have reached its limit. Overpumping of underground wells has drawn in seawater, tainting the water supply for farmers and everyone else.[22] In the heavily irrigated valley of the Sacramento River in northern California, farmers grow in the desert a crop native to monsoon-flooded jungles: rice. The cost is high for American taxpayers who foot the bill, and the wildlife of the river, which suffers from diverted water flows.[23] In Florida, the Everglades have been polluted by fertilizer runoffs from government-subsidized sugar farms. This huge swamp is a unique ecological treasure, and a critical source of water for all Florida, including not just farmers, but industry and city residents.[24]

In all these cases, change has been resisted politically by short-sighted agricultural interests, even though poor farming practices may ultimately undermine their own way of life. And in the case of California rice and Florida sugar, the damage extends well beyond the local environmental and financial impact. The U.S. government has badgered the Japanese for years to import rice from the California desert. To protect sugar grown in Florida at a cost several times the world market price, the United States has raised an insurmountable tariff wall to keep our imports from struggling Third World countries and is destroying the unique Everglades in the bargain.

Perhaps organic farming can restore the fortunes of agriculture and eliminate some environmental damage as well. In an experiment run by Rhône-Poulenc, Europe's largest agricultural chemical maker, a wheat farmer in England saw his gross margins jump when he abandoned conventional farming.[25] John Reganold of the Washington State University Department of Crop and Soil Sciences compared sixteen conventional and organic farms in New Zealand. He concluded that the organic farms had better soil and were as successful financially as their conventional counterparts.[26] In Germany, the fabled vineyards of the Rhine and Mosel have been hard hit in recent years due to tough competition and changing tastes. The sweet Rieslings of Germany have lost favor to the drier Chardonnays of France and California. Some German vineyards have responded successfully by experimenting with new grape varieties grown organically.[27]

Organic farming also offers new opportunities to hard-pressed farmers. For most, food is a commodity. They sell their milk, for example, by the ton, and each farmer's milk is mixed with that of all other farmers. Under these circumstances, there is no such thing as "quality." Rather, the lowest common denominator prevails. There is no good reason—and certainly no financial one—for one farmer to improve the quality of his milk. He gets the same price per ton.

Organic farming places renewed emphasis on the quality of soil, plants, and produce. Quality is particularly important for winemakers, since wine is sold by the ounce, not the ton. Unlike a dairy farm, Buena Vista must look beyond sheer quantity. If organic farming improves the quality of its product, the vineyard can charge a higher price. If it also lowers costs, so much the better. Any farmer—any businessman—can benefit from lower costs and higher quality.

Around the world, people are concerned about what goes into their food. In Japan, the biggest export market for American agriculture, consumers worry about chemical additives in imported beef, rice, and fruit. Japanese government polls measuring these concerns are no doubt self-serving: they help justify import restrictions (and Japan is certainly not the only government up to this trick). Nevertheless, the concerns themselves are genuine, and no different from those in the United States, where many consumers are alarmed by pesticides in juice for children, growth hormones in milk, and genetically engineered tomatoes. Such consumer fears are even stronger in Europe than in other parts of the world.

Opportunities are great for those developing biological alternatives to chemical farming. One by one, governments are banning pesticides and herbicides because of the damage they cause to foods and the environment. For those they keep on the "approved" list, regulators raise the burden of safety-rule compliance to increasingly onerous—and costly—levels. New methods that obviate the need for chemicals without tainting food in the process will find ready markets. This new industry will grow most quickly in those countries where the demand for organic food is strongest.

Agriculture is one of America's most productive industries, but American farmers may have gone as far as they can through the application of ever-increasing amounts of capital and chemicals. Other countries are catching up; during the past generation, Europe has become a major exporter of food, and organic farming may become the cutting edge of competition worldwide.

PARADIGM SHIFT OR PUBLIC NUISANCE?

We know the manager of a forty-acre farm in Dutchess County, about 100 miles north of New York City. Our friend and his partners started their farm in the late 1980s with the idea of growing vegetables organically for sale locally and in New York. To avoid chemicals and to keep costs down, they need compost, and lots of it, so they set up a large-scale composting operation. They found neighboring farmers, food processors, towns, and even a cooking school willing to pay them to take compostable material off their hands.

Their organic vegetables and compost were in demand. But after a strong start, they ran into a brick wall. Not long after they started up, they found their organic farm tarred as a "toxic waste" site in town hall meetings and in the local weekly paper. Apparently many of their neighbors decided that anything more than a lonely spotted cow on a hillside was not their idea of country living.

Fighting your neighbors is never any fun, no matter how just your cause. But taking on New York State is another story. New York has a "right to farm" law that protects farmers from harassment by neighbors who don't like the looks and smell of farming—as long as it's conventional farming. But since our friend wanted to truck in "waste" to be composted, they were treated like they were stockpiling rusting drums of plutonium from dismantled ICBMs. After five years, they did get the state permits they needed to compost food scraps. But the financial toll was high: legal bills reached $20,000 per month.

At a time when agriculture in New York (and many other places) is taking a beating, our friend's farm offers a new paradigm for profitable, small-scale organic farming. What's more, their farm helps get rid of mountains of organic waste that would otherwise be landfilled. This model could be replicated outside metropolitan areas across the country—this is the "farm of the future." Traditional farmers in their area have started imitating their methods.

TO CERTIFY OR NOT TO CERTIFY

Organic certification is a very specific process, much like the ISO 9000 standards for manufacturing. In both cases, producers invest a significant sum to prove to an independent authority that their operations meet certain quality standards. Such certification, really just a piece of paper, provides consumers with a level of comfort that their purchase will meet expectations. For the producer, independently administered standards also provide a source of pressure to maintain quality.

There are many vineyards that employ organic methods without obtaining certification. For most, the writing is on the wall—they have to change. The future is not about spraying the vineyards every week, repairing erosion with bulldozers, and pumping as much water as they want from the rivers and wells. Like many other farmers, these vineyard managers see the benefit of some organic techniques but want to keep their options open, to spray pesticides in a pinch, for example. If you are an alcoholic, reducing your drinking by half is a good idea. Likewise, selectively adopting organic farming procedures helps the environment and no doubt saves some money. But does radical improvement in business performance result? Or does an alcoholic remain an alcoholic even on half a bottle of bourbon a day?

Fewer farmers are applying for organic certification than did a few years ago (although the number of acres farmed organically continues to increase).[28] At the same time more farmers are adopting "sustainable" farming techniques. Many are switching to no-till farming, planting new crops right over last year's stubble, rather than plowing everything under. This helps keep topsoil in place and reduce fuel consumption, but government research shows that no-till farmers use more herbicides to control weeds.[29] Two steps forward, one step back. One vineyard manager told us, "We agonize over this. We're not that interested in getting organic certification because it's not necessarily the best thing for the environment. . . . In some cases it may be more sustainable to throw down a little Roundup [a commercial pesticide] than to cultivate and have more erosion." Perhaps. But the experience of Buena Vista and those in other industries who aim for zero emissions, just like those who adopt extremely high-quality goals, is that objectively verifiable standards are necessary to effect real improvement.

HARD SELL

Quality sells wines, but the organic label does not. There may even be a negative connotation to organic wines: the hippie factor. Some consumers seem to think there is an inverse relationship between health and taste. And, in fact, many organic products often taste flat. One of us recently tried to substitute organic "Fruit Loops," a children's breakfast cereal, for the real thing. The kids were not fooled—or amused. According to Buena Vista, organic grapes don't necessarily make for better wines. The vineyard does not expect to get a higher price per bottle of wine as a result of going organic, and it has no plans to label its wines "organic" or "made from organic grapes."

Consumers respond strongly to scares about pesticide poisoning, and are wary about high-tech foods like genetically engineered tomatoes and milk made with bovine growth hormone. Over the past decade, eating habits have become healthier as consumers shifted to leaner meat and fresher fruits and vegetables. Nevertheless, the organic food industry has been slow to get off the ground. Organic products usually cost more; perhaps people just don't want to pay more for food that is not dangerous. In any case, building a business on a fad, like organic food, is risky. If to survive you must charge a premium for your product, you are doubly in danger. Selling quality is a safe bet, especially if you do not charge extra for it. Buena Vista's strategy is to sell quality wines; organic farming is the way to get there.

Environmental correctness cuts two ways. If you tout your organic grapes, what about the nonorganic ones? Buena Vista is unusual in that it grows over 80 percent of its own grapes. Others, including the biggest names in the business, buy the bulk of the grapes they use from others. So even if all their own grapes are organically grown, they don't make a peep. Companies that base their marketing on "green" frequently end up in hot water. In effect they are challenging the public to judge them by a higher standard. Someone from a combative environmental group inevitably rises to the challenge. And that can get ugly.

RETRAINING THE WORKFORCE

To go organic, managers at Buena Vista discovered that more than a shift in the way they grow grapes was necessary. They had to rethink the whole process of making wine. In particular, they had to retrain their workers by involving them more in the management of the vineyard.

Using conventional methods, Buena Vista's workers just drove around spraying everything. To farm organically, they had to understand what was going on. Which rows need to be mown this week to keep beneficial insects around the vines? How should the vines be pruned to take advantage of prevailing breezes? In short, the workers had to be trusted to make decisions that managers had previously made exclusively. One manager explained it to us this way: "When we started out, we expected the workers to say, 'You guys are crazy,' because it was so complicated. But they didn't. They embraced the new system. They are more like craftsmen, more involved in operations." He went on, "If you had to choose between a job that involved high-tech chemical methods and one that was environmentally sound, what would you do?"

Now there is a two-way flow of information between workers and managers, less command-and-control. Managers need to hear from those in the vineyard when conditions change. As one explained, "If workers find some problem, they tell their supervisor. Sometimes we ask the guys to look out for something in a certain area." There is no quick, chemical fix for every problem that arises. As a consequence, the value added by labor went way up; the workers' knowledge of the vineyard became critical. Under these circumstances, workers are no longer interchangeable drones, but trained specialists integrated into the business. Training is the way knowledge was substituted for chemicals at Buena Vista.

Turning labor from a liability into an asset: this is what reindustrialization is all about. The great strides made by the manufacturing sector in the past decade come in large measure from empowering the workforce. The challenge now is to reinvigorate other sectors of the economy. With millions of workers, who are mostly low paid, agriculture is a good place to start.

For the past few generations, the best jobs for those aspiring to a middle-class way of life were in factories. Rapid productivity increases made these jobs pay well, but also reduced the number of jobs available. While manufacturing has accounted for a steady share of total economic output for the past couple of decades in the United States, employment in this sector has fallen steadily, and will keep going down. And so it is throughout the industrialized world; fewer workers are needed to produce more and more goods. When industrialization began, manufacturing jobs paid poorly. But rising factory wages later drew workers off the farm by the tens of millions. Now, by applying knowledge to farm work, by substituting organic procedures for chemical solutions, perhaps agricultural productivity and wages can be raised.

THE LESSONS

In an extremely competitive market, Buena Vista was able to improve its product and lower its costs by adopting strict organic farming methods. There are several lessons:

Focus on your strengths. First and foremost a vineyard, Buena Visa used organic methods to focus on its most important activity: growing grapes. Many of its competitors, which buy most of their grapes from others, are winemakers and marketers first. Buena Vista has differentiated itself.

Make a leap of faith. Inspired by two managers with an unconventional view of wine-making, Buena Vista was able to make a break with traditional farming practices. This is never easy. Fortunately for Buena Vista, its owners were also willing to take a chance. Conventional wisdom says organic farming is an uneconomic fad.

Tally the indirect dividends. Measuring unexpected benefits (and problems) is perhaps a contradiction in terms. Nevertheless, no shift in thinking can take place if indirect benefits are not accounted for. In Buena Vista's case, a shift from technology to knowledge resulted in better organization and management.

Set high standards. Organic certification, a rigorous process, galvanized Buena Vista in a way that good intentions alone would not. Many other vineyard managers have adopted some organic methods, without obtaining certification. They are not enjoying the full benefits of real change.

PART TWO

FIGHTING EURO-SCLEROSIS

EUROPE SEARCHES FOR
A BIG GREEN FIX

By conventional environmental measures, Europe is at the head of the class. Tough recycling laws and high gasoline taxes keep consumers on their toes. Strict packaging and pollution regulations ensure that industry operates to the highest standards. Indeed, the countries of northern Europe, like Denmark, Germany, and Holland, are probably the most "environmentally correct" in the world. But for all of Europe's environmental successes, the Green Wave has not improved the competitive performance of Europe as a whole. Environmental gains have not resulted in the efficiency gains Europe needs to maintain its standard of living.

As economic circumstances shift, the relative competitiveness of Europe, Japan, and the United States constantly change. But in one area, Europe always stands out: quality of life. American business may have restructured itself to productivity leadership, but in terms of education, life expectancy, infant mortality, crime, and divorce, the United States trails Europe badly. While the social fabric of America seems to unravel dangerously, Europe remains a place where no one is abandoned. "From each according to his ability, to each according to his need," may no longer be the communist rallying slogan it once was, but in Europe at least, the least powerful members of society are not forgotten. And while the United States gets strip-malled from one end to the other, its highways crumble, and its public services fray, Europe nourishes the majesty of its history and invests relentlessly in its unparalleled infrastructure. No American who has visited the beautifully maintained cities of France or experienced the dazzling efficiency of Germany's train system can depart unawed.

And yet the tough question cannot be ignored: How can the Europeans pay for this marvelous quality of life? After a brief period of economic glow following the decision to forge Europe into a single market, European industry then appeared routed across virtually every front by competitors from America and Japan. For a decade or more, unemployment rates have been creeping up, reaching double digits in the mid-1990s—rates that would have been considered revolutionary a generation ago. At the same time, government debt expanded to unsustainable levels, even in thrifty Germany. Money for all these high-profile government works had to come from somewhere. The expansion of the public sector has reached its limits in Europe, which is now facing a sobering truth: the European Union has not created a single new private-sector job *in thirty years.*

In 1993, German Chancellor Helmut Kohl put it this way: "It seems as if there is still nothing more important than thinking about how we can expand our recreation time. . . . If we want to secure Germany's future, we cannot organize our country as if it were one big recreation park."[1] The continent is turning into a giant Euro-Disney, complete with fairytale castles, futuristic monorail trains, lots of people on vacation, and a potful of red ink.

All of Europe's cultural and social advantages come at a cost, one that Europe may not be able to afford much longer. Government largesse depends on high taxes, which in turn depend on high wages. But high labor costs are driving business out of Europe. In the early 1990s, wages in Germany, for example, leaped ahead of those in the United States and Japan, driving German manufacturers to shift production abroad, in some cases to the United States. Labor costs, including benefits, in Italy and France also pulled ahead of the United States during this period; even in Britain, once the poor man of Europe, paychecks rose nearly to U.S. levels. Militant unions in Germany and France kept pushing for raises despite sky-high unemployment rates.

There is no reason why Europeans should not be paid more than others—as long as they produce more. Currently, they do not. The surplus of wealth needed to maintain the level of services Europeans take for granted depends on productivity growth. BMW and Mercedes-Benz opened factories in America not because workers in Germany are paid too much per hour, but because they produce too little in return for those fat paychecks. German labor productivity lags behind the United States and Japan in virtually every type of manufacturing. In services, German workers don't do much better.[2]

In addition to its quality of life, Europe has many other comparative advantages. By forging the continent into one free-trade area, Europe could create the richest, largest, and most dynamic market in the world. But interminable fights over currency and political union suggest that it will be business as usual in Europe as high-paying jobs continue to slip away to other parts of the world.

Environmentally driven productivity improvements could help reverse this trend. Europe has some of the toughest environmental standards in the world. Many forward-looking companies are indeed riding the Green Wave, using waste reduction to close the productivity gap with Japanese and American competitors. But European politicians—and too many businessmen—seem more interested in using pollution laws as barriers to foreign competition than as incentives for reducing waste and costs. Europe stands ready to grasp defeat from the jaws of victory.

THE HIGH-PAYING JOBS OF THE FUTURE

One of Europe's strengths should be environmental technology. Governments and voters in Europe have repeatedly demonstrated their green credentials, spending lavishly on the environment. And this investment, now running at well over $100 billion per year, has produced results. By almost any measure, Europe is cleaner than other industrialized areas. Europeans use less water and less energy than competitors in other parts of the world. The skies over Europe are clearer, with lower levels of pollution like sulfur oxides (generated by power utilities), less nitrogen oxides (from cars, trucks, and industry) and greenhouse gas (from the combustion of fossil fuels). One of us remembers walking along the main canal in Bruges as a child in the early 1960s; the waterway was little more than an open sewer, however picturesque the setting. Today, the waterways of Europe are much cleaner, even those like the Rhine that flow through heavily industrialized regions. In France and Germany, there is now nearly as much forested land (as a proportion of the total) as in the United States, despite much greater population densities.[3] In short, investment has undoubtedly improved the European environment. Sky, land, and water are much cleaner than they were even a generation ago, and by many measures conditions are better than in the United States and other industrial nations.

All this makes a beautiful place even more beautiful. But what about jobs? Western Europeans now spend more on the environment than any other region, recently pulling ahead of the United States. Environmental outlays grew throughout the recession of the early 1990s; spending in Germany alone doubled in the past decade. Growth has been boosted by the harmonization of pollution laws throughout the European Union and by the opening of bidding for public-sector projects to companies from all over Europe. Naturally, European companies stand to benefit most from this healthy environment, and they have been responding to demand. Germany is already the largest exporter of environmental technology, with particular strength in air-pollution controls, where Germany's engineering skills shine.

Much environmental spending, like construction of water-treatment plants, industrial-site remediation, and trash disposal, favors local companies. But when the application of technology is involved, the market is more open to competition from other countries. For end-of-pipe solutions, like wastewater treatment and air-pollution controls, European suppliers have held their own. But how will Europe fare in the market for environmental technology (ET) that prevents waste and pollution in the first place?

If Europe's experience in information technology (IT) is anything to go by, the future in ET does not look good. In information technology, as in ET, the European market is now the world's largest. Many of the original developments in computers took place in Europe, particularly in Britain—the English produced the first electronic computer at Cambridge University during the war. Many advances in telecommunications originated in France (and Alcatel remains the world's largest supplier of telecom equipment). Even in semiconductors, European players once vied for leadership. Whatever their contributions, however, European companies do not set the agenda in IT; their American and Japanese rivals do. And Europe pays for this in jobs.

HIGH INFORMATION PRICES DESTROY ENVIRONMENTAL PRODUCTIVITY GAINS

When the price of information falls far enough, industry can replace mechanical effort with knowledge, a process central to translating green strategies into productivity gains. But while the price of information falls around the world, policy-makers in Europe try to prop up the cost of information. Much like the Community Agricultural Policy, which keeps food prices in Europe high, restrictions on the flow of information forcibly prevent European industry from fully exploiting the productivity potential of the Green Wave.

The challenge for business, government, and labor is to exploit the fall in information costs, not to get slam-dunked by it. This means observing what we call the "Iron Laws of Information." Gresham's Law says that "cheap money drives out good." We say cheap information always drives out expensive information. Its corollary states that information always flows to the least-regulated economy. Generally, therefore, less regulation will mean better environmental performance.

With notable exceptions like the United Kingdom, most European governments, believe, however, that the good of the state is best preserved if state-owned companies keep the price of information well above costs, and demand monopoly rents from their citizens. Germany, for example, extorts billions this way from telephone customers. Far from doing Germany any good, however, this policy keeps down telecommunications usage and forces German companies to move their computer operations and other value-added services to other countries, such as the United Kingdom. France actually restricts the use of foreign languages by its citizens, and limits their exposure to foreign culture.

In the European Union as a whole, market-unification plans usually mean extending German and French policies of state control to other countries, like the United Kingdom, that don't want to get caught behind the information cost curve. This, the Germans and the French seem to think, will level the playing field. It may, for a while, but at a very high price.

The United Kingdom sees great advantages to Franco-German policy. So long as France and Germany keep the price of information high, the United Kingdom can use the Iron Laws to attract their information business. As a result, the United Kingdom is becoming the information entrepôt of Europe. Britain is the Heathrow Airport of the European information business, the place where all European information goes to be collected, managed, and then redistributed piecemeal to the other members of the European Union.

The consequences of the United Kingdom's policy for the continentals is incalculable. Riding its low-cost information strategy, Britain is emerging as the dominant force in services in the Union. It could easily wind up controlling EU banking, advertising, accounting, and insurance markets by early in the next century. A new age of British knowledge imperialism will have begun. Britain's information costs are lower and its overseas connections are wider and deeper, giving it significant economies. Using the Iron Laws, Britain keeps itself less regulated than its neighbors and is thus better adapted to exploiting the markets of the twenty-first century.

By keeping the cost of information artificially high, Europe keeps its citizens from riding the Green Wave. On the Continent, the cost of information may *not* be cheaper than natural resources or labor. In the U.K., industry, and competitors from other countries that locate there, can still exploit the low cost of information. Indeed, this poses so great a problem for Britain's EU partners that some of them—notably France—want EU laws that will force the British to reregulate.

Continental governments are trying desperately to regain control, trying to offset the high cost of information with lavish subsidies elsewhere. In everything from the Common Agricultural policy to high-tech R&D programs (including many environmental technology projects), the European Union is pouring money into a dike that simply cannot be held. All the while, European industry is losing its competitive position. Flagship companies are falling by the wayside despite rising government R&D expenditures. There is something fatally Quixotic in EU policies.

CLIMATE CHANGE AND ENDANGERED SPECIES

What makes capitalism work is what Joseph Schumpeter called "creative destruction." New markets force organizations, managers, and workers to change. Companies that don't respond go out of business; workers who lose their jobs find new opportunities at new companies. There has been no greater demonstration of creative destruction than the massive restructuring of American industry that has been taking place over the past decade. Household names like IBM, General Motors, and Sears Roebuck veered toward collapse. Millions of people—first factory workers and then managers—lost their jobs. Yet millions of other new jobs were created, largely at new companies. A harsh environment, no doubt, but American industry transformed itself without creating an enduring mass of chronically employed workers. As this book demonstrates, organizations need to change to capitalize on efficiencies that come from the Green Wave.

A climate in which organizations can adapt is key to capturing the benefits of the Green Wave. Wal-Mart revolutionized retail distribution by eliminating all the middlemen (except itself) between factory and consumer. As a result, Wal-Mart has steadily reduced the amount of transportation required for everything it sells, cutting costs, fuel use, and emissions as a result. With this strategy, Wal-Mart helped the environment and its bottom line far more than, say, buying new trucks that got 10 percent better fuel economy. Eventually, home shopping via television on the Internet may eliminate the need for Wal-Mart, furthering the transportation efficiency of the economy. In Germany, these kinds of changes are not permitted: blue laws and other regulations strictly enforce the way retailers can operate, and government control of broadcasting effectively rules out commercial channels for home shopping or any other purpose.

High severance costs make layoffs expensive, so productivity increases cannot be quickly translated into labor savings. At the same time, a crushing burden of payroll taxes makes workers expensive to hire, so employers are reluctant to take them on even if conditions improve. And there is far less labor mobility in Europe than in the United States, even within countries; people simply don't move as much for new jobs or anything else. Between countries, there is essentially no movement of workers, except at the highest levels of business.

Most European countries have excellent schools. Their workers are well educated and well trained once on the job. They do indeed have the skills to change cheap information into valuable knowledge. But too many European governments continue to restrict the flow of information among citizens, artificially propping up its cost. This reduces the potential for the cost-effective substitution of information for other resources. The Europeans have cleaned up their environment, and have created a huge local market for environmental technology. But under current conditions, they will not enjoy the breakthroughs in productivity that come from the application of environmental technology.

Ironically, Europe has the training and education to revector workers displaced by layoffs, and to do so at good wages. But the high cost of information prevents this adjustment from happening. By contrast, in the United States and the United Kingdom, information flows freely, but the education is not there to keep people working at jobs that will sustain the middle class. In the United States, the market clears and people find work, but at wages that may not support their families.

One of the principal purposes of the European Union is to prop up industrial dinosaurs with lots of employees. As a result, the biggest companies in Europe don't need to adapt to market forces or to make the organization changes necessary to benefit fully from the productive potential of environmental and information technologies. And we're not just talking about coal mines, steel mills, and post offices: in 1992, the EU announced a program to save 2 million jobs in the *computer industry*.[4] If computer companies can be paid to ossify, then no industrial policy is too reactionary. Eventually, economic realities forced many companies to lay off workers in the recession of the early 1990s, but much market share had already been lost.

The worst consequence of Europe's turn-back-the-tide policies is lost opportunities to improve productivity. This is precisely the medicine Europe needs to raise paychecks and thereby pay for the social services it now enjoys. But in addition, the Europeans have created an environment in which old companies, not new ones, are encouraged. These new companies are needed to create the jobs that are inevitably lost in the old ones.

The real advances in environmental technology (as in information technology) come from small, entrepreneurial companies.

Over the past decade, small and medium-sized companies, not the largest ones, have led America's export boom.[5] But high-growth start-ups and new high-wage jobs are endangered species in Europe. Despite its current problems, Europe has enjoyed strong productivity growth since the Second World War. But the Europeans have not created a climate in which innovation, in environmental technology or anything else, can thrive. The Europeans, especially the Germans, have demonstrated their ability to improve existing ways of doing business; they have not done well inventing new ways of operating.

After decades and hundreds of billions of dollars, America's investment in information technology began to pay off in the 1990s. While American companies had raised manufacturing productivity through automation, they had long resisted efficiency improvements in white-collar jobs, in services, and in corporate management. Then computer networks began to break down the hierarchical structures common to most organizations. With "groupware" and other forms of direct communication between those producing information and those requiring it, the need for layer upon layer of management to "process" information quickly vanished. Redundant middle managers paid with their jobs, but the productivity of the survivors improved, often dramatically. As the examples in this book show, environmental technology can work the same way, if organizations adapt. Otherwise, expenditures on pollution controls keep regulators at bay and little else.

In Europe, such shifts will not come easily. Strong unions and backward-looking governments stonewall change, but so do attitudes. Executives in France, graduates of the *grandes écoles polytechniques,* run their businesses the way Napoleon ran his army. They demand respect from their subordinates, and get it. Informality is not accepted; only fellow graduates of the *polytechniques* address each other by first names or in familiar forms of speech. In Germany, a similar rigidness, a "this is the way we do things" attitude, prevails. Of course this is a generalization, and attitudes are more relaxed in Italy and Britain. Still, there is an inertia in European business that resists the efficiency improvements that can spring from new technology.

The big government, big company regime is reinforced by the EU's R&D policy, which further subsidizes yesterday's winners. The European Council of Ministers spends lavishly on high-profile research programs, including big budgets for environmental projects and new energy technologies. These outlays are no more likely to produce a viable ET industry than the Council's even more lavish spending on IT. In fact, special treatment by the EU could be the kiss of death for the environmental technology industry, which started out strongly on its own in Europe. In the past, industrial policies have not worked any better in Europe than they did anywhere else (including Japan). There are variations between national governments (France being the most dirigiste, Britain the most laissez-faire), but the EU as a whole leans toward constant meddling.

LOST OPPORTUNITIES

European environmental regulations often push industry in the wrong direction. Led by Germany, for example, many European companies passed laws to force more recycling. Eventually producers will be required to take back virtually all packaging from consumers. As a result, EU recycling rates shot up to over 40 percent in the mid-1990s for glass, cardboard, and paper. This change is environmentally correct, and has pushed manufacturers to rethink their ideas about packaging. But the economic sense of this "command and control" approach is doubtful. Within several years of its introduction, Germany's ambitious program had completely trashed the European market for recycled materials and upset otherwise sensible plans for incinerating waste. While there may be "make-work" jobs here sorting wine bottles from soup cans, it is difficult to see the kind of employment opportunities needed to sustain Europe's standard of living. The confusion of new packaging laws does serve, however, as a potentially useful nontariff barrier to keep out American and Japanese products.

While talking a good game about competitiveness and environmental policy, the EU continues to regulate with a heavy hand. In 1992, the European Commission issued a communication outlining its commitment to least-cost solutions for environmental problems and to the development of a competitive environmental technology sector.[6] In one important respect, with high taxes on gasoline and diesel fuel, Europe has improved transportation efficiency in the least intrusive way. A philosophical shift from regulation to taxes (which enforce environmental standards more efficiently) seemed imminent early in the decade, but has since fizzled. Italy, for example, sensibly imposed a tax on plastic shopping bags rather than create a complex recycling scheme. Some European leaders proposed a carbon tax in 1992, to improve energy efficiency and ward off global warming, but the idea soon died.

During the past few years, the Commission's environmental directorate, known as DG-11, has issued hundreds of directives. Vigorous environmental action by the EU has been popular throughout Europe, and has produced results (i.e., cleaner air and water). But rapid policy shifts have also produced uncertainty for business. Much of the confusion results from the years of wrangling among national governments about the harmonization of Union standards. Generally speaking, the richer countries of northern Europe, like the Netherlands and Germany, have tougher standards than those in the poorer south, like Greece and Portugal. EU policies have also sharply increased compliance costs both for business and member countries, which are already swamped by budget deficits.

Facing high unemployment, high taxes, and high budget deficits, Europe needs all the help it can get. With the environment, as with information technology, there is an opportunity to create many new jobs in a new industry and improve the productivity of virtually all workers in every sector. Better productivity alone can get Europe out of the high-wage hole it has dug for itself. Given the commitment of European voters to green policies, and the kind of money being spent in Europe to clean up the environment, this should be an area of competitive advantage.

Others are moving more quickly, and not just in the United

States and Japan. Countries like Hong Kong and Singapore are using their environmental policies to help launch themselves into the ranks of industrialized nations. Mexico may not be far behind; the North American Free Trade Agreement (NAFTA) is already raising environmental standards as well as worker productivity and manufacturing efficiencies. Poland and other Eastern European countries may pursue the same course.

Nothing underscores the relationship between pollution and costs than the remains of the Soviet Empire, until recently the second most powerful nation on earth, a genuine superpower of enormous military might. The old Soviet Union had some of the cheapest wages in the world and a complete absence of pollution controls. In what is left of this empire there is no competitive industry of any kind. Its satellites in Eastern Europe are no better off. The collapse of the iron curtain has revealed an industrial landscape scarred almost beyond belief and populations suffering all the wretched health problems that go with decades of unbridled waste and inefficiency.

If lax pollution laws and competitiveness went together, Russia, Poland, and the other countries that made up the old Soviet bloc could be the industrial juggernauts of the 1990s. They are not, and the shocking state of the environment there is stark proof of what happens when pollution costs are not factored into the economic equation. Emissions of air pollutants in all these countries far exceed those in Western Europe. Rivers are dead, toxic-waste sites abound, and great stretches of land are radioactive (especially in Russia).

The industrial collapse of Eastern Europe along with communism itself reduced pollution levels early in the 1990s, and reindustrialization is taking place with greener and more efficient processes. The only way these countries (and others like Mexico and Brazil) can compete is by *raising* their environmental standards—and they know it. With their rock-bottom wages, these countries are already siphoning off jobs from Western Europe, especially Germany. As productivity improves—and higher environmental standards will help—the flow of jobs could turn to a flood.

RIDING THE BIG GREEN TSUNAMI

JAPAN TARGETS ITS NEXT EXPORT CAMPAIGN

Japan is driven by efficiency, not environmentalism. Fortunately for Japan, efficiency is almost always better for the environment than any alternative. During the two decades after 1975, Japan's economy expanded rapidly, but its oil imports fell steadily, as did emissions of most pollutants. Throughout this period, the Japanese government kept pressure on industry to reduce energy use. This efficiency push is what makes Japan so dangerous to its competitors: efficiency means lower costs and higher quality.

Japan is an isolated island nation without natural resources, driven since the mid-nineteenth century by its need to secure raw materials for production. With the rapid industrialization that followed Commodore Perry's arrival in 1853, Japan's leaders first became obsessed with their lines of supply. For the past fifty years, Japan has maintained an aggressive export strategy to cover huge imports of everything from wood to fish, iron ore, and oil.[1]

Small and isolated, crowded and bereft of natural resources, Japan must export or die. Exports give Japan a sense of security and economic self-sufficiency in a hostile and capricious world.

And export it does. Japan may sell twice as much to the United States as it buys, but its balance of trade with the rest of the world is not so favorable. Indeed, Japan's much-mooted surplus with the United States barely covers its fuel bill.[2] Without exports, Japan would face a threat to its security and prosperity. Sixty years ago, such fear drove Japan to secure its sources of oil and other raw materials by military force.

Compared with the United States, Canada, and parts of Europe, which are richly endowed by nature, Japan has virtually nothing. Japan is a trading nation, which must sell its wares (most of which are luxuries like cars and cameras) to buy the necessities, without which Japan cannot survive. Nobody ever froze to death because he didn't have a cassette tape player. Many outside Japan don't appreciate Japan's predicament.

Along with Japan's success has come an increasing propensity to consume. The postwar generation of savers and workers is being replaced by a new breed of consumers and relaxers—or so it seems to the old guard. In truth, the Japanese remain thrifty and diligent by world standards. Nevertheless, the Japanese are enjoying at least some of the rewards of their past efforts. They want to travel, spend more time with their families, drive new cars. As a result, less of the country's output is available for exports. This change comes at a time when Japan's long-term growth rate is declining.

The truth is, Japan must export to pay for oil and other natural resources. That is why the Japanese are extremely sensitive to protectionist sentiments in the United States and Europe. Pressure to reduce its trade surplus persists, and will only get worse. But no amount of Structural Impediment Initiatives and jawboning at the World Trade Organization about rice imports will change the facts. Japan cannot abruptly shift production overseas or open its markets to a flood of imports without threatening its security. Admittedly its trade position leaves quite a bit of room for error, but given what is at stake, Japan needs a healthy buffer.

The only alternative Japan has is to cut raw-material imports. The less Japan imports, the less it will need to export. In this way it can achieve "harmony" with its trading partners. Dematerialization of industrial production offers Japan a way out.

Perhaps more than any of its Western competitors, Japan needs to sever oil consumption from growth. The oil *shokku* of 1973 brought the Japanese industrial juggernaut to a screeching halt. The Japanese saw themselves running on empty, the eventual losers in a *Mad Max*–like scramble for the few remaining drops of oil in the world. That's why the greatest advances in fuel efficiency in the industrialized world during the past two decades have been in Japan.

While many Third World producers of raw materials have suffered remorselessly from falling commodity prices over the past decade, most countries have benefited from the dematerialization process. None more than Japan, where the effects have been dramatic.

The Japanese do not seem overly concerned about the environment, particularly outside of Japan, if their track record for drift net fishing, whale killing, and rain forest destruction are anything to go by. And anyone who has witnessed Japan's historical treasures surrounded by seas of vending machines, its postwar construction, which is truly horrible even by the standards of modern architecture, or Tokyo's beautiful Imperial Palace grounds bisected by a six-lane highway knows that environment aesthetics have not been a top priority.

Indeed, Japan seems willing to take grave environmental risks to secure its energy independence. The country has embarked on the world's most ambitious plan to generate nuclear power, stockpiling plutonium (a by-product of conventional nuclear reactors and one of deadliest substances known) in the hope that a fusion power breakthrough can be achieved.

Whatever its green credentials, Japan will only eliminate its trade problem if it can reduce its raw-material consumption and imports. In other words, get rid of oil and the trade problem will take care of itself. Exports could even decline without reducing Japan's wealth.

So Japan will ride the Green Wave. With the running start

that began in the oil crises of the 1970s, Japan already sets energy-efficiency standards. Its challenge now is to squeeze even more waste out of its products and processes. Japan's overseas customers are ready for these changes; many of its competitors are not.

FROM IT TO ET

Japan's success in getting the natural resource monkey off its back has been mixed. After the U.S. oil embargo in 1941, Japan attacked Pearl Harbor and grabbed the rich oil fields of Indonesia, a strategy that ultimately proved futile. In response to the Arab oil embargoes of the 1970s, Japan made energy efficiency the "moral equivalent of war" (in the immortal words of Jimmy Carter). In a tactical sense, Japan's efficiency drive paid significant dividends, wringing more steel and cars out of every barrel of oil. But so far, Japan's grand plan to move up the industrial food chain have not worked well.

Nowhere has failure been more conspicuous than in information technology. Despite decades of heavy government subsidies and dogged determination to engineer a "breakout" from Japan Inc.'s beachhead in cars and TVs, Japan's electronic giants, including Fujitsu, Hitachi, NEC, and Toshiba, have a few stunning victories and many expensive losses to show for their efforts in computers and telecommunications.

In the United States, by far their biggest export market, Japanese companies dominate one large market—cars—and several smaller ones, notably consumer electronics, cameras, and copiers. But these markets are mature. For a decade, production in Japan of each of the following products has declined or stopped growing: calculators, cameras, motorcycles, stereos, tape players, trucks, TVs, and VCRs. Passenger-car production expanded during this period, but exports from Japan fell. Consumer electronics—Japan's first real success—have been particularly hard hit.

In short, Japan is coasting, after a home run and a couple of base hits early in the game. To maintain rapid growth, Japan needs another big hit like cars. And the Japanese know it.

Japanese business leaders understand that information will dominate the world economy in the twenty-first century. As the first industrial revolution substituted mechanical power for manual labor, the second will substitute information for mechanical effort. This structural shift in the economic order will require a massive investment in information infrastructure, which is now underway. Perhaps best of all, information does not use the natural resources Japan does not have. So Japan has developed a simple strategy to maintain growth: go where the money is—information technology.

Unfortunately, thirty years and billions of dollars of government and private investment have made Japan the Saudi Arabia of memory chips—and little else. Japan is also strong in a few other commodity hardware markets like fax machines, laptop computers, printers, and disk drives, but prices for these products go nowhere but down, and competitive pressures from Korea and Taiwan (not to mention the United States and Europe) are relentless. In more complex systems, like workstations and communications systems, which account for the bulk of the market, Japan's role is marginal. At home, a program of rigorous import substitution has guaranteed a big and protected information technology market for Japan's electronics giants, but exports pale in comparison. In high-growth areas like services and software, Japan is nowhere.

Poor results in information technology, as close to resource-free as you can get, have left Japan chugging along in the same resource-intensive industries it first staked out thirty and forty years ago. Nevertheless, there remains plenty of room to make its manufacturing more efficient, and to increase the "knowledge-intensity" of its cameras, bread makers, and pickup trucks.

In response to pressure from its trading partners, Japan is shifting production overseas. To do so without hurting domestic living standards, Japan must shift low-value-added production offshore and focus on capital and knowledge-intensive opportunities at home. Information technology was going to make all this happen. But IT, which at the crack of the bat sounded like it might be a grand slam for Japan, has started looking like a single, a double at best. Environmental opportunities are now Japan's best shot at bringing everyone in before the inning is over.

HOW JAPAN WILL RIDE THE BIG GREEN WAVE

Japan is developing its environmental opportunities the way it attacked information technology, mobilizing government and industry from top to bottom toward a single, well-defined objective.

Japan's obsession with R&D and technology explains, in large measure, its success in recent decades. But a survey taken by Dentsu Institute asked Japanese CEOs what they expected their main concerns to be in the future. At large companies, the environment headed the list, along with R&D.[3] Technology plus efficiency make a powerful combination.

After the energy shocks of the 1970s, the government of Japan turned the screws on big business, particularly the heavy users of energy like railroads, steel mills, and electric utilities. This pressure was maintained during the 1980s. In 1993, Japan raised the stakes again for industry with the implementation of its tough new Basic Environmental Law.

The government has done more than pass laws. MITI (Japan's Ministry of International Trade and Industry) also added energy efficiency projects to its R&D investment list. Recently, MITI broadened its environmental portfolio from energy efficiency and pollution abatement to sustainable development. Indeed MITI has a *100-year* environmental plan for Japan that places much emphasis on energy-related technologies.[4] Perhaps more to the point, MITI has the bankroll to make these dreams a reality. You can be sure any new technologies that result from research will be available for export. Japan got a big shot in the arm in the 1970s when its fuel-efficient cars were suddenly in demand in the United States. Green exports could provide the next burst of growth.

In 1991, the *Keidanren,* Japan's club for major corporations, released its Global Environmental Charter, guidelines to encourage good environmental behavior among its members. Japan's business leaders can see that its overseas consumers are looking for change. Being green is good for business. Taking its cue from MITI, Japan Inc. will pressure suppliers to meet high standards for environmental efficiency. In this way, the Green Wave will probably roll over Japanese industry faster than elsewhere.

Japan will also wring whatever it can out of international organizations. At the Earth Summit in Rio in 1992, Japan had an unusually high profile, clearly indicating that the environmental wave is one that Japan would like to ride. While the Japanese government was fanning the "technology transfer" flames, Japanese companies were front and center, flogging their wares. And who can object to Japan's self-serving calls for the transfer of environmental technology to the Third World when the ends are so worthy? Japan is investing heavily in environmental technology and wants to exploit its advantage.

Japan is likely to use development aid aggressively to build environmental markets. The Third World and Eastern Europe (the region most in need of environmental cleanup) can expect a helping hand—if they buy Japanese. And there's nothing sinister about this approach; this is the way government aid works.

Don't be fooled by any offbeat public relations campaigns. You will be reading such hard facts as "the harmonious coexistence of our product and nature." One ad we saw spoke of "new links within families, new links between businesses, new flows of information between people and the environment, a new sense of connection between our individuality and the world we inhabit."[5] This may sound like terminal California-style New Age dementia, but it is not. Japan means business.

OPPORTUNITIES FOR JAPAN

The worldwide market for environmental technology is huge, and growing rapidly. Japan is ready. Honda, Nissan, and Toyota are developing high-performance, high-efficiency, low-emission engines. Perhaps the most practical purchase any environmentally minded customer can make is a high-mileage car. Sony and NEC are eliminating CFCs from their production processes. Hitachi and Toshiba are trying to reduce the carbon dioxide emissions of their power plants. Japan is maintaining a strong position in technologies for eliminating, treating, and preventing industrial and municipal pollution. The country is also investing heavily in alternate energy sources like solar panels and hydrogen cells.

But these are not the real opportunities the Green Wave offers Japan. The relentless pursuit of cost reduction and quality improvement, in response to environmental pressures from many quarters, will reinforce Japan's commanding position in its traditional markets, and may help offset some of the setbacks suffered in new areas like information technology.

In a sense, Japan's accomplishments to date are based on re-exported American inventions like the transistor and statistical quality control. Achieving the goals of zero emissions will require a complete rethinking of management and manufacturing strategy, akin to the challenges of "zero defects" production, but much more difficult. If Japan Inc. embraces zero emissions as its target for the next decade, a genuinely Japanese accomplishment will have been achieved.

Redoubling its efforts to reduce emissions will enable Japan Inc. to set new standards in manufacturing. Many competitors remain focused on quality alone (measured in defective parts per million, for example) which all too often ignores the waste involved in achieving high levels of quality. Even the Deming Prize, the apex of achievement in manufacturing in Japan, recognizes quality without regard to the waste it may take to get there. In future, this quality must be achieved without waste. For the smartest competitors, first-rate quality will be the *result* of eliminating waste.

Many think of environmentalism as a cost; for Japan it is an opportunity. As Michael Crichton wrote in *Rising Sun,* "Conservation is not synonymous with diminution of life style. It is synonymous with more wealth, power and freedom."[6]

Waste reduction will not end at the factory gate. Japan Inc. has fine-tuned just-in-time delivery like a Stradivarius. Not only are parts delivered to factories exactly when they are needed, but even convenience stores in Japan receive their deliveries many times a day, moments before consumers are expected. All these trucks delivering everything from spark plugs to sushi are choking Japan's highways—and its air. A significant challenge, and one to which the Japanese will no doubt rise, is to eliminate the environmental by-products of the just-in-time system.

CAN JAPAN SUCCEED?

Lacking outside natural resources, having returned after defeat in World War II, Japan has always run "lean" compared to its industrial competitors. Furthermore, as a densely populated island, Japan felt the ill effects of industrial pollution early, enacting strict environmental regulations in the 1960s. The oil crises of 1973 and 1979 destroyed whatever illusions Japan had about its ability to waste energy. Japan maintained its momentum during the 1980s with relatively little backsliding compared to its competitors. So Japan has a running start at riding the Green Wave.

Environmental pressure, particularly the risk of dependence on the Middle East for oil, is largely external. During its history, Japan has responded most effectively to external pressures, rather than internal ones. Waste reduction and industrial efficiency is the kind of agenda that MITI can get behind foursquare. After the war, Japan's government and industrial leaders mobilized the country for reconstruction. A clear new goal is needed, and environmentalism fits the bill perfectly.

Information technology was not the right challenge. While it achieved certain well-defined objectives (with the VLSI Project, for example), MITI could not drive all of Japan on a forced march to victory in computers. The reason was simple: Japan wanted to solve the problems of foreign customers from afar, without talking to them. Riding the Green Wave, Japan will be solving its *own* environmental problems, dealing with matters over which it has control. The automobile industry met Japan's need for small, fuel-efficient cars, for which there was a ready market overseas. The next Fifth Generation Project will involve energy and resource efficiency, and it may well succeed.

Many of Japan's industrial giants diversified with unrestrained ardor into information technology during the 1970s and 1980s. Most of these investments have been disasters, largely because they served the needs of Japan Inc., not its customers. Nippon Steel will find it much easier to sell clean steel-production processes, with which it is intimately familiar, than laptop computers, about which it knows nothing more than scores of faceless competitors. Japan Inc. will be serving real customer needs in environmental technology—its own. A short step will take these companies and their expertise into the open market, at home and abroad.

Much of Japan's success in manufacturing has been attributed to *kaizen,* the art of incremental improvements. Focused on quality and efficiency, *kaizen* has produced successive generations of better and cheaper cars, TVs, and cameras. This kind of management is well suited to the Green Wave, since waste reduction and resource efficiency are a natural extension of *kaizen.* Companies that reduce their emissions to zero do so through the relentless pursuit of small improvements, not the application of blockbuster ideas or technologies.

The financial shocks of the early 1990s forced Japan to reconsider the freewheeling years of the 1980s. Extravagant living is not the Japanese way, and many were uncomfortable with the excesses of the previous decade. They come much more naturally by economy, and their country has already proven its capacity to reduce waste, to operate efficiently. The Japanese can turn the slogan "less is more" into reality if any society can.

THE OIL-FREE BARONS OF TOMORROW

A uniquely Japanese system of business administration, well adapted to their lack of natural resources and concomitant need to be frugal, may do for Japan what thirty years of exports has not achieved: reduce its dependence on unstable sources of oil and other raw materials, improve its antagonistic trade relations, enable production and management to move overseas, and finally allow Japan Inc. to embrace foreign customers.

If it can successfully ride the Green Wave, Japan, for the first time in its history, will be secure, able to act with confidence, free to find a new role commensurate with its economic achievements. Riding the Green Wave may be this new role, a part scripted just for Japan to play on the new world stage.

The potential is there for the Japanese to become the "oil-free barons" of the postindustrial era, shifting the center of gravity in the energy world from Riyadh to Tokyo. As the environmental leader, Japan can have real political clout without threatening anyone. At the moment, Japan finds it difficult to flex its muscles militarily, or even politically, because of its history and fragile position as a trading nation. Japan understandably did not want to rock the boat during the Gulf War, for example, since most of its oil came from the Middle East.

As Japan improves its manufacturing, techniques and equipment developed for internal uses will find ready markets overseas. In addition, Japan can reinforce its position in key industries, especially cars, by driving down costs with a zero-emissions strategy. Even in information technology, steady cost reduction will pay the best dividends in the commodity hardware markets that Japan has staked out. "Lean and green" management will open up new markets in countries with tough environmental standards, and will give Japan Inc. a leg up with many new products and technologies not yet fully developed. And, as suppliers of advanced green components and processes, Japanese vendors can get their hooks into customer companies that need "environmentally correct" suppliers to help meet their own legal and market requirements.

As waste is eliminated from all activities, Japan has an opportunity to revolutionize its service industries. Poor productivity in services is a problem in all countries, but in Japan more than most. An obsession with waste elimination may be the catalyst needed to shift service productivity onto a new plane.

THE SECOND MEJI RESTORATION

In the early 1990s, the Japanese export juggernaut ran aground, particularly in high tech, where the high-wage, high-growth opportunities of the future lie. This poor performance has little to do with a high yen or the bursting bubble economy. Rather, structural flaws in their organizations made it difficult for decision-makers in Japan to connect with overseas customers.

Can Japan restructure? In Tokyo, they certainly have their doubts. Japan's business leaders have always looked to their American counterparts for inspiration, and they don't like what they see in America: layoffs, layoffs, and more layoffs. By the early 1990s, many thought these painful dislocations were a thing of the past, since productivity was rising rapidly in most sectors. Instead, to maintain their edge, American companies, even the most profitable ones, continued to lay off tens of thousands of employees. For the Japanese, this "take no prisoners" approach to labor relations has always been shocking. What they find even more horrifying is that they might have to take the same bitter medicine in Japan in order to turn their companies around.

We were struck on a recent visit to Japan by the number of times we heard the phrase "hidden unemployment." This refers to the millions of workers, particularly in white-collar jobs, who are kept on the payroll even though their employers could get along without them. Many companies have allowed their management ranks to balloon. The president of one large electrical manufacturer told us, "When I started working at this company as a young man, there were four layers of management in the factories, from machine operator to plant manager. Today there are nine." In the past, redundant salarymen kept on till retirement time were called "window-watchers." In the no-growth 1990s, Japan has run out of windows.

Without sharp cuts in costs, Japanese products will remain uncompetitive on world markets. Detroit has taken back market share from its Japanese competitors not solely because of quality improvements, but also because of sticker shock. One of us recently priced new minivans; the Japanese ones were thousands more than a similarly equipped Dodge Caravan. At some point, buyers will put up with a few remaining quality problems.

To cope with its cost handicap, Japan Inc. needs to do more than cut golf-tee and take-out sushi budgets. The "restructuring" mantra is repeated everywhere in Japan. For some companies, this means moving production offshore, to Malaysia for TVs or America for cars. Most managers hope that a combination of belt tightening and a heavy dose of technology will carry their companies through to sunnier days. It's not likely. Japan will not recover until it changes its thinking. Business as usual will lead to further reversals in markets won through decades of hard work.

Japan must use the Green Wave to cut costs. But efficiency improvements alone will not help if the wrong products are sold in the wrong way. Which markets to abandon? Which products to cut? Which layers of management to eliminate? Which research projects to scratch? Choices like these cannot be made without close contact with customers, and this is where Japan's industrial giants fall down.

Most Japanese companies are not structured to absorb information efficiently from their overseas customers, to filter the kind of noise they get from chaotic world markets. To restructure their corporate bureaucracies, in effect to improve the productivity of white-collar workers, they need to know what their overseas customers want. Future success will require a profound change in how these companies are organized and do business. For Japan to exploit the opportunities that lie ahead, the country must go through what we call a second Meji Restoration.

The first Meji Restoration was a period of renewal for Japan after centuries of isolation, but it did not happen overnight. Rather, this process took from 1853 to 1868, with civil war battles far bloodier than those at Gettysburg. What ensued was a period of industrialization and growth unparalleled in history. Many think that the Japanese miracle took place after the Second World War. In fact it took place in the century before, when Japan transformed itself from a feudal society into an industrial superpower.

By turn of fate, Japan has a comparative advantage in environmental technology. And Japan's manufacturers have proven their ability to lower costs by wringing waste out of their processes. But Japan's advantages in these areas will be wasted if structural barriers to change are not removed. These barriers restrict the flow of information, in effect preventing the substitution of knowledge for natural resources, labor, and capital that must take place.

SINGAPORE AND HONG KONG

CREATING JOBS ALONGSIDE
TOUGH ENVIRONMENTAL POLICIES

No other countries have committed themselves to development with the single-minded purpose of Singapore and Hong Kong. Already, the people of these two small city-states enjoy a standard of living approaching that of Europe. For their policy-makers, the challenge is to maintain economic momentum in the face of competition from other Third World up-and-comers, particularly China. Singapore attracts the high-wage, high-tech jobs that were once the exclusive domain of the United States, Europe, and Japan, even turning away investment that does not match its profile of future opportunities. Yet a cornerstone of Singapore's industrial policy is to maintain the highest level of environmental quality in the world. Policy-makers there believe investors come to Singapore because of its tough pollution standards, not in spite of them. Hong Kong, which already produces more TVs than Japan and more watches than Switzerland, is on a forced march to high-wage, high-tech manufacturing. Environmental pressure is a catalyst.

For a visitor from New York, Singapore is a vision of paradise. The lush smell of tropical vegetation combined with the humidity and heat—a steady eighty-five degrees here at the equator—arouses primordial sensations in anyone raised in a northern climate. From any vantage, one is struck by the beauty of the landscaping. Riding the elevated train into the suburban reaches of the island-state, one sees endless neighborhoods of tidy houses and low apartment blocks set on tree-lined streets. Broad boulevards bordered with mature trees lead to the center of Singapore. On Orchard Road, in the main shopping area, a dense canopy of trees arches over lanes of traffic. Parks frame the old colonial area of government buildings on the waterfront, facing out to sea. Across the Singapore River is the central business district with its large, modern office buildings. Everything is spotless, beautifully landscaped, meticulously maintained, and safe.

Touring such a pleasant, ordered world, it is easy to forget that this small island off the Asian mainland is the most densely populated country in the world, with twice as many people per square mile as Hong Kong, half as many as the City of New York, and about the same as Chicago. It is also easy to forget what Singapore was until a generation ago: an impoverished, crime- and disease-ridden British colonial backwater that was virtually destroyed during the Second World War.

What got Singapore from there to here in such a short time was the resolve of its government. Such single-minded purpose is rare among nations. Singapore takes an equally unswerving approach to the environment, never forgetting the profitability of industry. By contrast, in Europe and the United States, regulations are often introduced irrespective of impact on profitability. Singapore's policy-makers know that waste reduction and efficiency go hand in hand, and they have been able to make business leaders see the light.

Tough environmental standards do not cost Singapore jobs. On the contrary: Singapore remains one of the most popular locations for multinationals in Asia. Even oil giants like Exxon and Mobil favor Singapore for their regional refining and petrochemical investments, despite the city's tough environmental standards.

With a deep but well-protected natural harbor, Singapore was settled by the British as a free port between China and India, and the city's current prosperity rests on trade. Singapore is first and foremost an entrepôt, for goods, money, and information. Indeed, foreign trade is more than three times the size of the total economy (compared to about 25 percent in the United States, for example). When founded by the British a century and a half ago, Singapore was not much more than a swamp ringed with a few fishing villages. Since independence in 1965, the city-state has rocketed into the ranks of industrialized nations. In the first decade after independence, per capita growth averaged 9 percent per year; in the second decade, just over 6 percent per year. By the early 1990s, the city's per capita wealth exceeded that of Spain and several other members of the European Union. It shows: there is no evidence of poverty in Singapore.

Singapore's beauty is not just skin deep. Its air and water are every bit as clean as its city streets. Levels of conventional air pollutants like sulfur dioxide, nitrogen dioxide, and lead are far below U.S. EPA standards. Carbon dioxide emissions are also relatively low. Despite a *twentyfold* increase in GNP, energy consumption per capita has remained constant over the past two decades. Use is now about half the American level, and roughly on a par with Japan's. Water quality in rivers and coastal areas also exceeds international standards. All sewage is treated. The Singapore River, which flows through the city center, was described as "little more than an open sewer"[1] not so long ago. The city completed a ten-year cleanup of this River in 1987.

Singapore attracts plenty of companies in clean, fast-growing industries like banking and communications. But the city is not just a postindustrial service economy. Singapore's prosperity is built on manufacturing, including heavy industry like shipbuilding and petrochemicals. The genius of Singapore's Green Wave strategy is not that it created a sanitized environment for software developers and investment banks in suburban office parks. Rather, it encourages rapid growth in the manufacturing sector. Basic industries, considered by many to be dirty and slow growth, prosper in Singapore cleanly and efficiently.

THE GREEN PLAN

In Singapore, nothing is left to chance, and the environment is no exception. At the time of independence from Great Britain in 1965, Singapore's "environmental" concerns were on an elemental level: clean water, food, shelter, and basic health care for its people. Nevertheless, in 1967, Singapore began one of its most far-sighted and successful environmental programs: the Garden City campaign. Since then over 5 million trees have been planted in this small country, creating Singapore's current beauty and special character, and contributing in no small measure to air quality there today. In the 1970s and 1980s, prosperity led to the kind of pollution-control programs found in the industrial world.

By the late 1980s, environment officials believed that Singapore had gone as far as it could with infrastructure improvements and end-of-pipe solutions. They decided they had to get people involved—up to that point it had just been government action alone. They had to promote clean technology and environmental technology. In 1990, officials announced a splashy Environmental Week campaign (which became an annual event). Then in 1992, the government announced "The Singapore Green Plan: Toward a Model Green City."

With the same drive that pulled it out of the Third World and into the First, Singapore decided to make itself the green capital of Asia. Environmental technology has big sales potential around the world. As suppliers improve their manufacturing, techniques and equipment developed for internal uses can be sold to others. In addition, Singapore can reinforce its position in key industries by driving down costs with a zero emissions strategy. "Lean and green" management will open up new markets, and will give Singapore a leg up with many new products and technologies not yet fully developed. And, as suppliers of advanced green components and processes, competitors from Singapore can get their hooks into customer companies that need "environmentally correct" suppliers to help meet their own legal or market requirements.

The Green Plan is nothing if not comprehensive. According to officials, Dr. Ahmad Mattar, the minister of the environment, wanted to chart a new course for his ministry, to answer the question, What do we do for the next ten years? But always sensitive to international competitiveness, Singapore is tightening standards in stages, looking to developments in other advanced economies. When asked about Singapore's environmental goals, one official commented, "We want to be as good as or better" than Singapore's industrial competitors. Singapore wants to stay ahead of OECD averages, but to do so in a way that helps industry. Every move is evaluated for its effect on industrial efficiency. For example, with sulfur dioxide emissions, one official told us the environment ministry was concerned about the ability of industry to comply, and wanted to determine "whether it's better to control sulfur in fuel or simply to regulate SO_2 emissions—we did a study to see which way is most efficient."

For solid waste, Singapore's policy is to incinerate everything that cannot be recycled. Already 85 percent of refuse is incinerated at three waste-to-energy plants, with the resulting ash disposed of in sanitary landfills. In the long term, to conserve landfill space, Singapore wants to reduce the amount of waste generated per capita through greater efficiency. Without any minimization program, the government estimates that the amount of trash per person per day would go from 1.1 kilograms to 1.3 kilograms; Singapore's target is 0.9 kilogram. Because of the concern about the effect on business, however, Singapore has no plans for the kind of draconian packaging and recycling laws popular in Europe (and favored by many environmentalists).

For wastewater, Singapore collects and treats all effluent before discharge offshore. Treated water meets quality standards high enough for discharge into lakes and rivers, even though it actually goes into the sea. For air pollution, Singapore's goal is to achieve "good" air quality (by U.S. EPA standards) every day of the year by 2000, up from about three-quarters of the year in the early 1990s. To do so, the government is setting increasingly strict standards for industry and limiting the sulfur content in fuel oil.

To control car and truck pollution, emission standards move in step with the United States, Europe, and Japan, backed up with tough emissions testing. Unleaded gas has been required for all new cars sold after July 1991, and electric car use is encouraged. Singapore also draws drivers out of their cars with its superb mass transit system, which is being steadily expanded and upgraded.

Singapore's automobile policy illustrates its seriousness about car pollution, and its preference for market-based solutions. Gas prices are kept high (at about US$3.00 per U.S. gallon) to make driving expensive, although taxes on unleaded fuel were lowered to encourage drivers to switch from leaded gas. In addition, drivers must pay a toll to enter the central business district during rush hour, an incentive to switch to mass transit. Most intriguing are the "quota premiums" charged car buyers. Every year the Ministry of the Environment figures out how many cars the island can support if air quality goals are to be reached; the right to buy a car is then auctioned off to the public. In 1993, "quota premiums" ranged from about S$15,000 (almost US$10,000) for a minicar to S$20,000 (US$13,000) for a luxury car. The quota premium for cars only used on the weekend was S$13,000 (US$8,500), and for a motorcycle a mere S$1.[2] On top of the quota premium, new-car buyers pay an excise tax that can double the cost of their purchase. These fees are pretty stiff, but nobody tells people in Singapore when or where they can drive. There are few traffic jams, even on the busiest streets at rush hour, and the air is clean.

Singapore's no-nonsense approach to cars goes a long way toward keeping energy consumption down. Energy use and greenhouse-gas emissions are extremely low compared to other countries. But ever sensitive to business needs, Singapore has kept electricity rates cheap. Other countries, including Japan, add more value for every pound of CO_2 released into the atmosphere (even if emissions per capita are higher). But Singapore does not want to push too hard. We asked one official if Singapore could reach Japanese levels of energy efficiency. He said no, adding that the Japanese "have lots of flexibility in what they invest in; they can move energy-intensive businesses offshore, to Malaysia and elsewhere. We don't have this luxury. . . . We can't afford to shift to finance; maybe Japan can."

The government has developed a patchwork quilt of incentives and subsidies to encourage businesses to reduce electric consumption, rather than relying on high prices to do the job. For example, accelerated depreciation rates help landlords to upgrade air-conditioning equipment, which can count for 70 percent of commercial electric bills in this tropical climate. Other incentives encourage the use of energy-efficient devices, as well as renewable energy. The environment ministry considered a carbon tax but decided that companies would just pass the cost on to consumers, defeating its purpose.

Singapore encourages businesses to do environmental audits, acting as productivity consultants when companies request help. Indeed, the government is so confident of its abilities in this area that it set up an independent company (Singapore Environmental Management and Engineering Services) to sell its expertise in other parts of the region. Officials describe environmental audits as the "software" and environmental technology as the "hardware" of its green strategy. The government encourages ET companies to locate in Singapore.

Big oil and computer companies already do audits, and the environment ministry uses them as examples to sell smaller companies. To ensure that the right infrastructure is there, the government develops multistory industrial buildings for small companies and works closely with them through industry organizations like the Singapore Manufacturers Association. For example, when the country wanted to clean up its watercourses, small-boat repair and textile mills were relocated to these multistory buildings where pollution could be controlled. Those that didn't want to make the move were compensated and shut down.

Normally, the government is not so directly involved, preferring instead to set prices and quotas and let the market do the rest. For example, polluters can exceed organic limits for sewage for a fee, paying the city to treat their waste. The role of the environment ministry is to introduce new environmental technology as fast as possible, to encourage waste reduction at the source.

Clearly, Singapore is sensitive to business concerns, despite its success in the past. Singapore is an easy place to start a business—and just as easy to leave. The government, therefore, believes it must convince managers that its aggressive environmental policy is in the interests of industry. There are plenty of good reasons already for avoiding Singapore, particularly for manufacturing. For example, the city has high wages for the region, and an acute labor shortage. Workers can commute from nearby Malaysia, but employers must pay S$300 (US$180) per month for each foreign laborer, subject to quota limits. Already 30 percent of the workers in Singapore are foreign.

We asked one official if this scares off investors. His response: "For high-tech companies, we offer a disciplined, educated workforce and good infrastructure." As for environmental regulation, he said, "One investor in Indonesia was worried about the *lack* of pollution controls." Take the case of Mobil, an oil company that could locate its refineries anywhere. Most other countries in this part of Asia have bigger markets, lower wages, and laxer pollution standards. Instead Mobil continues to expand its refinery and petrochemical complex in Singapore.[3]

Singapore welcomes industry with open arms, but companies do have to play by Singapore's rules. The government has been screening newcomers for twenty years, discouraging those that are heavy polluters, particularly in industries that require lots of fresh water, which Singapore does not have. But these policies do not keep out heavy industry. Singapore is one of the biggest oil-refining centers in the world—and it doesn't smell like New Jersey. Shipbuilding is a major industry. We visited the spic-and-span Juron Shipyard, which sets international standards for environmental performance, yet manages to meet head-on low-wage competitors in nearby countries. In addition, hundreds of electronics companies do manufacturing and final assembly, activities that are not nearly as clean as many believe (see chapter "Alcatel Telecom Sends a Message").

Singapore has relied more on the carrot than the stick to build its industrial success. By recognizing that markets work better than regulations, Singapore rides the Green Wave, reaping efficiency benefits at the lowest cost.

When Singapore wants landlords to put in efficient air conditioners, depreciation schedules are accelerated; when it wants industry to meet tougher organic sewage levels, it charges fees for exceeding standards; when it wants to reduce car pollution and traffic congestion, it auctions the right to own a car and charges for rush-hour driving. People can continue to pollute, but they *pay* for it.

Compare this approach to that in the United States, for example. Government efficiency standards force air-conditioning manufacturers to improve their products; building codes mandate efficiency standards for new buildings. Cost is no object. As for sewage waste, if you exceed government standards, you get fined or sent to jail. And when it comes to car pollution, the government has tried every trick in the book—gas-mileage standards, reformulated gasoline, bus and multipassenger-car lanes, deadlines for electric vehicle sales. Every trick, that is, except the simplest and cheapest: high prices. Who says central planning died with the Soviet Union?

Singapore's strategy has the merit of effectiveness and efficiency. By simply charging for the cost of pollution, Singapore has greatly reduced the burden of regulatory compliance. Regulation, Singapore reasons, is ineffective and inefficient and therefore stands in the way of the country's industrial profitability and development.

Perhaps the smartest thing Singapore does is permit the easy flow of information. Singapore has, by some measures, the lowest telecommunications costs in the world. While other countries talk about the information superhighway, Singapore is already wired. Furthermore, its people are educated to the highest world standards. In short, Singapore has created a climate in which business can profitably substitute knowledge for natural resources.

THE CITY THAT NEVER SLEEPS

In Hong Kong, a visitor from New York feels right at home. Where Singapore is the picture of landscaped serenity, Hong Kong is a dense, urban environment of barely contained chaos. While Singapore grew out of a swamp, Hong Kong is perched on a rocky outcrop at the edge of the sea. In Singapore the swamps are gone, but in Hong Kong, the spectacular beauty of mountains and sea endures. Like the city itself, the harbor in Hong Kong teems with activity, and remains the soul of the city. Nevertheless, however arresting the scenery in Hong Kong, the visitor soon realizes what the business of Hong Kong is: making money.

Like Singapore, Hong Kong has British roots and was just as poor after the Second World War, with little or no manufacturing. Immigrants from southern China are in the majority in both cities. And like Singapore, Hong Kong's prosperity was built on free trade with the world, developing its industrial base in textiles, electronics, and, ultimately, services. Today, it's hard to believe that just thirty years ago these two cities were as poor as dozens of other Asian and African nations. With free trade, Singapore and Hong Kong enjoyed the fastest rates of growth over the past generation among developing countries. Both countries have similar levels of wealth. But where the government of Singapore has masterminded every step of that country's path of growth, the approach in Hong Kong is strictly laissez-faire.

Unfortunately, Hong Kong's laissez-faire attitude has until recently applied to the environment along with everything else. By the late 1980s, it was apparent that this approach could not continue. Air quality was unacceptable in most areas, and probably dangerous for a large segment of the population. At least 50 percent of Hong Kong's wastewater flowed into the ocean without treatment of any kind. Water effluent included municipal sewage as well as industrial waste that was often highly toxic. Hong Kong's offshore waters were a giant cesspool. One investigation of local shellfish turned up oysters with fecal contamination up to

100 times internationally accepted safety standards. Assorted other contaminants like heavy metals were found, and traces of hepatitis viruses were suspected.[4]

In this hotbed of capitalism, government regulation is simply a nonstarter. While big companies drive Singapore's prosperity, the entrepreneur is king in Hong Kong. Multinationals are comfortable with Singapore's rigorous environmental regime; Hong Kong's small businessmen are much more jealous of their prerogatives. A hearty "I'm from the Environmental Protection Department, and I'm here to help you" would simply not play well with Hong Kong's small manufacturers, a principal source of the territory's wealth—and pollution.

In the early eighties, Hong Kong, with a population of just 6 million, was losing tens of thousands of manufacturing jobs to southern China, where wages were far lower. The last thing the government could afford was to hasten this migration with heavy-handed environmental regulation. As one environmental official put it to us, "The big question is: If we clean up industry, will it all die? Will we kill the goose that lays the golden egg?"

Hong Kong wants to maintain its position as the leading Asian "dragon." Since 1971, output per worker has grown more than 2½ times, even faster than Singapore. Much uncertainty surrounds the return of control over Hong Kong from the British to China in 1997, but the outlook for this city remains bright nevertheless. Hong Kong is the gateway to China, and will remain so. But the giant sucking noise everyone hears in Hong Kong is the flow of jobs going across the border into southern China. The people of Hong Kong struggled to build middle-class lives. Will it now all slip away?

To offset this loss of jobs, Hong Kong must make a rapid transition from low-wage, low-tech, low-quality production to high-wage, high-tech, high-quality—but still low-cost—industry. The only way to make this shift is to boost the productivity of Hong Kong's workforce. Reducing waste is integral to this improvement.

When the Hong Kong government released its ten-year environmental program in 1989,[5] the first priority was infrastructure.

With its hellbent growth philosophy, the government had long neglected the pollution-control infrastructure. Since then, investment
has skyrocketed in sewage and solid-waste disposal projects. Hong
Kong developed a massive network of sewage collection and treatment facilities for the city and outlying areas. To begin with, Hong
Kong focused treatment on removing heavy metals and on the limited processing of sewage discharged into the sea. Hong Kong has
also moved away from incineration of municipal waste to a combination of recycling and sanitary landfills. The government has
contracted with private industry for the incineration of Hong
Kong's toxic and other hazardous wastes.

By bringing its infrastructure up to First World standards,
Hong Kong will eliminate its most offensive pollution problems.
But billion-dollar sewage plants do not prevent pollution, they
clean it up. Like their counterparts in Singapore, officials in Hong
Kong know they have to convince manufacturers, thousands of
them, that it is in their best interest to eliminate waste before it is
generated. Hong Kong officials realize also that they have an opportunity here to help to catapult the territory into a high-wage,
high-growth future. But to do so, the Environmental Protection
Department (EPD) must wage a block-by-block battle to bring
businessmen around.

SMALL IS BEAUTIFUL

In the industrial districts of Hong Kong, grimy, multistory loft
buildings stretch as far as the eye can see. These are home to the
small and medium-sized companies with 100 employees or less
that account for 70 to 80 percent of businesses activity in the territory. In each of these concrete high-rises, there are dozens of
firms with products as diverse as printed circuit boards, costume
jewelry, and men's suits. The environmental impact of each activity is different (although the drains may be shared). And small
manufacturers in such cramped quarters have little space for
wastewater treatment even if they have the money to pay for such

systems. The enforcement challenge for Hong Kong's Environmental Protection Department is monumental.

With the first round of legislation in the 1980s, existing industry was "grandfathered," that is, not covered. But in 1990, after public pressure increased, pollution standards were applied to all companies. Traditionally government has been probusiness, but by the end of the decade politicians began attacking industry as constituents complained about pollution. Now laws cover all discharges, even those from commercial establishments, like restaurants. In 1990, with the new legislation, the EPD set up a committee with input from industrial associations that could negotiate the details of regulations. Before, the government had tried to control by fiat, with little success. One official explained, "We set total objectives and spread around pollution allocations like slices of a cake."

To manage the enforcement task, the government applied increasingly strict pollution regulations to one neighborhood at a time. Before a pollution "control zone" was declared, the EPD had staff in place for six months. During that time, inspectors went door to door, asking each company about its activities, working with them, trying to get them to cooperate with others in the building to manage any environmental problems they identified. In some areas, the EPD had to wait until infrastructure development caught up; there was no point in pushing people if the sewage capacity wasn't there.

We asked one official how business responded. He replied, "They told us that they had no incentive to save water and electricity. It may be money down the drain, but they don't care." We asked him why the city didn't increase water charges to create an incentive, and he told us that government policy is to keep water charges low in Hong Kong. A big user will only spend HK$200,000 (US$25,000) per month; a smaller company, like a textile manufacturer, only half that. Industrial water is cheaper than domestic water to help business, and the government did not want to change its water pricing. An official recounted a visit to one factory, where they just left water running all the time. "We've always done this," they told him.

Many companies tell the EPD that they have no incentive to save on the raw materials they use. To cut waste, these companies would have to make process changes they don't care about. So the EPD decided to charge at the back end, for treating the sewage. This, the EPD reasons, will drive polluters to cut sewage fees by changing the front-end process that created the pollution in the first place.

Payback from these changes has to be fast. Since the territory reverts to Chinese control in 1997, "long term" is not a concept that plays well in Hong Kong. Nobody really knows for sure what the Chinese will do with Hong Kong when they take over. As one observer in Singapore remarked, "Hongkongers' strength lies in creatively wearing down a piece of machinery."[6]

All key sectors of manufacturing are now in flux. Textile companies are moving to China largely because of the low labor costs there. In addition, owners can sell their land in Hong Kong, which is very expensive, then move to China, where land is cheap. In short, the successful ones move, and the unsuccessful ones go down the drain (most likely in a flood of filthy wastewater). There are also many small food processors in Hong Kong preparing such Chinese dishes as noodles, peas, dim sung. These companies vary their production every day, which complicates treatment. Electroplating companies (jewelry makers, for example) are often marginal, and are generally very small. They usually have no place for waste treatment, even if they can afford it. Nevertheless, the EPD found that for electroplating companies, simple housekeeping changes solved a lot of problems. For example, they have pipes that are not expensive to fix leaking corrosive chemicals. Generally speaking, one official told us, 70 percent of waste can be avoided by tinkering around the edges. The next 20 percent can be eliminated inexpensively; the last 10 percent starts to cost real money.

One of Hong Kong's most successful sectors is printed-circuit-board makers. Some of the biggest ones in Hong Kong have become world leaders. As they grow, they have more space and money to spend on cleanup. The bigger companies can comply; smaller ones have difficulties. The EPD prosecuted one large company, which then went to closed-loop systems, reducing its water consumption by 2 million liters per year. This company was so pleased with the results that they now sell processing services to other PCB manufacturers, handling 10 percent of the etching solvents generated in Hong Kong.

We asked an EPD official if his people had been able to sell the link between clean production, costs, and quality. He told us that the experience of the large PCB company was typical, that companies resist at first, but they come around after they get going. Others realize that they have a competitive advantage once they get ahead of compliance; they wouldn't mind if competitors opt out of market because of tighter controls.

The EPD has found one card very effective to play against Hong Kong's entrepreneurs, who are ever sensitive to the value of their assets. Overseas buyers sometimes ask EPD for a list of companies with environmental treatment systems, so they can avoid those with problems. They don't want to buy a company that will cause bad publicity. This goes right to the value of an entrepreneur's company, and hits them in the pocketbook. Many see the light when they realize that the value of their companies is at stake. As small businessmen ourselves, we know the power of that message.

Many countries in Asia have tough environmental laws, but they don't have the resources to enforce them. Hong Kong has a different philosophy: don't enact a law until you can make it stick. As a result, the city has slipped from some of its 1989 goals, despite public pressure to reach them. The rapid schedule for infrastructure development has been hard to meet. When companies realize that the wastewater sewers won't handle the volume of water they produce, they connect instead to storm sewers, which run right into the sea. Just adding inspectors has been tough. In 1980, the EPD had only 100 employees; by the early 1990s there were over 1,000, growing at more than 10 percent per year.

A big new toxic and hazardous-waste center caters to small and medium-sized companies, taking their by-products at concessionary rates. The EPD wanted to make disposal free, but to attract a private operator the government had to guarantee revenues for fifteen years. To do so, they had to charge polluters; the problem is that if Hong Kong charges too much, companies will just dump their waste down the drain.

To clean up the air, Hong Kong switched to low-sulfur fuel, but the big problem now is cars. In 1992, the government mandated the use of catalytic converters for new cars, using U.S. and Japanese standards. Gas prices are high, at HK$7.00 per liter (about US$3.50 per gallon). But during the past decade, energy consumption in the city has risen with GNP; energy use has not been a big concern. Electricity, like water, is cheap in Hong Kong, as a matter of policy.

SAVING THE GOOSE THAT LAID THE GOLD-PLATED EGG

Industry in Hong Kong includes pollution controls on their lists of reasons for leaving the city. And while many business leaders admit in private that environmental regulations will not force them out, they are using whatever leverage they can to keep the business climate in Hong Kong friendly.

For EPD officials, this means trying to co-opt the companies they regulate, using a carrot rather than a stick. One official explained Hong Kong's approach to polluters: "Legislation says we don't have to give warnings; but we work with them. If they can give us a schedule and stick to it, we let them. . . . Of course, if they slip from the schedule without good reason, we prosecute. . . . We give them notice, and the chance to change, before we prosecute."

In free-market Hong Kong, industry convinced regulators to permit companies to, in effect, subcontract waste treatment to the government. Textile manufacturers can opt to release untreated water (within certain limits), paying higher sewage rates. The government will then take responsibility for treatment. As a result, businesses can "make the choice about whether it's cheaper to do it yourself or not."

Still, the EPD gets a lot of resistance, especially from the textile industry. As a result, the government has been forced to act like engineering consultants, trying to find the most palatable solution for each type of manufacture. "We look to Japan, the U.S., wherever, to find technology we need," one inspector said. Inspectors visit each company half a dozen times a year, monthly if there is a problem.

We spoke with W. T. Siu, a consultant at the Environmental Management Division of the Hong Kong Productivity Council, a government agency. The HKPC is an environmental crusader, but one for whom economic success is the Holy Grail.

Siu showed us a system developed by the HKPC for electroplaters, to recover nickel from their wastewater. A major industry in Hong Kong, electroplaters are leaving in droves—hundreds have already gone to China where the grass is greener (green as in money, not environment). We asked one woman we met in Hong Kong whether she was worried about life after Hong Kong comes under Chinese control in 1997. She told us, "I'm more worried about the nuclear power plant at Daya Bay that the Chinese are building than about nineteen ninety-seven." Talking about how poorly the project was constructed, she added, "They forgot to put in the rebar; they said they would put it in after the cement." No wonder she is worried.

In Hong Kong, if the government wants to push about pollution, it also must provide solutions. Siu's system pays for itself in eighteen months, after which manufacturers can sell the nickel they recover for a profit on the open market. The next challenge is copper, but the biggest problem, according to Siu, is cyanide, which is "very hard to get out—and we can't eliminate it without affecting quality."

For the textile industry, "thermal pollution" is a concern: wastewater is too hot for the sewer system. HKPC developed a heat-recovery system for one company that used 20,000 cubic meters of water per day. The multimillion-dollar system reduces the water temperature from 70°C to less than 45°C by reheating fresh water needed for the dyeing process. We asked Siu if there were any problems with heat recovery. He responded, "Not a technical problem, but with management; they have always just used cold water to cool down wastewater, so why change?" As everywhere, attitudes are the most important ingredient for making environmentalism pay.

Environmental officials in Hong Kong know that in the long term going green will make companies more competitive. But, to repeat what one told us, they don't want to get there by killing the goose that laid the golden egg in the short term. To resolve this trade-off, this official added, "Maybe some part of the goose will have to die."

No matter how much help each company can get from the government, eventually everyone must play ball. There's a certain environmental Darwinism at work here. Polluters are hounded until they clean up, or go out of business. Since the survivors improve their productivity in the process, Hong Kong is left with companies that compete successfully, while paying the kind of wages needed to maintain the city's standard of living.

OUT IN THE REAL WORLD

On a cold, rainy January day, we visited a small electroplating factory in Yuen Long, far from the glamour of central Hong Kong. The jewelry plater was located on the top floor of a relatively new, three-story concrete loft building, very much like a loft in the garment district of New York or industrial sections of Brooklyn. This day the windows were wide open, and the air was frigid. All the employees wore winter coats. Wooden pallets covered the floor, with running water underneath. Tanks of chemicals—a real witches' brew—held many types of jewelry in various stages of processing. Several dozen workers, without protective clothing, tended the vats, rapidly shifting containers of chemicals and racks of jewelry from place to place. The fire-exit door was covered with a locked metal gate. Welcome to Hong Kong.

In a cramped two-office suite at one end of the floor, amid half-packed boxes of merchandise, we spoke to the managing director. He told us that his company was talking to the EPD, but that they would have to spend HK$1 million (US$125,000) to comply with new laws, so he was moving to China by year's end—at least part of the factory. He told us that the "EPD said how we had to comply, not just that we had to have the results they want; in China, as long as we meet the results, they don't care how we do it." He told us that the outlays he needed here would not save money in the long run, because labor costs would be far higher than the value of the metal recovered. He added, "Space is a problem here; in China we can spread out."

This factory was not dumping untreated sewage. Already, the general manager told us, he was recovering nickel and gold, and he is trying to keep cyanide usage to an absolute minimum. He explained that with the nickel processing service from the HKPC, the value of the metal paid only half the cost of recovery. He had to take up the slack. He also spent HK$600,000 (US$75,000) for a gold-recovery system, with a five-year payback. And he said he was trying to solidify all these heavy metals, not dump them down the sewer, so they could be landfilled.

Nevertheless, the managing director complained to us, "We got a twenty-thousand-dollar [US$2,500] fine just because we were a little over the limit. Next time it will be ten times that amount. The Hong Kong government is giving us too little time. In other countries, these laws have been in place for ten or twenty years; Hong Kong wants us to comply now all of a sudden. . . . No bank will lend us money for this equipment, because there is no profit in it."

LESSONS FOR THE NEXT
GENERATION OF TIGERS

Singapore and Hong Kong are two countries that started without natural advantages, except as ports. Both countries have prospered by adapting to change. Both are riding the Green Wave to maintain that prosperity. In other parts of Asia, including such high-growth countries as Taiwan, the environment has been neglected. Eventually, the cost will be high in jobs as well as in ecological damage. On this forced march to high value-added growth, those that can't turn green will fall by the wayside.

After years of neglect, Hong Kong is cleaning up the environment. At the same time, the city is trying to raise productivity and position industry for the future. In a permeable economy like Hong Kong's (and Singapore's), citizens and business can vote with their feet if they don't like what the government is doing. The challenge is great, but judging by the continued growth of the economy in Hong Kong, perhaps the transition to cleaner, more productive industry is succeeding.

What Hong Kong and Singapore have learned applies to every policy-making authority in the world: don't regulate, bill them instead. Most governments opt for mountains of regulations and force industry into thousands of man-years of costly compliance. The simplest thing to do is to raise prices, and let the market look after the rest. Regulation almost inevitably increases overhead and stunts industrial growth. The lesson for other governments is simple: to enjoy rapid growth and good wages like Singapore and Hong Kong, raise the cost of polluting, and let the market take care of the rest.

THE REAL
INFORMATION
REVOLUTION
AROUND US

Since the invention of handwriting, the cost of information has been falling. Now with the advent of cheap and easy-to-use computers, it has fallen so far that companies are substituting information for labor, capital, and natural resources at an unprecedented rate. They can do this across a broad range of operations from manufacturing and distribution to customer service, achieving unheard-of improvements in quality and productivity. In other words, the work of machines and the natural resources that fuel them is being replaced by knowledge. The information revolution is driving the "dematerialization" or "greening" of production. What results is the remaking of the corporation for the first time in this century, preparing us for leaner and greener prosperity in the next.

Many changes can make information cheaper than raw materials. But today's advances in information technology are taking place at breakneck speed; the cost of information is now in free fall. The key to profiting from the Green Wave is unlocking the power of cheap information.

262

This extraordinary phenomenon of information substitution has happened many times before, most dramatically during the Protestant Reformation. Indeed, what is happening to business today is no different from what happened to the medieval Catholic Church once Gutenberg's press made bibles cheap and available for anyone to read. Suddenly everyone had access to information and could make use of it for themselves. This power shift swallowed whole large parts of the Church, several kings, and some entire nations. In the growth markets of the day, especially northern Europe, and later in North America, the Calvinists swept all before them with results we can still see.

Like the Church in the sixteenth century, companies the world over are being convulsed as inexpensive information fundamentally alters traditional measures of value and patterns of commerce. Perhaps most importantly, this change shifts power from producers to consumers, the modern "temples" of knowledge. Today's Protestants are the companies that know how to capitalize on the falling information-cost curve. While others are being torn apart like Europe four centuries ago, these companies are profiting from the diffusion of power that results from the new realities of cheap, accessible information. They ride the Green Wave by putting information to work.

FALLING INFORMATION-COST CURVE

To illustrate the information-cost curve, we have prepared a chart that shows the relative cost of information, energy, and labor. The cost of a three-minute, station-to-station telephone call from New York to Chicago is our proxy for information costs, while oil prices represent the cost of energy. For labor, we use effective wage rates. These are the average wages per hour paid, adjusted for changes in labor productivity. All figures are in 1990 dollars.

Since 1900, the cost of information has fallen precipitously, but the fastest decline has taken place since World War II, and especially since 1960. Effective wage rates have fallen steadily throughout this period, as higher productivity has boosted output. Oil prices have been surprisingly steady, except for a spike in the 1970s and early 1980s. Since then, oil prices have fallen back toward historical levels.

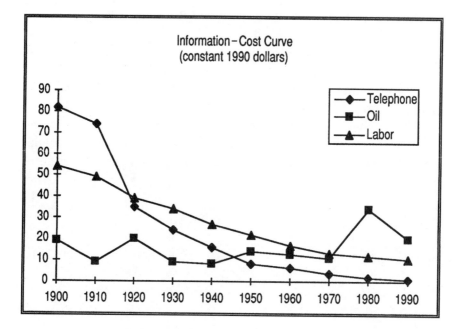

With the cost of information falling so rapidly compared to these other factors of production, business has a strong incentive to substitute information for natural and human resources wherever possible. This is the driving force behind the Green Wave.

A BRIEF HISTORY OF INFORMATION

For most of written history, information costs have fallen imperceptibly. Long periods passed between major cost discontinuities. The evolution from the invention of writing to the printing press took many thousands of years. But once discontinuities, like movable type, began, they occurred with increasing rapidity.

Progress from the printing press to the bill of exchange and other commercial instruments took only hundreds of years. Moving from this commercial revolution to the industrial revolution took only a century; from the industrial revolution to the telegraph, only half a century; and from the commercial computer to the personal computer, only twenty-five years. Now, seemingly daily announcements double the power of previous generations of microprocessors and associated hardware and software. Information costs are in complete free fall.

Information was once so precious it was sacred, far more scarce and valuable than labor, land, or other natural resources. Information on how to grow crops, when to plant them, and when the seasons were expected to change was painstakingly collected. Commonly it was held in temples and controlled by the religious with the full authority of the State.

Scarce and very expensive to acquire, information had great value to those who controlled it. From the earliest Mesopotamian king to Lenin and the *shacho* of Japan's industrial giants, rulers have recognized that information is power. Controlling it meant keeping power.

At the same time, high-cost information also made early civilizations vulnerable. Nothing devastated these societies more than the sacking of their temples: with the loss of that building went the loss of all knowledge from when to plant crops to how to rebuild the temple itself. A crude predator could eliminate thousands of years of carefully collected information at a stroke. And often did. Such "lost" civilizations are still being unearthed.

For millennia, information costs didn't fall by much. Information was expensive to collect, expensive to store, and, without machinery, it was even expensive to use. Empires and city-states rose and fell and knowledge increased, but the costs of acquiring, managing, and disseminating information stayed pretty much the same. Large empires in China, India, and Italy used bureaucracy and administrative skills to bring down information costs and widen information dissemination, but these efforts had little lasting impact. Information was managed similarly in Rome as it was in the earliest Sumerian cities thousands of years earlier.

Rome did, however, divorce the management of knowledge from temples by creating large libraries for civil administration and learning. But information was still tied to geography. You had to go to the library; it didn't go to you. Information dissemination remained a problem until relatively recent times.

Christianity made several important strides forward. One of Christianity's great gifts to civilization was the monastic system that preserved information following the collapse of the Roman Empire in the West. But the monasteries didn't do much to cut the costs of acquiring information or of increasing its dissemination. Indeed, for a time, monasticism may even have increased these costs. Illuminated texts were extremely laborious to reproduce.

The cost discontinuity in Christianity was the invention of the portable temple. When a priest can say a Mass anywhere, the temple goes to the people. Information, for the first time, was on the move, and Christianity became a portable, go-anywhere, cross-any-ocean phenomenon. This cut the cost of information dramatically.

It was also a major change in "software." Making temples portable and information mobile was a change in thought, not technology. Software changes like this one are essential to firms trying to apply knowledge to production instead of money to natural resources, machinery, and labor.

The next major software change, the translation of the Bible into the vernacular, allowed people to have the temple to themselves. This too brought down costs. However, information still had to be collected manually and recorded by hand, a very slow and expensive process. But the first hesitant steps in the secularization of information had been taken: information no longer had to reside in temples. It was losing its sacred character. A similar process has just recently taken place in many businesses. Restructuring means moving knowledge out of headquarters and into the field. The high priests of corporate power are finally giving way to their many followers abroad in the land.

The effects of secularization were explosive. Gutenberg's

fifteenth-century invention of movable type caused the most dramatic drop in the cost of information since handwriting was developed. It made books commonplace and universally available. People could leave the priest behind and take the book with them, anywhere. Computers have done much the same thing for today's line workers. They are empowered.

In the sixteenth century, information, and with it immense amounts of power that had resided with the Church and State, moved suddenly into the hands of individuals. Everywhere literacy moved, Church and State collapsed. We see the same thing today with the implosion of large corporate staff organizations.

Inexpensive books literally made the library at Alexandria available to anyone. Common people gained access not just to religious ideas, but to scientific knowledge and political ideas as well. Individuals for the first time appropriated the power to interpret information and to create it. They could print books. The power shift that followed movable type was indeed cataclysmic.

Just like the information revolution today, the Reformation spread across growth markets like wildfire. It flourished especially along major trade routes, following the business paper trail across northern Europe. This shift in control over information was naturally resisted by incumbent rulers, and dueling books were soon followed by dueling nations. Religious wars devastated Europe for centuries.

Then with the discovery of the New World, perhaps the most important event in history, the printing press had consequences that we can see today.

The combination of portable, secular information in the hands of the newly empowered and "reformed" colonists created a force that raced through the New World. These colonists saw their rights as "self-evident" and not bestowed on them by a Church or a State. Low-cost information enabled them to create a political process of their own and to assume, for the first time, an educated electorate. The secularization of information was complete. Low-cost information, in effect, created America.

It also created the modern corporation. Unencumbered by

churches or kings, the "reformed" had ideas of their own on how best to exploit their environment profitably. They found themselves, for the first time, in a position to organize and they did, creating one of the most endurable and adaptable organizations on earth: the publicly traded company.

By substituting information for craftsmanship, the industrial revolution made literacy a mass phenomenon. In the nineteenth century came improvements in printing technology that, among other things, lowered the cost of newspapers and made mass circulation achievable on a daily basis. With the invention of the telegraph, information became available everywhere instantly, rapidly "democratizing" stock markets, for example, and increasing their access to savings. Unprecedented social upheaval followed. While revolutions swept Europe, the United States was engulfed in a civil war of unprecedented gruesomeness.

By the mid-twentieth century, the burgeoning volume of information needed management. The computer age began. Computers cut information costs further than ever. Soon we had microprocessors, and the opening shots of the personal computer revolution were fired.

What makes PCs different from any other tool of information-cost reduction is that people aren't on the receiving end anymore. They can buy information, sell information, and most importantly, create information. Personal computers are the ultimate information-generation machine. The PC completes the shift of power from producers to consumers. The personal computer is a social force of unprecedented magnitude.

From the holy to the banal, the falling cost of information has meant the growing empowerment of consumers at the expense of producers. Knowledge today resides with consumers—educated ones at least. Information, now plentiful, has displaced other, traditional means of production: labor, land (or natural resources), and capital. Information also makes it easier for customers to voice, indeed to force, their preferences on producers.

On electronic networks of every kind from television to cyberspace, consumers exercise the new power they hold. Their reaction is instant: back through the media; at the polling booth; and most importantly, at the cash register. It is no coincidence, therefore, that the companies profiled in this book succeeded largely by improving customer responsiveness. We have concluded, in fact, that *profiting from the Green Wave and maximizing customer service are indistinguishable.*

HOW CHEAP INFORMATION TURNS PRODUCTS AND SERVICES GREEN

In the industrial age cheap information allowed us to substitute mechanical for human effort, but the costs were high in terms of natural resources. In the information age, knowledge is substituted for both mechanical effort and natural resources.

A computer program that improves pickup and delivery scheduling for Wal-Mart substitutes knowledge for drivers' wages and for diesel fuel. Everyone benefits: customers get better service and lower prices, management enjoys improved profits, workers maintain bargaining power with better productivity. And of course the environment improves with reduced emissions. On the farm, better cover-cropping can supplant expensive chemical pesticides. In the factory, better design can reduce purchasing requirements.

For all the talk about PCs, therefore, the information age is not about computers. It is about substituting knowledge for other resources. Information does not mean technology; it means experience, knowledge, and understanding. Computers can be the tools that facilitate the flow of information. But their misapplication can *slow* the change, institutionalizing structures that are inefficient, wasteful, and costly. Paving cow paths does not speed the flow of traffic.

To ensure optimal use of information, we have to harness the power of those in the best position to turn it into knowledge. This requires a radical shift in management. In the industrial age business adopted the only model that then existed: the army and its command-and-control management style. Like the army, information flowed from the top down to the foot soldiers. And like the army, this method created layers of bureaucracy to filter information up and down.

In the new model, organizations must be more organic. They are flatter, with many more direct reports to each manager. But most important, knowledge flows to where it is needed: from the line to management rather than the other way around. Shifting from the hierarchical to the organic model causes problems, though.

There are tools that can help. The first law of thermodynamics, for example, tells us that energy and mass cannot be created. For a business, this means that input (capital, labor, materials) equals output (products, services) plus waste (pollution). Therefore, if waste is reduced, output increases. The company that does this best will be the low-cost producer. Waste indicates where inefficiencies and frictions occur. Waste is like the canary in the mine shaft—it tells you when you have a big problem.

Organizing a firm to watch the canary is not always easy, as the examples in this book show. Since front-line employees are the ones who know where the pockets of waste are, and how they can be eliminated, harnessing their knowledge through information technology is vital. The farm worker in the field knows more about where tilling is needed than the farm manager. Similarly, the assembly-line worker knows what steps can be eliminated in putting a door on a car.

LABOR CONFRONTS CHEAP INFORMATION

The most serious threat to growth in any country is illiteracy: the illiterate cannot access, manage, or disseminate information. They cannot ride the Green Wave and are fast becoming unemployable. Moreover, they are a permanent drag on national productivity improvement and thus on growth in the standard of living. In the industrial age, any able-bodied person, regardless of race or sex or ability to read, could find work. Only the literate can control and process information. All the advantages of falling information costs go to the educated. The illiterate will become a new form of industrial "waste."

Labor has a key role to play in successfully exploiting the Green Wave. In the machine age, the role of unions was to extract monopoly rents from capital by withholding labor. In the information age, labor has learned the hard way that withholding services doesn't work. Strikes are greeted as another opportunity to move production offshore, or, more frequently, to substitute knowledge for labor. Cheap information means that market power is now so diffuse and machine age jobs declining so fast that unions offer little or nothing to their members. The struggle between labor and capital has become a sideshow, occasionally inconvenient but rarely of any consequence.

To profit from the Green Wave, labor has to reestablish its bargaining power and its ability to guarantee high-wage jobs. Since the standard of living of workers depends on their ability to improve productivity, labor needs to get into the productivity-enhancement business. The only way labor can benefit from the substitution of knowledge for raw materials is to make their workers more knowledgeable. Labor could then become an agency of the upwardly mobile, instead of a rear-guard action in an industrial Dunkirk.

Information, like oil, is a raw material; it creates value only when it is transformed into something useful, namely knowledge. This is well understood in Singapore, Hong Kong, and Japan, where education is taken seriously and produces results. These Asian countries that propelled themselves into the ranks of industrialized nations after the Second World War invested heavily in education and training. They have been able to capitalize on cheap information flowing from other countries, like the United States.

The United States is probably farthest ahead in permitting the free flow of information between citizens. It is less regulated than most of its trading partners, and has fewer government-owned companies. Yet serious barriers to information flow exist. The Federal Communications Commission and protectionism restrict the flow of information. A more serious threat to the full exploitation of cheap information is the sorry state of public education in America. There is no way to measure the impact of poor education on the use of information: illiterate people cannot turn information into knowledge.

Europe should have an edge here. Most European countries have excellent schools. Their workers are well educated, and well trained once on the job. They have the skills to change cheap information into valuable knowledge and ride the Green Wave to industrial success and higher-than-ever standards of living. However, their governments by and large do not believe in the free flow of information between citizens, preferring instead to monopolize electronic communications. This stunts labor's advantages, depriving workers of the opportunity to add real value.

Many Third world countries are being hurt by the falling information-cost curve. On the one hand, the substitution of information for natural resources has diminished the market for the commodities they sell, from aluminum to oil to zinc. On the other, the need to exploit the sudden wealth of information places a premium on education. The uneducated masses of the Third World, like their counterparts elsewhere, are seeing the value of their labor plummet.

HIGH STAKES
FOR AMERICA

2000 AND BEYOND

For two centuries, cheap natural resources were a competitive advantage for American industry. Since John D. Rockefeller struck oil in Pennsylvania 100 years ago, plentiful and inexpensive oil has driven America's economic expansion. At one time, perhaps before the invention of the transistor, unlimited natural resources helped many businesses, but today cheap oil holds U.S. industry back. With the level of competition now experienced in every marketplace, the United States cannot afford to squander resources—environmental, financial, or human.

In recent years, American industry has reemerged as an export powerhouse, achieving a level of competitiveness in world commerce not experienced since the immediate postwar years. Market share is up, profits are up, and—most important—productivity is up. These achievements are real, but the price has been high.

During this period of industrial rejuvenation, one national champion after another, from General Motors to IBM to Sears, responded to overwhelming market pressure by completely overhauling operations. In consequence, tens of thousands of Americans at a time—white-collar workers for the most part—got the ax. This was not just another economic downturn, or another boom-bust cycle. It was a profound reshaping of the American economy. No one can insulate American companies and American jobs from global competitive pressures anymore. For many managers and workers unable to survive the harsh reality, this may be the end of the American dream.

Whatever the cost, American business has literally stripped down into fighting form. But any lead on overseas competitors remains precarious. No business can long afford to be complacent about its competitive standing. Many Japanese and European companies put off their own day of reckoning, but recessions in the early 1990s finally forced them to face up to the kind of restructuring that has been so widespread in the United States. Models of Japanese and European economic power, from Toyota to Philips, have had to face the music as well, shutting plants, laying off workers, and shedding unprofitable divisions. More and more American business leaders are keeping a sharp eye on their rearview mirrors.

For all the pain endured by working Americans, much of the country's new competitiveness is based on favorable exchange rates. For a decade, the value of the U.S. dollar fell against the Japanese yen and the German mark. That's the good news: in effect, the value of the yen doubled compared to the dollar, making life a great deal easier selling Detroit-made cars, among other products. This change more than anything else has boosted America's relative productivity. The risk, however, is that, given the volatility of exchange rates, this advantage can evaporate overnight.

A cheap dollar also helped American exporters—at least in the short term. And so did cheap energy prices, oil and electricity. The last decade has been a time of weak commodity prices, particularly for oil. Like exchange rates, however, commodity prices can also swing quickly and violently. Rapid industrialization in Asia and Latin America may boost demand for natural resources and push prices up for a long time. Many American companies now enjoying gasoline at $1.50 a gallon would see their cost advantage evaporate.

Cutting manufacturing costs remains more important than ever. Japanese car and electronics companies have used the high yen to drive down costs like never before. And because natural resources are scarce in Japan, they are preparing for higher commodity prices, too. It's no coincidence that four of the companies profiled in this book are Japanese. These organizations live and breathe efficiency improvement.

For enduring success, American companies must keep the pressure on all across the productivity front. Blessed with an abundance of natural resources, the United States has been wasteful compared to other countries. As a result, cost cutting and waste reduction remain the mother lodes of opportunity to retain and expand America's current competitive edge.

THE COLOR OF MONEY

Environmental technology is becoming big business in America. Already, industry spends more on environmental compliance than on computer hardware, and American companies are leaders in many areas of environmental technology. Innumerable processes and technologies (frequently from small and medium-sized companies) are reaching the market in the United States. These are high-tech, high-growth opportunities, with the creation of many well-paying jobs. An added plus: this industry has been recession-proof.

Much of this activity is occurring in response to the new Clean Air Act and other legislation, but change also signals a more supportive view of environmental responsibility. Venture capitalists and mutual funds are now scouring the field for these new investment opportunities, facilitating the development of new ideas and products.

Many advances have taken place in the areas of greatest concern to Americans, such as toxic wastes, recycling, and ozone-destroying CFCs. American manufacturers are spending billions of dollars to clean up old sites contaminated with toxins. Companies large and small have responded with innovative solutions for removing chemicals from contaminated soil and groundwater. Recycling, as anyone who has children in grade school knows, has become a cardinal civic virtue. An entire industry has grown to turn garbage into cash by removing and reusing recyclables, from plastics to heavy metals.

To eliminate CFCs from manufacturing, suppliers have brought a host of new and more benign solvents to market. Water-based formulas using the acid found in lemons are replacing dangerous petroleum-based solvents. And everyone from start-up inventor-entrepreneurs to multinational chemical companies are finding ways to take CFCs out of cooling systems. On the energy front, American companies continue to lead the development of cogeneration technology (producing heat and electricity at the same time). Diesel-engine manufacturers are setting world standards for efficiency and cleanliness. And in such specialized areas as thermal recycling of old tires (i.e., burning them to produce power), Americans are putting technology to work to clean up thousands of local dumping grounds.

Americans have brought on the technology and the hardware, but they've also created the "software," the new thinking, necessary to make zero emissions a profitable reality. Environmental technology is becoming a commodity, just as computers have. Some of today's high-tech environmental solutions will become the mainframe dinosaurs of tomorrow. Already state-of-the-art incinerators are having problems getting enough garbage; recycling has reduced the need for their services. In the mid-1990s, toxic disposal companies had to scramble to find enough drums of poisonous chemicals to maintain growth. Better production techniques are reducing the need for these kinds of "end-of-pipe" solutions.

Here is where American industry shines: putting new ideas to work. The country's entrepreneurial climate brings good ideas to market quickly. And more American managements today adapt quickly to changing circumstances. The pace at which industry has shifted from pollution treatment to prevention demonstrates this capacity.

America's commanding lead in information technology also provides the tools needed to make environmental efficiency a competitive leader for the next decade. Where the United States could stumble, however, is in turning low-cost information into knowledge. Knowledge can be substituted for natural resources, but it is produced by educated workers, not computers. American public schools are not yet catching up with those in Asia and Europe. But the imperative is there: the revolution now underway in American education will eliminate this disadvantage.

YANKEE INGENUITY

After years of political wrangling, the federal government completely overhauled the original Clean Air Act in 1990. The new law mandates tough new standards for cities and industrial polluters, requires lower new-car emission levels and the introduction of clean-fuel vehicles, and phases out chemicals that deplete the ozone layer.[1] The revised Clean Air Act is the most important new environmental legislation in the United States in two decades.

Old-line business fought passage of the revised Clean Air law tooth and nail. American car makers, for example, successfully argued against emissions standards, as they were originally proposed, by calculating the additional costs in the billions of dollars and thousands of jobs.[2] Similarly, Detroit resisted higher car mileage standards (although in fairness, the car companies advocated higher gas taxes as a better means of reducing fuel consumption). Opponents estimated the cost of compliance with the act at $25 billion per year.[3] Even the EPA estimated that the act would force U.S. business to increase spending for pollution-control activities to $185 billion by the year 2000, up from $115 billion in 1990.[4] These kinds of figures are sobering, but the profiles in this book show how the smart companies are turning regulation to advantage.

Smart managements seized the challenge and opportunity of tough new environmental laws to make waste reduction their new philosophy: to turn their companies into low-cost producers by voluntarily exceeding any standards set by government. These forward-looking firms use environmentalism as a catalyst to transform their companies. They are ushering in the next stage of industrial development, sharply redefining production for the next century.

For some rigidly managed dinosaurs, the environment remains no more than a public relations or legal problem. Rearguard environmental battles account for a significant share of legal costs in the United States.[5] By some accounts, more is spent on legal fights about who is responsible for the so-called Superfund toxic dump sites than on actual cleanups. Ossified companies are simply fire-fighting, responding to a legacy of environmental battles with the EPA and state regulators, trying to stay one step ahead of their next fine. Since permitting, compliance, and pollution fights are legal affairs, responsibility frequently falls in the lap of the legal department. No one expects lawyers to improve sales or create jobs.

Occasionally, a flurry of environmental activity results from bad publicity. Headline-grabbing catastrophes often force old-line companies into a new approach to the problem. But getting from "problem" to "opportunity" remains a big step. An environmental engineer at one electronics firm told us that his company did not take CFC emissions seriously until environmentalists started marching outside the CEO's office with black balloons. As the area's largest employer, this company had not worried about bad press regarding the environment or anything else.

Fortunately, many forward-looking American companies have risen to the environmental challenge before them. But often their targets are far too modest, for example: "to reduce the generation of all waste 50 percent by the year 2000." But improving efficiency by half over ten years probably means falling behind the averages—even in the United States.[6] The toughest competitors are looking for these kinds of cost improvements *every year*. Companies that ride the Green Wave successfully set their sights high, so they can compete year after year.

A few years ago, the U.S. Environmental Protection Agency challenged industry with its "33/50" program, a voluntary effort to cut toxic emissions by 33 percent by 1992 and 50 percent by 1995. About 250 companies, accounting for a large share of the country's toxic output, signed on.[7] Meeting this "challenge" is a step in the right direction, but when numerous competitors are cutting emissions right to zero, America's cost position will continue to be undercut by a money-losing margin, sometimes fatally so. In today's global markets, "50 percent better than we were in 1988" won't cut it. Few will survive for long as high-cost producers.

TOXIC AVENGERS

When it comes to pollution control, the United States sets the standards in many areas. Air and water in the United States are generally cleaner than in the more densely populated countries of Europe and Asia. With the attention given to toxic wastes in the past decade, American industry has cut chemical emissions substantially. In the first four years that the EPA required companies to report all data, total chemical releases and transfers fell by one-third.

The United States has also cut energy use faster than all other major industrial countries except Japan and Great Britain. The United States made great strides after the oil crises of the 1970s in reducing the energy intensity of its economy.

Between 1970 and 1990, the amount of energy it took to produce each dollar of output fell by 25 percent. However, because Americans used so much energy to begin with, they still consume twice as much energy as the Japanese (and 50 percent more than the Germans).[8] That means every dollar of output generated in the United States requires twice as much coal, oil, and electricity as in Japan. During the past twenty years, the gap between American and Japanese energy efficiency actually increased.

As long as prices were rising quickly (in the 1970s) or people were afraid they would start rising again (in the early 1980s), American companies increased energy efficiency rapidly. But by the late 1980s, when real prices had fallen to postwar lows, the country was backsliding. U.S. energy consumption is currently stuck at a level well above those of its industrial rivals.[9]

There is a silver lining in America's lagging energy performance. If the country burns too much gasoline and coal, it means that there are deep pools of cost that can be eliminated. If the United States improved its energy efficiency by 25 percent, the country would liberate $200 billion for investment in growth each and every year. Waste reduction drives productivity growth. As the companies in this book show, these pools are hidden under rocks—old practices and old management habits—and can only be found with new thinking.

EXPORTS, EFFICIENCY, AND THE ENVIRONMENT

There is much that government can do to help business find these profitable pools to tap for greater efficiency. The simplest approach is to tax activities that are wasteful and environmentally undesirable. If government's objective is to reduce pollution and create good jobs, market pricing has to come to the fore. Good policy is not about spending more money—quite the opposite. The most effective laws are those that simply tax environmental "bads" like gasoline, toxic waste, and sewage, and allow business to figure out the best way to cut back.

It's no wonder that the Japanese use less energy: electricity and gasoline cost two to three times as much in Japan as in the United States.[10] Gas costs $1.50 per gallon in New York, so the United States burns lots of foreign oil and runs up its trade deficit. Gas costs $4.50 a gallon in Tokyo, so Japan runs energy-lean and it turns a trade surplus year in and year out.

In the short run, low gasoline taxes might reduce costs for

Americans. But any company that does not meet the efficiency standards of its toughest rivals is just putting off the inevitable. In the near future, companies with their heads in the sand will get blindsided from overseas. If Americans want to protect jobs at home, government policy must encourage efficiency above all else. Quality is the best tariff; raise environmental standards, and efficiency, productivity, quality, and wages will all improve.

Higher gasoline prices would hit business hard. Americans have greater distances to cover to go to work and to get to market compared with rivals in Japan and Germany. But this disadvantage should make decision-makers *more* concerned about wasting energy, not less. Higher prices would also affect Americans who are having difficulty making ends meet, and who have few choices in the way of public transportation.

There is a way around these problems. Revenues raised from gas taxes could be used to insulate those with lower incomes, by cutting Social Security contributions for low-wage earners, for example. The effect would be to discourage pollution, rather than to discourage job creation, which is the effect of high employment taxes. On a grander scale, high carbon taxes could raise enough money to lower the federal deficit significantly, thereby reducing interest rates and the cost of capital. All employers would benefit, including the efficient producers that reduce their energy use.

For certain types of pollution, where there is a limit to the amount that is considered acceptable, the government can auction the right to pollute. This approach works well for many industrial pollutants, but it can also motivate consumers. Singapore sets a limit on the number of new cars that are acceptable, and auctions new-car permits. The right to buy a big polluting car can cost more than $10,000.[11]

In 1925, Calvin Coolidge said, "The chief business of the American people is business." When it comes to pollution, legislators have generally viewed government's role as a counterweight to big business, to protect the individual from the big interests. Today the business of America is good jobs, but current policy still reflects the old David and Goliath attitude of government. In the past, environmental laws tried to strike a balance between the need to clean up pollution and a desire to insulate voters from the costs of doing so. The idea was to shift costs to industry through regulation. Instead of raising gas taxes, for example, the federal government set fuel-efficiency standards for automobile manufacturers.

This "let-business-pay" approach might have worked back in the fifties when foreign trade was insignificant and big business was seen as the enemy. Today exports drive growth.[12] U.S. manufacturers export more of their output than their Japanese counterparts. Almost one out of three jobs in the United States is directly tied to foreign trade. In other countries, the costs of improving energy efficiency has been placed squarely on the consumer in the form of sky-high fuel taxes. This gives foreign companies an important advantage.

GETTING BEHIND THE WAVE

Experimentation with market solutions is starting to take place. To help ration water between agricultural and urban use, California allows farmers to sell their water rights to cities in the state. The Clean Air Act is headed the right way, as well. To reduce acid rain, for example, the EPA issues power plants sulfur dioxide pollution "allowances," which they can use or sell. Also, refiners making more reformulated gasoline than the law requires can sell their "credits" to those not in compliance. This is good, but like the vast body of pollution law before it, the Clean Air Act relies primarily on regulations emanating from Washington. Perhaps the public needs to be sold on market solutions, although it seems strange that faith in Washington's central planning continues even after the collapse of the centrally planned Soviet Union.

To meet its global treaty commitments, the United States must reduce carbon emissions in the United States by the year 2000 to their 1990 levels. To do so through regulation will not be easy. A tax on the carbon content of fossil fuels (the main source of CO_2) would do the job, but by one account, levies stiff enough to have any real effect on U.S. carbon dioxide would cut GNP by $5 trillion over the rest of the decade.[13] But carbon taxes would not necessarily hurt the economy. The experience of other countries with high energy taxes indicates that business will do whatever it can to reduce fuel consumption when and as taxes go up. And judging by the experiences of the companies profiled in this book, efficiency would improve, as would quality.

Another regulatory trend may have an even more profound effect on energy efficiency in the United States than a gas tax would. In state after state, regulators are ending the monopoly formerly enjoyed by electric power utilities. Deregulation will allow individual electric consumers (generally businesses) and independent producers to harness the power of energy now wasted. When electricity is produced at traditional large power plants, as much as half of the energy in the coal or oil is lost as waste heat before it reaches the consumer. Cogeneration (used by several of the companies in this book) captures much of the heat that is now simply vented into the atmosphere.

SUSTAINABLE DEVELOPMENT IS HERE

We are at the dawn of a new industrial age, when the substitution of information for natural resources will make sustainable development a reality. There is no reason why America should not lead the way. There was a time when abundant resources were the biggest advantage the United States had. Today, this dwindling legacy works to the disadvantage of American industry.

If the United States does not maintain a rapid pace of waste reduction and efficiency improvement, the restructuring of the economy that took place over the past decade will seem like a picnic. If the United States fritters away the gifts with which it was so fully endowed, productivity growth will remain disappointing. And without better productivity, industry cannot pay the rising wages needed to sustain the American dream.

The United States is a job-creation machine. Unfortunately,

too many of those jobs don't pay middle-class wages anymore. It doesn't make much sense to create jobs by becoming the First World's sweatshop. With cheap energy, low-cost wages, and abundant—if poorly educated—labor, the United States may be the perfect location for low-tech manufacturing that its Asian and European counterparts no longer want. But Americans may find themselves fighting with Mexico and Indonesia over these jobs, while the opportunities needed to support a large middle class shift to Japan, Western Europe, and Asian centers like Singapore and Hong Kong. Wasteful industrial practices are associated with the Third World, not the First.

Americans are now choosing the direction they wish to take. The United States has everything necessary to succeed in this new world: environmental technology, information technology, flexible workers, entrepreneurial spirit. The country has many strengths, and retains its economic leadership. The American worker remains the most productive in the world. In services and in most manufacturing sectors, U.S. productivity remains well above that in Europe and Japan.[14] If Americans want to remain the world's most prosperous people, they must keep raising the world's standards for efficiency. It's happening now. More will follow if industry and government act wisely.

RIDING THE
INFORMATION-
COST CURVE

ADVANTAGE AMERICA

The relentless fall in the cost of information is undermining the economics of many industries. This change is similar to the effects of rapid construction of the railways in the mid-nineteenth century that occasioned industrialization in Europe and the United States. The substitution of knowledge for human, financial, and natural resources is causing the reindustrialization of the economy. Railway construction created many fortunes—and destroyed many others. The frenzy of investment and acquisitions in multimedia, wireless communications, entertainment, and third-world telephone networks will paper the world in the twenty-first century equivalent of railway bonds. Who will be the winners and losers this time around?

There are a billion middle-class consumers in the world today and there are thousands, if not tens of thousands, of companies who want nothing more than to suck cash out of their pockets. The company that can dominate direct, electronic access to these consumers will be the most formidable industrial empire

285

ever known. Trillions will be made. Direct access will be *the* growth market of the next quarter century.

To find the losers, just look over any list of the world's biggest enterprises. In country after country, companies with electronic access to consumers, telephone companies such as Nippon Telephone and Telegraph, British Telecom, and AT&T, rank first or second and occasionally third. NTT is ranked first in Japan and in the world. Collectively, these companies employ millions in well-paid jobs. Clearly, investors have placed a very high value on these companies. Indeed, the top eleven firms of this kind have a combined capitalization of some $500 billion. That's half a trillion dollars of shareholder money, a significant portion of the world's entire wealth. If something wipes out a large part of this value, every stock market in the world will be shaken to its core.

That "something" is about to happen. The same forces that tore apart IBM and Digital Equipment are about to strike these direct-access giants. Many are companies burdened with excessive costs and unhealthy balance sheets. Their ability to adapt to change is limited. They are highly vulnerable. Many are likely to implode.

In the United States, eight of the top fifty companies—total market capitalization: $250 billion—are telephone companies (for the most part the remnants of the old Bell system). Several of these companies will be gone by decade's end. A few will be bought up. Some will be acquired. But collapse is inevitable. Already, carriers across the United States have combined their cellular operations in a process that is still going on. Soon these talks will broaden to cover full integration.

The direct impact of this change on the environment will be profound. Right now, for example, the telephone system is the world's largest copper mine: U.S. telephone companies have 1.5 billion miles of wire in the ground and strung from telephone poles. This "outside plant," as it is called in the industry, is very expensive to build and labor intensive to maintain. Within a decade, much of it will be pulled down and recycled, just as thousands of miles of rail lines were abandoned and pulled up after

World War II. That is, if anybody can find a use for that much copper. The concentration of natural resources once required for this infrastructure is rapidly becoming unnecessary.

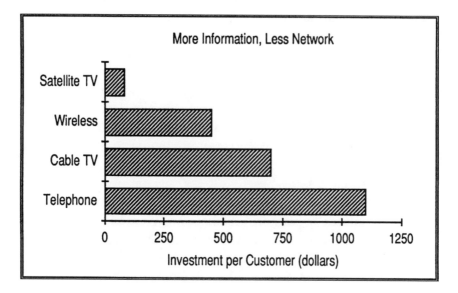

The economic forces that will devastate the telephone industry (and the copper market along with it) are compelling and irresistible. The above chart shows the investment in equipment necessary to provide different kinds of communications links to consumers. Telephone is by far the most expensive. Phone companies have well over $1,000 of plant for each customer. Cable companies are not much better off, although they can provide much more information over the wires that reach their customers. Wireless alternatives, like cellular, personal communications systems (PCS), and satellite communications are, well, wireless. They don't require the same investment; they are far less resource intensive. For telephone companies with a hundred years' worth of copper baggage, the challenge is big, to say the least.

As daunting as the problem is for existing players in the United States, it is worse in many other industrial countries. While American carriers have been shedding jobs for a decade, those elsewhere have been slow to respond. Germany, for example, is privatizing Deutsche Bundespost Telekom, the government-owned telephone system. The Bundespost is in no shape to be privatized, and neither the German government nor the Bundespost itself—let alone its powerful unions—appears to be in any hurry to trim the beast.

Telekom has twice as many employees per customer as the average American carrier, and four times as many as a typical cable TV company. Put another way, to compete with the American telephone company Bell Atlantic, Telekom needs to cut 100,000 employees off its payroll. To compete with cable operator TCI, Telekom would have to cut 150,000 employees. But to be a real contender—lean and mean enough to survive the multimedia wars—it will have to ax nearly 200,000 people.

Such change would be unprecedented in modern Germany, and is not politically possible. Telekom has granted full, protected civil service status to three times as many employees as it needs to compete. So they *can't* be fired, no matter what. Investors could be stuck with a pig in a poke. More likely, German taxpayers will pick up the tab for unnecessary jobs, just as they did when highway construction threatened railway workers.

For a customer, shareholder, or employee of the New York Central Railroad in 1920, it would have been inconceivable that this industrial juggernaut would find itself on the scrap heap in just a few decades. If you've ever walked down an abandoned railroad line you'll understand what's going on, and how quickly fortunes can change.

PERSONAL COMMUNICATIONS SYSTEMS

PCS is a new form of wireless communications, much like cellular, but cheaper and better. While cellular is convenient, it is also expensive. For most users, cellular complements ordinary telephone service, but does not replace it. PCS will be different: it slashes the cost of network operations and maintenance. Indeed, the cost pressure from PCS may be what finally forces telephone companies to abandon their existing "wireline" plant. When PCS can reach consumers for less than the cost of junk mail, all that aging telephone gear will look pretty fragile.

Many in the investment community regard PCS as a me-too technology that will slug it out with cellular in a zero-sum game neither can win. Initially, PCS will compete with cellular, and in terms of quality and price, will provide a formidable challenge. The real opportunity, however, lies in providing all telephone customers with a cheaper alternative to the expensive and inflexible copper plant now in place. PCS will do to the telephone what truckers did to the railroad: decimate it.

The ubiquitous telephone network is now a financial drag. One regional Bell operating company president told us, "We can't lower the costs of maintaining the network. There might not be enough cash flow to pay for upgrading our network." Cellular, now a cozy duopoly, will not be able to respond much faster.

In 1983, AT&T predicted that by the year 2000 there would be 900,000 cellular phone users in the United States—a big number at the time. At the end of 1994, with six years to go, there were already 20 million users. AT&T (and others) underestimated this market by a wide margin. Over the next decade, many millions more will be cut loose from the wired telephone system.

In the United States, once the new PCS networks are built, there will be a dozen or more wireless, wireline, and satellite options for each consumer. There will be as many as half a dozen PCS operators in every area. All these carriers will have computers capable of giving consumers fingertip access to the best network, at the best price, for whatever type of communication they have in mind.

One of these new alternatives could be from electric power utilities. Like cable TV providers, power companies want to use the wired connections they already have going into every house to offer telephone service. Once these two-way links are in place, however, they will have other important benefits.

Power companies must build (or purchase) enough electric

capacity to meet the maximum daily needs of their customers. This demand might peak in the morning during the winter when hot water heaters come on, or late in the afternoon during the summer, when people start flipping on their air conditioners. For the rest of the day, capacity exceeds demand, often by a very wide margin. If peak demand can be cut, large capital and operating expenditures can be avoided.

Two-way communications with customers can help. For a discount, utilities will offer customers interruptable electric service for major appliances like hot water heaters and air conditioners. When demand peaks, an energy management system starts shutting off some of these devices for a few minutes at a time. While barely noticeable to individual customers, the impact on peak generating requirements can be significant. The need for new coal burning plants or hydro-electric dams is reduced: better for customers, the utility, and the environment. As a bonus, these systems can also read electric meters, eliminating the need for workers to visit each house.

SATELLITE TV

While PCS will render the telephone network obsolete, satellite TV will have the same effect on cable. In a matter of months in 1994, satellite TV signed up half a million customers, many of whom canceled cable subscriptions. With its vast improvement in quality and variety, satellite TV also captures consumer dollars now flowing to Blockbuster Video and other similar rental outlets. Furthermore, the newest generation of satellite TV was designed for two-way communications via a link with regular telephone lines should interactive applications develop.

TV broadcasting from satellites has been around for years. Originally designed for distribution of network feeds to local stations around the country, satellite TV was then offered directly to consumers. The service never appealed to a market beyond those in remote locations because of size and cost. Until recently, the receiving dishes were 8 to 12 feet in diameter, and cost a minimum of $2,000. With the latest generation, price and size shrunk sharply to $700 for an 18-inch dish capable of receiving 150 channels for a monthly fee in line with cable service. Competition is likely to push dish prices down along the kind of curve that brought us $99 VCRs.

What is most remarkable about satellite TV is that it shifts almost the entire cost of infrastructure to the consumer in the form of a satellite dish. The information provider rents base station and transponder time, the cost of which is tiny when spread across all customers. With cable, the operator bears the entire cost of stringing wires by each house, whether its residents sign up or not. Furthermore, cable networks will require billions of dollars in upgrades to compete with direct TV and telephone company offerings. We fully expect there will be tens of millions of satellite TV subscribers in the United States before decade's end; the service is already a big success in the United Kingdom. Satellite TV growth will come out of the hide of cable companies, and those telephone companies that think they can grab a big share of the entertainment market.

If PCS eliminates the last mile or two of cable to the consumer, satellite TV gets rid of it all altogether. Already, over 60 percent of American households have cable TV, and there are some 27,000 video stores in the country. There are miles of cable and lots of bricks and mortar that will be replaced by a simple 18-inch satellite dish. In short, satellite TV offers everything you want from your communications network, and less.

BRANDING WARS

With all these electronic channels delivering similar menus of communications and entertainment to consumers, competition will be brutal. To differentiate themselves, and to avoid slugging it out on price alone, competitors will rely on branding of their new media.

Bell Atlantic started the land rush for direct electronic access to consumers late in 1993 when it announced that it would acquire Tele-Communications, Inc. (TCI), the world's largest cable carrier, for a cool $33 billion. Bell Atlantic unleashed a gigantic wave of mergers, acquisitions, and joint ventures now rolling across the industry, a wave that is getting bigger and stronger by the day.

The TCI deal would have been one of the biggest mergers in history (if Bell Atlantic had pulled it off). What stunned other carriers around the world was the brilliance of the concept: that a network giant with global access can project its brand into every home in the world, seizing control of consumer spending habits and shutting local carriers out of their home markets completely.

Bell Atlantic hoped to dominate this business using "Star-Gazer," a platform for entertaining its customers. TCI would have broadened StarGazer's reach from a few mid-Atlantic states to most of the United States and several key European and Asian countries.

StarGazer's mission is simple: to manage customers' experience of the network and its services. Simply gaining access to customers—buying TCI—was not enough. To make that access pay, Bell Atlantic had to control the customer's interaction with the network and manage how customers "experience" the services they buy. In other words, telecommunications has become the business of brand management, Disney style.

If Bell Atlantic had succeeded in getting brand dominance with consumers, all the other big players from AT&T to NTT, from Microsoft to Apple, and from Sega to Nintendo to Sony, would have been shut out of living rooms around the world. This would have turned them all into evolutionary dead ends, the failed species of market evolution. Competitors worldwide suddenly realized that if Bell Atlantic could rapidly duplicate Disney's success with Mickey Mouse, a cartoon character recognized instantly in every consumer home the world over, it would have administered a stunning blow from which they might never recover.

In the aftermath of the failed Bell Atlantic–TCI merger, Disney itself started working with Ameritech, BellSouth, and SBC

Corp. And Disney's ambitions are global. In one joint venture, for example, Disney will launch a German-language satellite television channel, specializing in family entertainment, that will be available to one third of German households. This combination of cheap computing and alternate access technologies will cut off the German phone company, Telekom, from its customers.

The genius of Disney, or Coca-Cola, or any of the world's great brand managers, is that their products are not just recognized, they are understood. A Coke means the same thing to literally billions of consumers, irrespective of language and culture. Indeed, the image of "Coke" *is* language. It expresses a common set of values, a "virtual" culture, understood by everyone who sees the image, whether or not they actually drink Coke or even like it.

Coca-Cola and Disney go to great lengths to protect their brands, and to manage how consumers experience their products. Disney World is just that: an entire world of Disney in which Disney controls the whole environment and meets every need.

Bell Atlantic's vision was no less breathtaking. The company believed that using StarGazer and similar ideas, a virtual Disney World could be projected through the network, locking on to the imaginations of consumers everywhere.

To old telecommunications hands, this sounds pretty farfetched. But it is not to those on the leading edge of consumer marketing, who are accustomed to the power of media and well-managed brands. Immediately after the TCI announcement, every major player in consumer electronics and video services started to move. Blockbuster, the video rental giant, perceiving a threat to its very existence, has started work with IBM and Sega to download the Sega experience to eager "Segaddicts" the world over. Entertainment and communications will be remade in a few years. There is simply too much money at stake for it to be otherwise.

THE BATTLE SHIFTS TO THE INTERNET

In 1994, the release of a recording on CompuServe by Aerosmith, the popular rock band, showed just what the impact of these forces will be. These recordings were exclusive, since you couldn't buy them in stores. But they can be used by anyone with a PC, a modem, and a big enough hard drive to store the music. CompuServe, an on-line service provider, showed that with good brand management, control of consumer purchasing can move rapidly from carrier to carrier.

Aerosmith has been around a long time—long enough to be remembered by the parents of the young teens who now flock to their concerts, watch their videos, and buy their records. In other words, Aerosmith may be long in the tooth, but the band has broad cross-segment appeal. Selling the music in this way, CompuServe has accomplished several things at once. It has reinvented the business of making and distributing records, slashed costs and lowered prices, and initiated a process that will eventually divert billions away from existing retail channels. CompuServe may have unleashed the billions of dollars needed to make on-line services profitable in a big way.

With a stroke, CompuServe reinvented record production and distribution. Recordings can be sent from Aerosmith's studio directly to your home the minute they are finished, and charged to your Visa, MasterCard, or American Express. By eliminating everyone in the food chain from the record company to the retailer, CompuServe has created a wealth-generating machine with fabulous potential.

CompuServe has substituted cheap information for discs, tapes, and the whole distribution system that supports them. An entire industry could implode, eliminating layer after layer of cost. Losers include retailers, obviously, but also the endless numbers of agents, publishers, labels, manufacturers, and distributors that come between you and the recording artist and studio.

CompuServe has demonstrated conclusively that consumers will redirect spending from existing channels into the network.

A similar process is also taking place in computer software, which has traditionally been distributed on disks, much like records. A small developer called id Software, from Mesquite, Texas, created a market for itself overnight by distributing millions of free copies of its "Doom" game over the Internet. When the company released a new version, "Doom II: Hell on Earth," paid sales were expected to top a million copies. Another software distributor, CyberSource, sells computer programs over the Internet on a trial basis. If you don't pay after 30 days, the program deletes itself from your hard drive.[1]

CD distribution over the Internet, like that which CompuServe and Aerosmith tried, will take a while to develop, since each song can take up to half an hour to download using the typical modem. But satellite TV, which now offers CD-quality music channels, has the capacity to deliver an entire CD in less than thirty seconds. You can see where all this is going: with high-powered, multimedia PCs now available for home use for less than $2,000 (and falling), demand can only grow.

This should be good news for telephone companies, except that they cannot afford the cost of rebuilding their networks to take this kind of traffic any time before the next century. The big question for those providing electronic access is who will control the network interface with their customers? In 1993, Bell Atlantic thought carriers themselves could do this and was prepared to bet $33 billion that it could be done. Less than a year later, carriers had been pushed aside, probably for good. This is bad news for telephone company management, employees, and shareholders. Without carrier control over the customer interface they will have a hard time cashing in on the surge of demand that lies ahead.

With its Aerosmith release, CompuServe showed how the game will unfold. There are already millions of kids who use CompuServe weekly, if not daily, to do homework. They are familiar with its intricacies and know how to make it work for them. Kids even talk "CompuServe." With Aerosmith recordings at the touch of the same key, they are already won over. So, for that matter, are their parents. Talk about value: CompuServe keeps the kids from hanging out at record stores in the mall.

And Aerosmith recordings are environmentally clean. CompuServe has demonstrated that services with real cash potential can be distributed over the network without leaving a trace. Products on the Internet eliminate the physical product itself, and its packaging and all layers of distribution, including record stores. Some 1.5 billion CDs, tapes, and records are sold every year around the world, 800 million in the United States alone. There's a lot of oil taken out of the ground to make those CDs. A few years ago there was a debate over the environmental friendliness of the CD "jewel" box, the plastic flip-open case each CD comes in. A number of recycled and recyclable alternatives were bruited about. These are a dead letter now: CDs over the Internet cut out the jewel box, the CD, the stamping factories, the oil wells, and everything in between.

THE BIG BANG

If the telephone companies are loosing their grip on communications, will control then shift to brand builders like Disney? Or the providers of entertainment like Hollywood producers? Many players are worried about what's going on. They can see the writing on the wall: Who needs record companies if the Internet connects customers and musicians directly? Others are trying to adapt, as we have seen, with mixed success. Disney, for one, has found CD-ROMs a tough business to crack.[2]

In fact, control is shifting away from producers of all kinds to consumers. Perhaps for the first time in history, consumers, not businesses, are driving change now. Microprocessors are making it happen. In the United States today, more PCs are being shipped than TVs. Over the next decade a billion PCs could be sold around the world.

Recently, a watershed was reached in information. Computing power is measured in MIPs, or millions of instructions per second. Historically, computer performance was valued in dollars paid per MIP. In 1995, the "dollars per MIP" barrier was crossed, and a MIP could be purchased for less than a dollar. We call this event the "big bang."

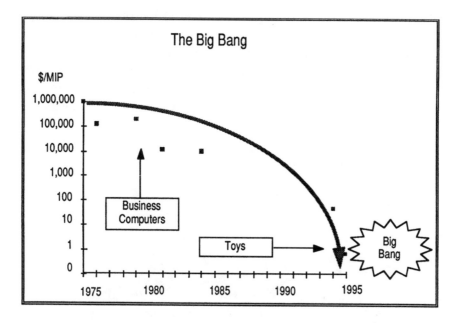

In the future, cheap and powerful microprocessors will allow toys to do to personal computers what PCs did to mainframes: completely restructure the market for processing power and network through-put. The sudden emergence of toys as powerful as mainframes running loose in homes around the world will allow consumers to dictate the volume and direction of network traffic.

Nintendo, Sega, and others have introduced toys so powerful that you can trace a network from one machine to another clear around the world without ever encountering another processor as powerful. These toys place extraordinary centrifugal forces on the carriers connecting them. The rate at which networks expand— and how they expand—will now be dictated by the software in toys. Moreover, each Sega will be a wormhole into another network of unknown size and dimensions.

The big players in communications must confront an ugly truth: for several decades the cost of owning a computer has been dropping much faster than the cost of owning a network. Computer owners, not the carriers, now drive the network, and they have all the cost advantages to make this dominance stick, permanently.

Unfortunately for the telephone companies the cost of providing a telephone circuit has not fallen as fast as computer prices (see chart). Saddled with the communications equivalent of mainframes, they are trying to compete with PCs. That's a losing proposition.

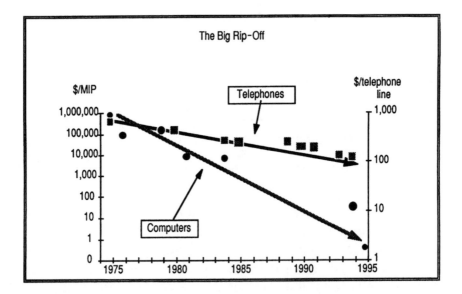

Two-way video could cause bandwidth demand to explode even faster than high-powered games. The companies that now dominate entertainment cling to the one-way broadcast model, with interaction limited to placing orders for merchandise or movies. Declining information costs are turning the tables. Over three million camcorders were sold in the United States alone in 1994.

Eventually, every home will turn into a TV station with immense transmitting capability.

Two-way broadcasting is not the same as video conferencing, a market waiting to happen since AT&T introduced the Picturephone at the 1962 World's Fair. Innumerable large companies as well as start-ups continue to pour vast resources into R&D for this application. For a variety of reasons, including lack of standards and transmission quality, but most importantly for lack of demand, this business is going nowhere.

Education could be the "killer application" that causes video conferencing to finally happen. For example, software developer Interactive Learning International of Troy, New York, has combined video conferencing with interactive training programs to create a very powerful learning model. With the ILInc system, students and trainers can be anywhere on a network while communicating and working together. This is actually more interactive than a live class room, since the PCs make sure that each student is participating all the time.

In a traditional class, even a small one, students can daydream as they gaze out the window. They can't when they are plugged into a computer. Such interactive learning may eventually solve the "education crisis" in the United States, bringing to public schooling the kind of restructuring and productivity improvements experienced in business over the past generation.

Few telephone companies are ready for these seismic changes. NTT in Japan is the only one we have heard of with a plan for two-way video communications from every home. In its plan called "NTT's Basic Concept and Current Activities for the Coming Multimedia Age," the phone company predicts video traffic in and out of its customers' homes. NTT wants to lay enough fiber cable to meet this demand, a big job to say the least.

France Telecom gave its video conferencing business a boost in 1995 with free trial calls for buyers of its PC video kits.[3] A decade ago, France Telecom created the world's biggest market for on-line communications by giving away millions of "Minitel" terminals to its customers. Minitel was a big success in France.

While originally designed as an electronic yellow pages, what sent Minitel off like a rocket were the electronic "chat" services (essentially on-line sex talk), which multiplied like Gaulois butts in a cafe ashtray.

Two-way video pornography certainly holds some interesting possibilities, and is already taking place on the Internet. Those with high-speed data connections can tap into the Internet's multicasting backbone, or "M-bone" as it is called. With PC video kits (like those sold by France Telecom), low-grade video conferencing and voice communications can take place on the M-bone between individuals and groups of people much more cheaply than is possible on phone company video conferencing lines. And, of course, the Internet offers anonymity.

TV set top boxes that simply allow carriers to broadcast lots of movies will fail. Systems that let consumers interconnect with their choice of carriers for everything from computers to camcorders will do very well. This suggests to us the set top winners will not be today's personal computer leaders—their products are expensive and rigid. What's more, their suppliers have agendas firmly rooted in the past. Look for newcomers with a more flexible and cheaper approach.

ELECTRONIC TOLL COLLECTION

The Internet and other communications channels deliver information, but they also connect buyers and sellers. In a sense, the Internet is one big marketplace. One of the most profound effects of this development will be on money.

Bank-by-phone, like most other on-line services, has been pretty much a dud. Since the early 1980s, banks have offered a variety of ways to check bank balances and move funds around by phone or by PC. Neither these nor any other personal finance–related computer products captured the imagination of consumers, until Intuit's "Quicken" program came along. Quicken is a cheap, simple, and powerful budgeting and bill-paying program that runs on a PC. With millions of customers, Intuit attracted the attention of programming giant Microsoft in 1994. Others, like American Express, are also attracted by the possibilities. In 1995, Amex entered a joint venture with America Online to offer an array of financial services to its cardholders.[4]

In combination with the marketplace potential of the Internet, software like Quicken could replace banks as we now think of them, and the employees who work there. In the United States alone, there are some 100,000 commercial banks, savings banks, and credit unions, with two million employees. Quicken can already pay your bills electronically. It would not be a big step for this software to surf the Net for the best deal on a car loan or a mortgage, or for the best interest rate on a deposit. In fact, a computer could go out for bids every night on a loan, and shift your business to the lowest bidder for 24 hours at a time.

As shopping develops on the Internet, and as it evolves on the home shopping channels, order entry and payment will be electronic. "Home page" product listings on the Net will evolve into interactive, virtual shopping. Information technology will reduce the need for many physical products, the stores that sell them, and the banks that finance them. From these broad brush strokes, the sustainable development landscape may be discarded. Economic growth can be uncoupled from natural resource exploitation without hurting our living standards. On the contrary, the way we live will improve.

One big question remains: Will all these new means of information access reduce the need for mobility? Or will car use, and the pollution and energy consumption that goes with it, just grow and grow like Topsy? Will the information superhighway replace real highways the way the interstates replaced the railroads? Perhaps we need to look back further: Railroads did not replace horses, but created demand for transportation that did not exist before. People simply did not travel, and goods did not move as much, until the railroads were developed.

One thing is certain: falling information costs will profoundly affect the way we live. Many of today's industrial leaders will wane, as newcomers push their way to the front of the line. But our lives will improve. We will be freed from the constraints of time and space to live, work, and play where we wish. With fewer demands placed on the planet for natural resources, the environment will improve dramatically. And companies will never control markets and lives the way they did in the past. In tomorrow's information world, consumers, citizens, people will call the shots.

NOTES

INTRODUCTION

1. See *USA Today,* February 23, 1994, pp. B1, D1.
2. "A greener bank," *The Economist,* May 23, 1992, p. 79.
3. "Cleaning up," *The Economist,* September 8, 1990, Survey, p. 26.
4. "Environmental spending," *The Economist,* October 12, 1991, p. 107.
5. In an advertisement, the state of Massachusetts ranked growth rates for four high-tech industries in that state in 1991 as follows: environmental manufacturing (30 percent), biotechnology (23 percent), software (19 percent), environmental services (15 percent), telecommunications equipment (15 percent); *New York Times,* May 31, 1992, p. D5.
6. "Cleaning up," *The Economist,* September 8, 1990, Survey, p. 5.
7. "The perils of greening business," *The Economist,* October 14, 1989, p. 75.
8. "How to prosper in the value decade," *Fortune,* November 30, 1992, p. 91.
9. "Pink-slip productivity," *The Economist,* March 28, 1992, p. 79.
10. "Small companies are finding it pays to think global," *The Wall Street Journal,* November 19, 1992, p. B2.

NISSAN DRIVES DOWN PLANT EMISSIONS

1. "Will Nissan get it right this time," *Business Week,* April 20, 1992, p. 84.
2. "Sudden death of a golden age," *Financial Times,* October 20, 1992, "World Car In-

dustry" p. 10; "Nissan closure shocks workforce," *Financial Times,* February 25, 1993, p. 3.

3. "Detroit's big chance," *Business Week,* June 29, 1992, p. 84; "Japan outpaced on car costs," *New York Times,* June 18, 1992, p. D2.

4. "Nissan Motor's U.S. sales chief Mignanelli quits," *The Wall Street Journal,* April 13, 1993, p. A4; "Nissan to lay off 115 employees at U.S. sales arm," *The Wall Street Journal,* April 20, 1993.

5. "Nissan marketing shakeup leaves Chiat unscathed, for now," *Adweek,* April 19, 1993.

6. "Nissan Performance lays off most of its work force," *San Diego Business Journal,* March 15, 1993.

7. *The State of the Environment,* Organization for Economic Cooperation and Development, Paris, 1991, p. 146.

8. "Nissan receives environmental excellence award," Nissan press release, November 13, 1992.

9. Ibid.

10. "Nissan develops paint removing technology to aid plastic bumper recycling," Nissan press release, December 3, 1991.

11. "EPA unveils plans to curb incinerators of hazardous waste by blocking growth," *The Wall Street Journal,* May 19, 1993, p. B6.

12. "Nissan receives environmental excellence award," Nissan press release, November 13, 1992.

13. "What BMW sees in South Carolina," *New York Times,* April 11, 1993, p. 5.

14. "Breakdown in the fast lane," *The Economist,* February 27, 1993; "Logez, chief of purchasing, is leaving GM," *The Wall Street Journal,* March 12, 1993, p. A3; General Motors 1991 Annual Report, p. 13.

15. Francis McInerney and Sean White, *Beating Japan* (Truman Talley Books/Dutton, 1993), p. 141.

16. "Driven back to basics," *Financial Times,* July 16, 1992, p. 10.

17. Francis McInerney and Sean White, *Beating Japan* (Truman Talley Books/Dutton, 1993), p. 141.

18. "Vehicle sales jumped during late May, reflecting a shift in production to U.S.," *The Wall Street Journal,* June 4, 1993, p. 2; "Will Nissan get it right this time?" *Business Week,* April 20, 1992, p. 83.

19. Robert Levering and Milton Moskowitz, *The 100 Best Companies to Work for in America* (Currency/Doubleday, 1993).

20. Ibid.

21. "Nissan and the environment," company publication, April 1991.

22. *Nissan 1991 Annual Report,* p. 6.

23. *Nissan 1992 Annual Report,* p. 9; "Nissan establishes recycling parameters," company press release, December 19, 1991, p. 1.

24. "Nissan to introduce safer refrigerant in 1992," company press release, December 19, 1991, p. 2.

25. "Quick, save the ozone," *Business Week,* May 17, 1993, p. 79.

EXXON REFINES ITS STRATEGY

1. *Exxon 1993 Annual Report,* p. 5.
2. *Environment, Health and Safety,* Exxon report, p. 27.
3. Ibid, p. 28.
4. U.S. Environmental Protection Agency, *1991 Toxics Release Inventory,* May 1993.
5. "Oil industry projects a surge in outlays to meet U.S. environmental standards," *The Wall Street Journal,* August 31, 1993, p. A2.
6. "A battle on many fronts," *Financial Times,* Oil and Gas Industry section, p. 6.
7. In 1993, Exxon environmental expenditures were almost $1.9 billion; see Exxon 1993 annual report, p. 4; *Environment, Health and Safety,* Exxon report, p. 28.
8. In 1993, exploration expenses totaled $648 million, while R&D costs were $593 million; see Exxon 1993 annual report, p. F3.
9. "Science and marketing mix in gasoline," *New York Times,* March 2, 1994, p. D5.
10. Ibid.
11. *Exxon 1990 Annual Report,* p. 23.

WAL-MART DISTRIBUTES THE WEALTH

1. Company press release, May 28, 1993.
2. Company press releases; "Wal-Mart Store comes in colors but is all green," *The Wall Street Journal,* June 11, 1993, p. B1.
3. "Groundbreaking new market," *Critical Trends in Environment,* June 1992, p. 18; "Biodegradable ballpoint pen debuts in U.S.," *Business and the Environment,* October, 1992, p. 10; "Buy Recycled Business Alliance adds members," *Business and the Environment,* May, 1993, p. 8.
4. "Learning to wrap products in less—or nothing at all," *New York Times,* January 19, 1992, p. 8.
5. "Suchard grazes on green pastures," *Financial Times,* August 25, 1993, p. 8.
6. See George Stalk, "Competing on capabilities: the new rules of corporate strategy," *Harvard Business Review,* March 1992, p. 57.
7. "The retail revolution." *The Wall Street Journal,* July 15, 1993, p. A12.
8. "Wal-Mart spotlights fast LANs," *Computerworld,* January 25, 1993, p. 16.
9. Wal-Mart letter to the editor, *The Lakeville Journal,* January 6, 1994, p. A6.
10. "Deregulation delivers the goods," *The Wall Street Journal,* June 29, 1993, p. A19; "Trucks keep inventories rolling past warehouses to production lines," *The Wall Street Journal,* February 7, 1994, p. A9A.
11. "Home shopping: the next generation," *The Wall Street Journal,* March 21, 1994, p. R11.

LUFTHANSA AIRLINES WORKS SMARTER

1. "Losing their way," *The Economist,* June 12, 1993, p. S4.
2. "Lufthansa managers buoyed by second-quarter results," *Aviation Week & Space Technology,* July 12, 1993, p. 1.
3. "Aviation and the environment," speech by Hans-Peter Reichow, Lufthansa in Sydney on October 30, 1992.
4. "Losing their way," *The Economist,* June 12, 1993, p. S9.
5. "Lufthansa says deficit narrowed in first six months," *The Wall Street Journal,* August 13, 1993, p. B5D. Note: In 1992, Lufthansa lengthened its depreciation schedule for aircraft from ten to twelve years, boosting profits, but its write-off of equipment remains extremely conservative by industry standards. See "Lufthansa chief plots turnaround strategy," *Aviation Week & Space Technology,* March 8, 1993; "Lufthansa AG loss narrows for the year," *The Wall Street Journal,* March 18, 1994, p. A7.
6. "Lufthansa chief plots turnaround strategy," *Aviation Week & Space Technology,* March 8, 1993, p. 2.
7. "Crash marriage," *The Economist,* October 9, 1993, p. 75.
8. "Losing their way," *The Economist,* June 12, 1993, p. S5.
9. Ibid, p. S18.
10. Press conference presentation by Dr. Klaus Schlende, deputy chairman, Lufthansa, May 13, 1993, p. 4.
11. "Aviation and the environment," Hans-Peter Reichow, Lufthansa, Sydney, October 30, 1992, p. 5.
12. *Lufthansa 1992 Annual Report,* p. 3.
13. "Aviation and the environment," Hans-Peter Reichow, Lufthansa, Sydney, October 30, 1992, p. 5.
14. *The Lufthansa Integrated Environment Concept,* company brochure, August 1992.
15. "Hush kits for Boeing 737-200s," Lufthansa press release, August 6, 1993.
16. "Getting competitive at Lufthansa," *Aviation Week & Space Technology,* March 8, 1993, p. 2.
17. *Lufthansa 1992 Annual Report,* p. 9.
18. "Managing the future," *The Economist,* December 19, 1992, p. 68.
19. "Lufthansa chief plots turnaround strategy," *Aviation Week & Space Technology,* March 8, 1993, p. 5.
20. *Condé Nast Traveler* and *Check-in* magazine surveys.
21. "Losing their way," *The Economist,* June 12, 1993, p. S15.

HITACHI PREACHES THE GREEN GOSPEL

1. "Setting new environmental goals," *Hitachi Today,* Summer 1992, p. 2.
2. "The different engine," *The Economist,* February 5, 1994, p. 85.
3. "The green giant? It may be Japan," *Business Week,* February 24, 1992, p. 74; "Technopolicy," *Look Japan,* May, 1993, p. 22.
4. "Setting new environmental goals," *Hitachi Today,* Summer 1992, p. 1.
5. Ibid.

ALCATEL TELECOM SENDS A MESSAGE

1. "Miscarriage risk from microchips," *Financial Times,* December 4, 1992, p. 6.
2. "Sematech's new environmental mission," *New York Times,* October 5, 1992, p. D2.
3. "The European Community," *The Economist,* July 3, 1993, Survey p. 10; "Balladur pulls a tough balancing act, managing France in its meager years," *The Wall Street Journal,* February 16, 1994, p. A13.

HOWE SOUND PULP AND PAPER

1. "Port Mellon comes clean," *Reader's Digest,* April 1992, p. 87.
2. The federal government closed Howe Sound to prawn, shrimp, and crab fishing in 1989 when high levels of dioxins and furans were found in shellfish off Port Mellon.
3. "Port Mellon comes clean," *Reader's Digest,* April 1992, p. 88.
4. "Attack is the best line of defense," *The Financial Times,* May 7, 1993, p. IV.
5. "A town loses jobs, then celebrates," *New York Times,* October 26, 1992, p. A10.
6. Ibid.
7. "Glory can be regained," *The Financial Times,* May 7, 1993, pp. IV–I.
8. "Port Mellon comes clean," *Reader's Digest,* April 1992, p. 86.
9. "Tree-lover, spare the woodman," *The Economist,* June 22, 1991, p. 19.
10. "Glory can be regained," *The Financial Times,* May 7, 1993, p. IV–I.
11. "Longer and deeper cycles," *The Financial Times,* December 14, 1992, p. 10.
12. "The worst may be over," *The Financial Times,* December 14, 1992, p. 11.
13. "Tree-lover, spare the woodman," *The Economist,* June 22, 1991, p. 23.
14. "Glory can be regained," *The Financial Times,* May 7, 1993, pp. IV–I.
15. "Misunderstood mess," *The Economist,* May 29, 1993, Environment Survey, p. 5.
16. Ibid, p. 4.

17. "Greens pick an enemy: chlorine, the everywhere element," *New York Times,* December 20, 1992, p. 2.
18. "Surviving under fire," *The Financial Times,* November 25, 1992, p. 10.
19. "Dioxin's health risks may be greater than believed, EPA Memo Indicates," *The Wall Street Journal,* October 16, 1992, p. B9.
20. "Ontario introduces bill to cut pollution by pulp, paper mills," *The Wall Street Journal,* February 3, 1993, p. A3.
21. "There may be no simple answers," *The Financial Times,* May 7, 1993, pp. IV–II.
22. "A self-inflicted wound," *The Financial Times,* December 14, 1992, p. 9.
23. "Glory can be regained," *The Financial Times,* May 7, 1993, pp. IV–I.
24. "Woodpulp industry is fighting for its life," *The Financial Times,* May 7, 1993, pp. IV–I.
25. "Boise Cascade may be out of the woods in first period," *The Wall Street Journal,* April 12, 1993, p. B4.
26. "Environment a high priority at HSPP," *Canfor News,* October 1990, p. 3.
27. "There may be no simple answers," *The Financial Times,* May 7, 1993, pp. IV–II.
28. "Ten-year shipping agreement signed," *Canfor News,* July 1990, p. 3.
29. "Glory can be regained," *The Financial Times,* May 7, 1993, pp. IV–I.
30. "Attack is the best line of defense," *The Financial Times,* May 7, 1993, pp. IV–II.
31. "Two sides face new realities," *The Financial Times,* May 7, 1993, pp. IV–II.
32. "There may be no simple answers," *The Financial Times,* May 7, 1993, pp. IV–II.
33. Ibid.
34. "Tree-lover, spare the woodman," *The Economist,* June 22, 1991, p. 23.
35. Ibid, p. 20.
36. "Attack is the best line of defense," *The Financial Times,* May 7, 1993, pp. IV–II.
37. "Forest industry under attack in Europe," *Canfor News,* June 1991, p. 3.
38. Interview with the authors.

BLACK PHOTO

1. "Fewer killings tallied in '93 in New York," *New York Times,* January 2, 1994, p. 19. According to the Metropolitan Toronto Police Department, 62 people were killed in Toronto (population 2,275,771) in 1993, down 10 percent from 1992. In New York (population 7,071,000) 1,995 homicides were reported in 1993, down 0.6 percent from 1992.
2. Preamble to the British North America Act, 1867. The BNA Act is Canada's founding document. It eschews all reference to American-style "life, liberty and happiness."
3. "Canadian technologies make for positive image in photo-finishing," *The Financial Post,* October 26, 1992, p. S41.
4. *Controlling Industrial Discharge to Sewers,* Municipal/Industrial Strategy for Abatement, The Queen's Printer, 1989. This document made water consumption a top priority of the government of Ontario.

5. Interview with company executive.
6. See Chapter 13 of our *Beating Japan* (Truman Talley Books/Dutton, 1993).
7. "The famous brands on death row," *New York Times,* November 7, 1993, Section 3, p. 1.
8. "Canadian technologies make for positive image in photo finishing," *The Financial Post,* October 26, 1992, p. S41; and "An environmental overview of Black's System Crystal," Black Photo Corp., July, 1992, p. 6.
9. "An environmental overview of Black's System Crystal," Black Photo Corp., July, 1992, p. 6.
10. "Canadian technologies make for positive image in photo-finishing," *The Financial Post,* October 26, 1992, p. S41.
11. "What's in a number," *Green Market Alert,* Vol. 3 No. 5., May 1992, p. 2.
12. "An environmental overview of Black's System Crystal," Black Photo Corp., July, 1992, p. 4.
13. "Canadian technologies make for positive image in photo-finishing," *The Financial Post,* October 26, 1992, p. S41.
14. *Water Conservation in Ontario—Implementing a User Pay System to Finance a Cleaner Environment,* Municipal/Industrial Strategy for Abatement Advisory Committee Technical Report, The Queen's Printer, May, 1991.
15. "Cleaning up the photofinishing business," *Critical Trends in Environment,* June 1992, p. 19.

INTER-CONTINENTAL HOTELS

1. *The Economist,* March 7, 1991, p. 67; *The Wall Street Journal,* December 16, 1992, p. B1.
2. "Inter-Continental launches phase two of worldwide environmental initiative," company press release, September 20, 1992, p. 3.
3. Ibid, pp. 1–2.
4. "Inter-Continental launches phase two of worldwide environmental initiative," company press release, October 1, 1992, pp. 3ff; "Inter-Continental Hotels recognized for environmental greening," company press release, July 24, 1993; *The Daily Planet,* Inter-Continental in-house newsletter, October, 1992; December, 1992, p. 4; May, 1993, p. 2.
5. *The Daily Planet,* Inter-Continental in-house newsletter, October 1992, pp. 6, 7, 8.
6. "Elegant earnings for an elegant property," *South Florida Business Journal,* May 28, 1993, p. 1.
7. "Saving by recycling: greening of the Grand Hotel," *New York Times,* August 8, 1992, p. 17.
8. *The Daily Planet,* Inter-Continental in-house newsletter, October 1992, p. 6.
9. See, for example, James Doherty's review of service in the capitals of Europe in "Service with a smile—if you're lucky," *Nation's Restaurant News,* August 23, 1993, p. 1.

BUENA VISTA WINERY TAKES THE NEXT STEP

1. Adam Smith, *The Wealth of Nations* (The Modern Library, 1937), p. 639.
2. "Buena Vista winery recognized as a leader in organic farming," Buena Vista Winery press release, August 31, 1992.
3. *Cable Network News,* September 29, 1992.
4. "Organic wine hits the mainstream," *New York Times,* November 19, 1991, p. D1.
5. "Grapes of wealth: Brown-Forman to buy Fetzer Vineyards," *Los Angeles Times,* July 18, 1992, p. 1.
6. "Wine is bottled in more shapes and sizes," *The Wall Street Journal,* December 9, 1993, p. B1.
7. "Passing the jug," *New York Times Magazine,* November 15, 1992, p. 48.
8. "California's double whammy," *Financial Times,* January 16, 1993, p. VIII.
9. "Certifiably Carneros," *California Farmer,* September 21, 1991, p. 10.
10. "Bugs, weeds, and fine wine," *Business Week,* August 10, 1992, p. 1x.
11. "Certifiably Carneros," *California Farmer,* September 21, 1991, p. 10.
12. "Buena Vista winery recognized as a leader in organic farming," Buena Vista Winery press release, August 31, 1992.
13. "Certifiably Carneros," *California Farmer,* September 21, 1991, p. 10.
14. "Organic wine hits the mainstream," *New York Times,* November 19, 1991, p. D1.
15. "Certifiably Carneros," *California Farmer,* September 21, 1991, p. 11.
16. "U.S. is expected to support reductions in use of methyl bromide, a pesticide," *The Wall Street Journal,* November 17, 1992, p. B4.
17. "Organic wine hits the mainstream," *New York Times,* November 19, 1991, p. D1.
18. "U.S. is steadily losing share of world trade in grains and soybeans," *The Wall Street Journal,* December 3, 1992, p. A1.
19. Ibid.
20. "Le déclin de l'agriculture allemande," *Le Monde,* December 10, 1992, p. 18.
21. *The State of the Environment,* OECD, 1991, p. 185.
22. "Future of big vegetable growing area in California threatened by salt water," *The Wall Street Journal,* July 1, 1993, p. A2.
23. "Environmental truce clears smoke in rice fields," *New York Times,* December 12, 1992, p. 8.
24. "U.S. and Florida lean on sugar producers to restore polluted Everglades," *New York Times,* January 16, 1994, p. 20.
25. "Organic profits go against the grain," *Financial Times,* April 30, 1993, p. 32.
26. "Soil quality and financial performance of biodynamic and conventional farms in New Zealand," *Science,* April 16, 1993, p. 344.
27. "Where Riesling is king, experiments and trouble reign," *New York Times,* November 25, 1992, p. C1.
28. "High prices, uneven quality, and fleeting consumer interest have taken their toll," *Boston Globe,* June 17, 1992, p. 1x.

29. "No-till farms supplant furrowed fields, cutting erosion but spreading herbicides," *The Wall Street Journal,* July 8, 1993, p. B1.

FIGHTING EURO-SCLEROSIS

1. "The United States economy, back in the driver's seat," *New York Times,* February 27, 1994, Section 3, p. 6.
2. "America the super-fit," *The Economist,* February 13, 1993, p. 67.
3. For comparative historical statistics, see *the State of the Environment,* OECD, Paris, 1991.
4. "Delor's rescue plan to save two million computer jobs," *The European,* November 5, 1992, p. 38.
5. "America's little fellows surge ahead," *The Economist,* July 3, 1993, p. 59.
6. "EC industrial competitiveness paper stresses least-cost approach," *Environment Watch: Western Europe,* November 20, 1992, p. 13.

RIDING THE BIG GREEN TSUNAMI

1. See also from the authors: *Beating Japan: How Hundreds of American Companies Are Beating Japan Now—and What Your Company Can Learn from Their Strategies and Successes* (Truman Talley Books/Dutton, 1993).
2. In 1989, for example, Japan had a trade surplus of $45 billion with the United States; its total fuel imports in the same year were $43 billion; *Japan Economic Almanac 1990.*
3. "New order," *The Economist,* August 25, 1990, p. 58.
4. "Japan sets an example for the world," *The Japan Times Weekly International Edition,* December 17, 1990, p. 12.
5. NTT advertisement, *Look Japan,* September 1991, inside front cover.
6. Michael Crichton, *Rising Sun* (Knopf, 1992), p. 227.

SINGAPORE AND HONG KONG

1. C. M. Turnbull, *A History of Singapore 1819–1988* (Oxford University Press, 1989), p. 304.
2. *Straits Times,* January 21, 1993, p. 3.
3. A Mobil advertisement in *The Wall Street Journal,* April 14, 1994, p. A15.
4. "Faecal contamination rife in oysters: study," *The Standard,* January 16, 1993, p. 1.
5. *White Paper: Pollution in Hong Kong—A Time to Act,* June 1989.
6. "A tale of two cities revisited," *The Straits Times,* January 20, 1993, p. 28.

HIGH STAKES FOR AMERICA

1. Environmental and Energy Study Institute, *1992 Briefing Book,* Summary of Laws, p. 39.
2. "Price tag is producing groans already," *The Wall Street Journal,* October 29, 1990, p. A7.
3. "For each dollar spent on clean air someone stands to make a buck," *The Wall Street Journal,* October 29, 1990, p. A1.
4. *Environmental Investments: The Cost of a Clean Environment,* United States Environmental Protection Agency, December 1990, p. v.
5. "Corporate legal costs in America," *The Economist,* August 17, 1991, p. 57.
6. By some estimates, energy intensity will fall by nearly 25 percent, or about 1.5 percent per year, without any change in current trends. See "Energy efficiency," *Financial Times,* November 17, 1992, p. I.
7. "Saving the planet," *Business Week,* May 11, 1992, p. 112.
8. "Growth vs. environment," *Business Week,* May 11, 1992, p. 74; "Back to conservation," *The Economist,* August 11, 1990, p. 27; "Who dares . . . and loses," *The Economist,* September 1, 1990, p. 61.
9. "Hot stuff," *The Economist,* September 15, 1990, p. 85.
10. "Energy and the environment," *The Economist,* August 31, 1991, Survey, p. 21.
11. "COE quota premiums," *Straits Times,* January 21, 1993, p. 3. [S]
12. For further discussion of misguided policy, see Peter F. Drucker, *The Frontiers of Management* (Truman Talley Books/Dutton, 1986), p. 71.
13. "Cheapest protection of nature may lie in taxes, not laws," *New York Times,* November 24, 1992, p. C8.
14. "U.S. comes top in services output," *Financial Times,* October 13, 1992, p. 6.

RIDING THE INFORMATION-COST CURVE

1. "Doom II is unveiled," *The Wall Street Journal,* October 11, 1994, p. B7; "CyberSource begins to offer software," *The Wall Street Journal,* January 31, 1995, p. B8.
2. "The movie was a hit, the CD-ROM a dud," *The Wall Street Journal,* January 23, 1995, p. A1.
3. "France Telecom starts campaign to promote video conferencing," *The Wall Street Journal,* February 1, 1995, p. 10.
4. "American Express goes on-line for card holders," *The Wall Street Journal,* January 30, 1995, p. A3.

ACKNOWLEDGMENTS

We owe our gratitude to many people at the companies profiled in this book. In particular, we wish to thank: at Alcatel, Dave England for his thoughtful comments, Maurice Kretz for a view from the front line, Susie DeVaris and Pam Tobiason for background information, and Xavier Woillez for the view from Paris; at Black Photo, Rob Buchelt and Alan Henkelman for showing us the ins and outs of modern photoprocessing; at Buena Vista, Sam Folsom for seeing two travelers on short notice; at Canadian Forest Products, Peter Moonen for bearing with us over a year of questions; at Exxon Chemical, Charles Emerson and Colin Chee for a generous amount of time and attention; at Exxon, Kate Corrigan for arrangements and follow-up, Ron Embry for his expert's perspective, and Ceasar Cuellar for a whirlwind tour; at Hitachi, Emi Takase and O'Patrick Wilson for much time and many arrangements, Tetsuro Fukushima and his team for their thoughtful presentation, and Yoshiyuki Ishii for sticking with us; at Inter-Continental Hotels, Reinhold Faller and Dale Dugan for their "green" customer service principals, Edward Andrews and Suzanne Gryner for showing us how things work in the real world, and Nell Barrett for pulling it all together; at Lufthansa, Franz-josef Darius and Maren Gatzemeier for a warm welcome and thoughtful discussion, Lucille Hoshabjian for coordinating activities on two continents, and Renate Sockolowsky for the bird's-eye view; at Nissan Motor Co., Fred Standish and Vicki Smith for a quick response to a big request, and Takashi Matsushita and Toyokazu Ishida for a warm welcome; at the Hong Kong Economic & Trade Office, Lawrence Chan for setting us in motion; at the Hong Kong Industry Department, Suzanna Ma for a charming tour of the Crown Colony. We would also like to thank Jared Zelmen for guidance on the economics of organic farming and Bill Hughes for his patience with our primitive understanding of pulp- and papermaking.

INDEX